The True Story of Alice B. Toklas

The True Story of
Alice B. Toklas
A Study of Three Autobiographies

Anna Linzie

University of Iowa Press, Iowa City 52242
http://www.uiowa.edu/uiowapress
Printed in the United States of America

Quotations from the Stein-Toklas papers held by the Beinecke
Rare Book and Manuscript Library at Yale University have been
used with the permission of Edward M. Burns.

The University of Iowa Press is a member of Green Press
Initiative and is committed to preserving natural resources.

Printed on acid-free paper

Library of Congress Cataloging-in-Publication Data
Linzie, Anna, 1971–.
The true story of Alice B. Toklas: a comparative study of three autobiographies /
by Anna Linzie.
p.   cm.
Includes bibliographical references and index.
ISBN 0-87745-985-1 (cloth)
1. Toklas, Alice B.   2. Authors, American—Biography—History and criticism.
3. Women authors, American—Biography—History and criticism.   4. Toklas,
Alice B. Alice B. Toklas cook book.   5. Toklas, Alice B. What is remembered.
6. Stein, Gertrude, 1874–1946. Autobiography of Alice B. Toklas.   I. Title.
PS3539.O23Z75 2006   2005055911
818'.5209—dc22
[B]

06   07   08   09   10   C   5   4   3   2   1

Contents

Acknowledgments

Many people in Sweden and the U.S. have contributed to the successful completion of this book: Rolf Lundén, Uppsala University; Danuta Fjellestad, Blekinge Tekniska Högskola; Susan Edmunds, Linda Alcoff, and Linda Shires, Syracuse University; Ann Fisher-Wirth, University of Mississippi; Petra Ragnerstam, Lund University; Pamela Marston, the University of Gävle; Prasenjit Gupta and others at the University of Iowa Press; my parents and brothers; my husband and baby boy; and many others. I am grateful to all of you.

I would also like to express my gratitude to a number of libraries: Uppsala University Library; Beinecke Library, Yale University; the John F. Kennedy Library, Boston; Bird Library, Syracuse University; and Baker Library, Dartmouth College.

Several institutions and foundations have provided crucial financial support for my project. I would like to thank the Fulbright Commission, the Swedish Institute, Syracuse University, Värmlands Nation in Uppsala, Munkfors kommun, Uppsala University, and the Wallenberg Foundation.

Materials from the Yale Collection of American Literature, Beinecke Rare Book and Manuscript Library, are reprinted by permission of Edward M. Burns, the copyright holder of the Stein and Toklas unpublished documents.

The True Story of Alice B. Toklas

The Toklas Autobiographies and the True Story of Alice B. Toklas

Now that I have written it twice
It is not as alike as once.
GERTRUDE STEIN, Stanza LXX, Part V, *Stanzas in Meditation*, 458

There would be no cause for concern if one were rigorously
assured of being able to distinguish with rigor between a citation
and a non-citation, a récit and a non-récit or a repetition within
the form of one or the other.
JACQUES DERRIDA, "The Law of Genre," 54

I wish once more to say that I know the difference between two.
GERTRUDE STEIN, Stanza LXXX, Part V, *Stanzas in Meditation*, 463

This study investigates three mid-twentieth-century texts written by a legendary Jewish-American lesbian couple expatriated to Paris. They are *The Autobiography of Alice B. Toklas* (1933) by Gertrude Stein and *The Alice B. Toklas Cook Book* (1954) and *What Is Remembered* (1963) by Alice Toklas. In a fitting image of the asymmetrical standing of the two women in cultural narratives and literary history, Toklas's name, birth date, and date of death are engraved in gold on the *back* of Stein's headstone at the Père Lachaise Cemetery in Paris, invisible from the cemetery path.[1] Richard Bridgman's 1970 comment on *The Autobiography* intimates its controversial status as a mock autobiography, as well as the difference in standing between Stein and Toklas, and may serve as a paradoxical leitmotif for the present study as a whole: "One possibility is sufficiently heretical that no one has dared advance it directly; but there have been hints that Alice Toklas composed her own autobiography" (209). As the above list of three Toklas autobiographies suggests, she *did*, at least twice. Nevertheless, while *The Autobiography* has been analyzed extensively in literary critical debates

I

ever since it was published, and subsequently canonized as perhaps the most significant woman-authored autobiography of the twentieth century, Toklas's own autobiographies relate in a very different way to discourses of literary history and criticism, the autobiographical canon, and standards of literary greatness—as an uninterrupted absence.

Very few articles and books deal specifically with Toklas apart from her indeterminate function in *The Autobiography*. Ironically, because it is not "her own," the drugged fudge recipe in the *Cook Book* is Toklas's only claim to fame besides her mythic role as Stein's eccentric companion. Naturally, one cannot expect a body of Toklas criticism comparable to the one concerned with Stein. But considering the fact that Toklas was indispensable to Stein's literary production from 1907 onward, and moreover published a number of her own books and articles, it can be argued that there is still a noticeable scarcity of critical interest. Although "her" first autobiography is among the most important works of literary modernism and continues to influence conversations on autobiography in general and lesbian autobiography in particular, Toklas and her work represent a striking omission in literary history and criticism. The aim of the present study is to indicate and perhaps partly bridge this gap. Just as she was indispensable to Stein's life and work until Stein died in 1946 and indispensable to the development and maintenance of Stein's literary reputation for the rest of her own life, Toklas should be indispensable to literary critical discourses on Stein and (lesbian) autobiography today.

My contribution to Stein scholarship and autobiographical criticism is an alternative take on and a new intertextual framework for one canonical autobiographical text and the very first extended consideration of two non-canonical and more or less obscure autobiographies. Instead of looking for dialogue only within *The Autobiography*, which a number of critics have done, I find it more interesting to also bring in the *Cook Book* and *What Is Remembered*, which constitute obvious intertexts for Stein's autobiographical writing. In my opinion, a critical engagement is called for that brings the Toklas autobiographies together for the purposes of analysis without automatically and prematurely granting any one of them priority or allowing the analysis to get stuck in the ruse of the "original." Therefore, my work brings these three texts together on the same plane of investigation, suspending the sense of absurdity and asymmetry in juxtaposing writers of such different rank in literary history as Stein and Toklas and texts of such dissimilar assigned literary value as Stein's *Autobiography* and Toklas's

What Is Remembered. This move should be seen as a strategic practice of critical license. License means excess, lawlessness, immoderation, abandon, a lack of control and responsibility. But it also means authorization or authority, warrant, privilege, or even carte blanche. As I authorize myself to talk about three Toklas autobiographies, my argument may seem excessive and irresponsible. My intertextual reading of three very different texts, my foregrounding of Toklas at the expense of Stein, and the enforced permeability between the sexual and textual levels of the Stein–Toklas relationship in my discussion are not necessarily appropriate gestures of literary criticism. In general, and with the scarcity of critical commentary on Toklas in mind, I define my own work ambiguously in relation to the recent renaissance in Stein scholarship, as an apprentice and a contributor, but also as a renegade, the proponent of a certain counterdiscourse.

As Bridgman's comment suggests, Stein and Toklas do not enjoy the same status in literary critical discourses. Stein is generally considered one of the most important writers of the twentieth century. Lately she has also become the object of a certain critical renaissance as her work has been reread through the critical frameworks of feminism and queer theory. Toklas, on the other hand, is rarely regarded as a writer or a cultural laborer in her own right, or even recognized as the enabler of Stein's literary production. Obviously, it is easier to treat Stein as one of the great modernist writers, her writings emanating from an independent mind, than to try to take into account the complicated structures of labor, pleasure, sex, and authority in the Stein–Toklas relationship. It is true that Stein's manuscripts are primarily in Stein's hand, with more or less extensive revisions and suggestions for changes in Toklas's red pencil, and it is unlikely that the two women ever engaged in actual cowriting. Nevertheless, I would like to argue that Toklas is indispensable to any consideration of Stein's work. A rigorous analysis of Stein's production as a whole—not only *The Autobiography* but above all her less accessible works—demands persistent critical attention to the contextual and intertextual framework for every text. This is another way of saying that a reassessment of Stein's work is called for that takes into account the way in which *Toklas's* work made it possible, the way in which she enabled Stein's genius through domestic and cultural labor. As Catharine Stimpson points out, "In 1907 Toklas, despite her brains and musical talents, had no vocation. *Stein became her work*. . . . She ended as the master of a special guild" ("Gertrice," 126, my emphasis). Toklas played a crucial role twice over in the production of Stein's writings and the simultaneous production of Stein as a writer. First, she enabled Stein's work in various ways at the time it was written, and then, after Stein's death, she continued the development and maintenance of Stein's literary reputation and protected the image of Stein as genius, even to the point of breaking up with old friends who did not subscribe to the same version of the legend (see Curnutt, "In the Temps de Gertrude," 122). Ultimately, as Andrea Weiss indicates, Toklas created Stein's oeuvre as we know it today: "On her death bed, Gertrude made her last request: that all her many unpublished manuscripts see their way into print. Alice was to outlive her by over twenty years, until that enormous task was accomplished" (99).

As I see it, an opening up of the analytical framework to include Toklas would at least provisionally displace the conventional reduction of Stein's oeuvre and literary reputation to a function of Stein's solitary authorship. Apart from her own publications (the *Cook Book, What Is Remembered, Aromas and Flavors of Past and Present* [1958], and various articles in journals and magazines) and translations and introductions (for instance, for Anne Bodart's *Blue Dog and Other Fables for the French* [1956]), Toklas's cultural and literary involvement includes the proofreading, editing, typing, and publishing she did for Stein; the management of the salon at 27 rue de Fleurus; and the development and maintenance of Stein's literary heritage after Stein's death in 1946. Beyond these clear contributions, there is also Toklas's elusive but inescapable influence on Stein's writing as such, impossible to theorize but discernible in the echoes of everyday life, intimate conversation, and erotic desire that find their way into the published texts.

My argument may appear strangely superfluous. Everybody already knows that the two women were inseparable and that there is no way of engaging critically with Stein without at least mentioning Toklas. For all the Stein scholars *mentioning* her, however, there are as yet no full-length studies of Toklas that account for her work, until now no dissertations written about her, and still very few articles that engage with Toklas beyond her uncertain connection with the namesake narrator in *The Autobiography*. Paradoxically, this seems to be exactly what Toklas herself would have wanted. As a foundational quandary for the present critical endeavor, it should be noted that all three Toklas autobiographies, and Toklas's every move from the moment she first met Stein in 1907 until her death in 1967, contribute greatly to the joint Stein–Toklas project of promoting Stein as a modernist genius and of keeping Toklas—and above all her sexual relationship with Stein—in the background. Making Toklas the primary object of analysis may not only be contrary to the inclination of Stein, who is reputed to have been childishly jealous of anybody else's claim to fame, and whose status as genius to some extent depends on the background position of her wife, but also contrary to the desire of *Toklas herself* to remain in disguise and under cover. Toklas was a fiercely private person, and obscurity (even after death) seems to have been her preference. It is not an easy task to deconstruct the Stein–Toklas genius/wife hierarchy, or to "save" Toklas from it, since she, the supposedly injured party in this asymmetrical relationship, both coauthored and helped to enforce it.

Despite the probable intention of the reluctant object of investigation to remain a mere parenthesis in Stein's story, the aim of my study is to insist, respectfully but surely offensively to the aforementioned object if she had been able to speak her mind about it, upon the critical recovery of Alice B. Toklas, not only as the quintessential "other woman" in Stein's world and Stein's word, Stein's sex and Stein's text, but also as a cultural laborer and a writer of her own books. In order to pursue this ambition, my study of the Toklas autobiographies draws heavily upon the legend of Stein and Toklas and various forms of biographical "evidence" but then continues beyond considerations of referential reality and authorial intention to construct a reading that moves into the realm of (inter)textuality. One example is the way in which I will first take into account Toklas's humble conception of her own role in Stein's literary production and low opinion of her own writing after Stein's death, and then *still* go on to read the *Cook Book* in relation to the category of literary experiment, construct *What Is Remembered* as a challenging act of mimicry, and place both texts in the same category as Stein's *Autobiography*, all critical ambitions that Toklas the historical person would most likely have abhorred. In relation to this ethical and theoretical dilemma, my critical agenda draws upon the insights of deconstruction but at the same time retains a provisional and rearticulated sense of agency, which reflects a certain feminist commitment to the woman writer as an entity who exceeds the limits of her text.

Judging by the relative stature of Stein and Toklas in dominant discourses of literary history, Toklas's attempt to place herself in the background was largely successful. Indeed, it is continued by literary critics and literary historians today, even beyond the expected level of asymmetry related to the quantitative and qualitative differences between Stein's writing and Toklas's writing. Toklas was resented by Stein's contemporaries, however, long before she was ignored by literary critics. The Stein–Toklas marriage was not easily accepted even among close friends, and almost everyone blamed Toklas rather than Stein for whatever acts of license and affront they found objectionable in this unique union. Above all, they worried about the way in which Stein developed a need for everything that Toklas provided, or, more grudgingly, blamed Toklas for *creating* those needs. Bridgman recognizes jealousy as part of the widespread aversion to Toklas and her position in Stein's life: "Some of Gertrude Stein's other women friends reacted with varying degrees of resentment to Alice Toklas' appropriation of the role of factotum" (110). Mabel Dodge Luhan is probably the most famous of these resentful women friends, complaining that Toklas "did everything to save Gertrude a movement—all the housekeeping, the typing, seeing people who called, and getting rid of the undesirables, answering letters—really providing all the motor force of the menage. . . . And Gertrude was growing helpless and foolish from it and less inclined to do anything herself" (quoted in Mellow, 179). Gertrude's brother Leo agrees, of course, professing to have "seen trees strangled by vines in this same way" (also quoted in Mellow, 179). Leo moved out shortly after Toklas's arrival at rue de Fleurus and almost entirely left Toklas out of his own autobiographical writing (*Journey into the Self*, 1950). Both Luhan and Leo Stein apparently felt rejected by Stein because of Toklas.[2]

The most interesting example of the tendency among Stein's contemporaries to blame Toklas for everything that went wrong in their relation with Stein may be Ernest Hemingway's hostility toward his mentor's partner. The friendship between him and Stein ended bitterly, as a result of the famous quarrel that is most obviously portrayed in *The Autobiography* and in *A Moveable Feast*, but also in a number of other texts by both writers. Hemingway, the best known of several promising young men initially accepted in and later expelled from Stein's circle, writes of *The Autobiography* that "the memoir writer will usually prove that a lady's brain may still be between her thighs" (quoted in Stewart, 121). Elsewhere, he slanders not only *The Autobiography* but also Stein's sexuality by saying of Joan Miró's "Farm" that it took nine months to paint, "as long to make as it takes a woman to make a child . . . and a woman who isn't a woman can usually write her autobiography in a third of that time" (quoted in Curnutt, "In the Temps de Gertrude," 131). What could be the reason for such unrefined, sexist reactions to Stein's text? Perhaps not only disgust at a literary work that explodes boundaries of both genre and gender, but also a wounded ego. In *The Autobiography*, Hemingway is called "a rotten pupil," "easily tired," "fragile," and someone who "looks like a modern and . . . smells of the museums," and the narrator complains that "whatever I say, Gertrude Stein always says, yes I know but I have a weakness for Hemingway." Stein in the text goes on, apologetically, by way of explaining such a weakness, to say that Hemingway "was the first of the young men to knock at my door" and that he is in fact an excellent pupil because he "does it without understanding it, in other words he takes training" (292–99).

Toklas is often left out of accounts of the legendary antagonism between the two celebrated writers, but, as Lawrence Stewart points out, she was an important "third party" in the conflict (117). The disaffection between Toklas and Hemingway was long-lasting—"Gertrude Stein in 1933 contrived to be utterly nasty about Ernest Hemingway; Hemingway waited thirty years for his revenge, and then contrived to be perfectly foul about Gertrude (who was safely dead) and Alice B. Toklas (who was not)" (Scobie, 125)—and most obviously mutual. The narrator of *The Autobiography* jokingly remarks: "Don't you come home with Hemingway on your arm, I used to say when [Stein] went out for a walk" (298). In her old age, Toklas turned down an offer to have *A Moveable Feast* read to her: "I never liked Hemingway" (Stewart, 119). When pressured for a comment in a 1960s interview, Toklas finally replied: "Oh, Hemingway was a horror" (quoted in Steward, 96). In a 1950 private letter, Toklas is more outspoken and precise in her disdain: "the whole Hemingway legend—which we saw him create and *soigner*—going to pieces as it is under one's eyes is the most pitiable embarrassing thing imaginable. . . . he is hopelessly 1890— and one can damn him no further. He wears like the new look but he is in the tradition of Kipling" (*Staying on Alone*, 210). It is interesting in this context to note that Toklas may have influenced extremely central aspects of Hemingway's literary imagination, although he could not and would not admit it. The narrator in *The Autobiography* points out that Hemingway "heard about bull-fighting from me. I have always loved spanish dancing and spanish bull-fighting and I loved to show the photographs of bull-fighters and bull-fighting" (295).

In various texts, Hemingway tries to erase Toklas from the traumatic story of having once been Stein's friend and then finding himself rejected. "The hatred Hemingway felt for Miss Toklas had become so consuming that even her name had gone up in smoke," Stewart remarks (120). "She was reduced to 'the friend who lived with [Gertrude Stein]' or 'her companion' or 'a companion.' The kindest mention was 'But we liked Miss Stein and her friend, although the friend was frightening'" (120). As reported by Stewart, Hemingway first misnamed his adversary "Miss Tocraz" and "eventually refused to give [her] any name at all" (117). Hemingway's aversion to Toklas produces glaring absences and telltale omissions in his work: "Alice Toklas . . . came to embody all that [Hemingway] detested in the Stein menage and work. And so frightening was the continuing memory of her that even when in *A Moveable Feast* he spoke of that local habitation (at 27 Rue de Fleurus) he could not bring himself to speak her name" (Stewart, 122). Even when Hemingway actually *does* speak Toklas's name, he unnames her. In the Hemingway Collection at the John F. Kennedy Library in Boston, there is a six-page unpublished text called "The Autobiography of Alice B. Hemingway." In this "revenge" piece we can see how Hemingway unnames Toklas in a very sophisticated and thorough fashion by appropriating her name for his text, turning another (reportedly very different, and obviously very straight) woman with the same first name into his wife, and reducing her to her Polish ancestry and the character traits that supposedly follow upon it, in a text that parodies and mimics her autobiography. Very few critics have paid attention to "The Autobiography of Alice B. Hemingway," but one exception is Kirk Curnutt, who in his article "In the Temps de Gertrude" not only mentions the way in which it has been overlooked in debates on Stein and Hemingway and their literary battle but also refers to it as a "mock memoir" (131).

"The Autobiography of Alice B. Hemingway" clearly parodies *The Autobiography*, opening with the same naming of a place of birth and the consequence of it, as well as an almost literal repetition of certain phrases in the first chapter of Stein's text. The ending, too, is a parodic and positively poisonous repetition of the ending of *The Autobiography*. The autobiographical "I" in this case is supposedly Hemingway's wife, who symptomatically does not exist by name until she becomes Mrs. Hemingway, and the text primarily describes what Hemingway tells her about his visits with Stein. The main part of their conversation concerns Stein's writing— as opposed to Hemingway's own—and the way in which she, according to him, has devised a way of working without risk or effort. Curnutt shows that not only did Hemingway "misread the circuitousness of Gertrude's prose as artistic sloth," but also, by "Equating the hard work of writing with his own sexuality, he suggests that Stein's lesbianism prevents her from properly valuing literary labor" ("In the Temps de Gertrude," 126, 132). Hemingway in the text indicates that Stein will soon need a best-seller and that she will then compromise her standards further (he is obviously talking about *The Autobiography*). Then he goes on to criticize Stein's infatuation with the English language, saying that it is a result of her non-English ancestry, and that she will never be a very good writer of English because of her ethnic background. This discussion seems to lead him directly to Toklas. When his wife asks him what her namesake is like, he describes Toklas primarily in ethnic terms, specifically as a Pole, which would then explain her brutal and callous character.

It is interesting to note that Curnutt, in his article on Hemingway's strug-gle with "recurring anxieties over [Stein's] influence" (123), suggests that "The Autobiography of Alice B. Hemingway" is relatively mild compared to other attacks on Stein by the younger writer and that it is characterized by a "conciliatory tone" (133). For one thing, Curnutt says, "this mock memoir eschews broad farce in favor of melancholy reflection, as if, instead of launching a cathartic counterattack, he were excising the lingering sadness of his 'temps de Gertrude'" (131). Moreover, "the most striking aspect of the sketch is its initial absence of malice, for rather than disparage Gertrude, he mourns her inability to measure up to his high standards" (132). It is true that Hemingway in this piece declares fondness for the older writer, despite her laziness, and that he only "indulge[s] in two highly personal insults" (132) aimed at Stein: one, equating her literary "laziness" with ignorance in relation to straight sex (a hetero/sexist slur); and two, "equat[ing] her abstract style with faulty translation" (an ethnic slur) ("In the Temps de Gertrude," 133). But "The Autobiography of Alice B. Hemingway" cannot be seen as anything but malicious and hostile in relation to Toklas, the bearer of the name that makes Hemingway's text signify as a parody. It is interest-ing, but not very surprising, that Curnutt almost completely omits Toklas from his discussion of the Stein–Hemingway disagreement and thus fol-lows Hemingway's example in unnaming her.

As Curnutt's article shows, the story of Hemingway's falling-out with Stein and Toklas proliferates in an extreme form of "almost the same but not quite" and includes gestures of both naming/blaming and unnaming in relation to Toklas as scapegoat for the conflict. For example, in "Letter of Exceptional Literary Importance," Hemingway expounds upon his version of the way in which he ended up among the ex-friends of Stein and Toklas:

"[Stein] had, *or Alice had*, a sort of necessity to break off friendships and she only gave real loyalty to people who were inferior to her. She had to attack me because she learned to write dialogue from me just as I learned the wonderful rhythms in prose from her" (quoted in Weiss, 98, my emphasis). In this instance, Hemingway does *not* unname Toklas but instead tries to name/blame her, despite the fact that, in his interpretation of the situation, *Stein* is the one with all the reasons (rivalry, prestige) to break up their friendship. He does so even to the point of making the grammar of the sentence seem off. When Curnutt leaves out "or Alice had" when quoting the same passage, the sentence immediately seems much less peculiar ("In the Temps de Gertrude," 121). In another Hemingway piece published in the *New Yorker* in 1927, Toklas is dropped altogether from yet another version of the "same" story (the "true story of my break with Gertrude Stein" this time, according to the title, and the "real story" of the same event according to the text). At least her *name* is not mentioned: "For a long time I had noticed that when I would come to the door of Gertrude Stein's house and ring the bell nobody would answer. Sometimes a window would open and someone would look out and then the window would shut again." The story grows increasingly absurd, but this time Hemingway's main impediments for trying to get access to Stein are the French maid and Stein herself, not Toklas ("The True Story of My Break with Gertrude Stein").

What is Hemingway's *reason* for alternately unnaming and naming/ blaming Toklas? It can be assumed that he, like many others, found Toklas frightening because of her lesbian sexuality, her strong personality, and the way in which she apparently dominated Stein. It has also been suggested that Hemingway secretly held Toklas responsible for Stein's abuse of him in *The Autobiography*. Officially, however, in the most famous passage of *A Moveable Feast*, Hemingway claims that the reason he was unable to remain friends with Stein was that he had overheard a conversation with overtones of lesbian sadomasochism between her and Toklas: "I heard [Toklas] speaking to Miss Stein as I had never heard one person speak to another; never, anywhere, ever. Then Miss Stein's voice came pleading and begging, saying, 'Don't, pussy. Don't. Don't, please don't. I'll do anything, pussy, but please don't do it. Please don't. Please don't, pussy'" (118). Hemingway reacts to Stein's and Toklas's conversation by panicking: "'I have to go,' I said and tried not to hear any more as I left but it was still going on and the only way I could not hear it was to be gone. It was bad to hear and the answers were worse."[3] It is arguable whether the incident that Hemingway describes ever took place, but this episode, whether factual or fictional, would seem to explain his sarcastic characterization of Toklas as brutal and cruel, and he was apparently so disturbed by this "reduction" of Stein to submissive lesbian lover that it "finished" his friendship with her.

In a characteristic move, Hemingway then laments Stein's appearance after Toklas cut her hair, and establishes his own recollection of her as more feminine, and another male artist's version of her, as the "true" Stein: "She got to look like a Roman emperor and that was fine if you liked your women to look like Roman emperors. But Picasso had painted her, and I could remember her when she looked like a woman from Friuli" (*A Moveable Feast*, 119). It seems absurd to imagine that Hemingway would even consider Stein as one of "[his] women," especially since he used to say: "Gertrude Stein and me are just like brothers" (Weiss, 71). This latter comment would seem to prove that Hemingway was well aware of Stein's homosexuality, and he also believed that Toklas's aversion toward him was grounded in sexual selfishness. In a letter, he mentions an understanding between him and Stein that he "always wanted to fuck her" and suggests that Toklas disliked Stein's male writer friends because she was jealous (1948 letter, quoted in Souhami, 153). The tangled gender implications of this conjecture are quite interesting, with Hemingway (of all people) expressing sexual desire for, and defining specifically as a woman, Toklas's husband and his own brother. With these complications in mind, it seems plausible to think that the obscure conversation that Hemingway overhears disturbs him to such an extreme extent not so much because of its actual content, but rather because it establishes as fact that neither Stein nor Toklas will ever be among "[his] women": a reality that exceeds the parameters for heterosexual convention, which is almost the same but not quite/not straight, is unfathomable and disastrous: "I could never make friends [with Stein] again truly, neither in my heart nor in my head. When you cannot make friends any more in your head is the worst" (*A Moveable Feast*, 119).

It seems as though the unusually strong bond between Stein and Toklas, their passionate *coupling*, is challenging not only to contemporaries who may have taken exception to Toklas's making claims on "their" share of Stein's attention. A tendency of resentment toward Toklas for being indispensable to Stein can be detected in literary history and criticism even today. As I see it, Toklas as "factotum" must be acknowledged. It is impossible even in the highly selective discourses of literary history and criticism to extricate the tree from the vine. At the same time, the hierarchical division of labor and the butch-femme role play in the Stein–Toklas marriage will be analyzed in relation to the probability that Toklas herself coauthored the public and private roles she and Stein played. In accordance with this perspective, and in an attempt to look beyond it, I suggest that Toklas's authority (or authorship) is present *precisely* to the extent that she herself appears to be missing from her own autobiographies. Critics and biographers agree that Toklas remains elusive throughout her life and beyond, not only in the accounts of others but also in her own life and work, where she carefully avoids establishing the semblance of a named "identity" for herself: "So often did Alice Toklas disguise herself— assuming the successive roles of maid, cook, wife, secretary, press agent, and publisher, making small talk with the wives of the famous, acting as a screen to keep unwanted visitors from boring Gertrude—that self-effacement and deliberately mistaken identity can be considered Alice's basic metaphor of self" (Adams, 5–6). I argue that it is possible, in relation to Toklas's predilection for self-effacement, to rethink her absence in terms of *authorial agency*.

Misnaming (deliberately adopting a mistaken identity) and unnaming (effacing) herself the way that others would misname and unname her, Toklas possibly deflects the violent effect of such actions. In other words, she refuses to construct and maintain a stable identity for herself that may then be denied and distorted by others and hides in a carefully crafted textual persona, designed to veil the secrets of her intimate life with Stein. A certain reverse discourse of "deliberately mistaken identity" could then be the provisional basis for a possibly heretical reassessment of the Toklas autobiographies. In this alternative version of the story, the category of agency resides in the double-speaking operations of deliberate (self)silencing and disorderly discourse, and in the quiet yet forceful resistance to readerly expectations for a "straight" account, in relation to both genre/textuality and gender/sexuality. By twice refusing to perform a straight autobiography, Toklas enacts her agency discursively in a performance of (non)identity. It is interesting to note in this context Stein's argument that identity "destroys creation" (355), whereas masterpieces derive from "knowing there is no identity and producing while identity is not" ("Masterpieces," 360). In relation to this theory, the suppression of Toklas's "identity" in the Toklas autobiographies may be the key to their particular version of genius. Ironically, then, investing the way in which Toklas hides her "real self" not only behind a "deliberately mistaken identity" but also behind Stein the genius with a different form of agency may make a provisional critical recovery of her possible.

My critical agenda entails an insistent shifting of the critical perspective, centering Toklas and pushing Stein slightly off center, as well as conceptualizing the Stein–Toklas sexual/textual relationship as being fundamentally *reciprocal*. Indeed, in Stein's own (unpublished) words, Stein and Toklas are not only "Gertrice/Altrude" (see Stimpson, 136, n. 1) but also "Mr. and Mrs. Reciprocal" (see Dydo, *Gertrude Stein*, 27). A new *double focus* on Stein and Toklas shifts the critical debate into a different gear, where questions of authorship and authority, sexuality and textuality, a certain division of labor, and a certain paradigm for writing literary history then take precedence. The (re)introduction of Toklas into the ongoing critical debate on Stein should be seen not only in general terms as a feminist critical practice, that is, as the recovery of a neglected woman cultural laborer and writer, but also, more specifically, as a way to extend the critical debate on Stein to include the spaces of the kitchen and the garden (rather than the bedroom, which is where most rearticulations of the relationship between Stein and Toklas have gone). A consideration of these spaces entails a new perspective on various discourses of domesticity, the hierarchies of race and class primarily visible in the *Cook Book*, another perspective on war and history, a heightened sense of social consciousness, and a reformulation of the modernist text as commodity, indeed Stein the genius as commodity. Furthermore, a sustained consideration of these aspects of the true story of Alice B. Toklas require a notion of the "true story" as a radically relative category that is necessarily multiple, provisional, and ever shifting.

Leigh Gilmore rightly points out that "Toklas' 'history' is dispersed across texts" ("Signature," 68). The (true?) story of Alice B. Toklas is presented not only in the three Toklas autobiographies but also in other Stein works, in letters written by Stein, Toklas, and others, in memoirs written by friends of the eccentric couple, in biographies, and in critical commentary (primarily on Stein). These intertexts, constructed as sharing the impossible referent of the "same" life, the "same" person, can be probed in such a way as to unsettle their boundaries, allowing us to take into account the fluidity of text, intertext, and writing in defiance of the regulatory fiction of "book." As Jacques Derrida puts it, "The idea of the book, which always refers to a natural totality, is profoundly alien to the sense of writing. It is the encyclo-pedic protection of theology and of logocentrism against the disruption of writing, against its aphoristic energy, and . . . against difference in general." (*Of Grammatology*, 18). As I see it, there is no way of assessing the relative truth value of different utterances signed by (or assigned to) Toklas in dif-ferent forms of text (autobiography, letter, interview), or even the relative truth value of *her* contributions to the legend as opposed to those of others. Instead, it becomes necessary to acknowledge that the individual utter-ances that make up "the true story of Alice B. Toklas" are many and varied, that Toklas (or Stein, for that matter) does not own or rule "her own" story, and that ultimately, there is no way of determining which installment of the "same" story is telling (more of) the truth. Monique Truong's recent and primarily fictional *Book of Salt* contributes to the ongoing narrative of Alice B. Toklas just like Stein's *Autobiography*, the "original" supposedly nonfic-tional installment of the story. Linda Simon's Toklas biography participates in the process of telling the "same" story as Toklas's "own" autobiographies, the *Cook Book* and *What Is Remembered*.

In the present study, I have decided not to claim precedence and authority for the "original" installments of the story, that is, the words of Toklas herself (and Stein), the "official" version. According to Phoebe Davis's reading of *The Autobiography*, this critical principle parallels Stein's own treatment of multiple versions of the "same" story: "Not only does Stein offer a variety of different, though equally valid, accounts of identical events, but more surprisingly, she also makes no claim for the authenticity of Toklas' version of the story" (24). In the following, I will make use of many types of text—autobiography, biography, fiction, let-ters, hearsay—and none of these relates more directly than any other to some authoritative dimension of extratextual truth. Chronologically, Stein's *Autobiography* would seem to constitute the most obvious starting point for the ongoing narrative of Alice B. Toklas. But this text itself destabilizes notions of originality and autobiographical truth and opens up the possibility that any subsequent installment or version of the "same" story might enjoy equal validity/invalidity or make equally false/authentic truth claims in relation to the genre as such. Moreover, "Ada" can be seen as another "Toklas autobiography," one that precedes *The Autobiography* by two decades. Significantly, the anecdote describing the occasion in 1910 when Stein showed her very first word portrait to its subject (Toklas) for the first time is one of the most famous parts of *The*

Autobiography. The story of this intimate everyday exchange between Stein and Toklas involves key concerns of my study: the juxtaposition and parity of food and literature, housekeeping and writing; the interplay of Stein's literary work and Toklas's domestic labor; and the subtle shifting of hierarchies and registers of authority:

> One Sunday evening . . . I called Gertrude Stein to come in from the atelier for supper. She came in much excited and would not sit down. Here I want to show you something, she said. No I said it has to be eaten hot. No, she said, you have to see this first. Gertrude Stein never likes her food hot and I do like mine hot, we never agree about this. She admits that one can wait to cool it but one cannot heat it once it is on a plate so it is agreed that I have it served as hot as I like. In spite of my protests and the food cooling I had to read. I can still see the little tiny pages of the notebook written forward and back. It was the portrait called Ada, the first in Geography and Plays. I began it and I thought she was making fun of me and I protested, she says I protest now about my autobiography. Finally I read it all and was terribly pleased with it. And then we ate our supper. (153–54)

This passage is interesting in several ways. Sandra Gilbert and Susan Gubar argue that it proves their point about the violence of Stein's appropriation of Toklas: "The cooking and eating of Alice are interrupted by a telling that is a forced feeding which Stein's Alice can only feebly protest" (252). It is true that, on this occasion, as an exception to the rule that *the couple eats when Toklas pleases*, Stein insists on having Toklas's "autobiography" read (consumed, digested) by its subject immediately, in other words "served as hot as I like." Toklas's protest about the food cooling and her protest "about my autobiography" are placed on the same plane. As Harriet Scott Chessman puts it: "Literally, the account of Stein's writing of 'Ada' becomes inseparable from an account of how Alice Toklas receives 'Ada.' . . . Reading occurs on a continuum with eating, as an act of subtle and nourishing communion" (63–64). This interpretation brings to mind Sarah Sceats's *Food, Consumption, and the Body in Contemporary Women's Fiction* and its views on "food as a language, eating an exchange." Sceats concludes her study by saying that women writers in particular have always used and will without doubt continue to "use food and eating to explore and convey philosophical, psychological, moral and political concerns" (184–86).

The anecdote quoted above is also interesting because of the use of pronouns in the penultimate sentence: "*I* protested, *she* says *I* protest now about *my* autobiography" ("I" is Toklas). This passage is confusing in a significant way. Earlier, Stein's speech is represented directly, rather than "translated" through Toklas, her interlocutor: "Here I want to show you something, she said." (In this case "I" is Stein.) Because of the fundamentally ambivalent authorial imprint of *The Autobiography*, the mix-up does not stop here: "Further, as we must remind ourselves, this Toklas is not Toklas at all, but Gertrude Stein, who names herself Toklas. The figure Gertrude Stein assumes the voice of Alice B. Toklas, who quotes Gertrude Stein" (Chessman, 64–65). In relation to this (con)fusion, Chessman helpfully indicates that it is possible to make use of the very *title* "Ada" to conceptualize the union of Stein and Toklas as irreducibly double, yet asymmetrical: "A kind of mirroring occurs here, where the two figures reflect each other and appear often to be identical, yet where enough asymmetry remains to reveal the fact of doubleness (Irigaray's *'living* mirrors'). The title, 'Ada,' offers an image of this half-symmetry, where the two 'a's represent the same letter, yet where one letter at any point is capital, the other small" (70). Similarly, the Toklas autobiographies represent the "same" story, but only one of them is regarded as a "capital" work of art.

In a highly simplified compression of the official history of textual production, Stein writes her companion's autobiography in the 1930s, which makes Toklas say in the 1950s that her autobiography is "done" already, but she can do something else (namely, a cook book with "memories"), and then in the 1960s Toklas goes on anyway to produce *What Is Remembered*, a memoir that to a considerable extent repeats material and echoes the autobiographical "I" from the "original" *Autobiography*. The first Toklas autobiography is followed by one text that seems to (passively) distance itself from it and then one that seems to authenticate or corroborate it. The ongoing autobiographical text of Alice B. Toklas would seem to have come full circle, connecting back to the original after a detour into hybrid antiautobiography. But both the *Cook Book* and *What Is Remembered* supplement *The Autobiography* in such a way as to not only modify the original text but also unsettle the very concept of originality. At the same time, this particular form of supplementarity creates a paradox, or perhaps more correctly a double take, since the first Toklas autobiography *itself* dispensed very thoroughly with the notion of originality in autobiography.

The return of the "I" from *The Autobiography* in *What Is Remembered* invites critical engagement by way of a modification of the concept of mimicry that has been deployed in postcolonial theory and criticism, primarily by Homi Bhabha in his essay "Of Mimicry and Man," where he argues that colonialism "often produces a text rich in the traditions of *trompe-l'œil*, irony, mimicry and repetition" (85). In the colonial situation there is a tension, identified by Edward Said, between the "synchronic panoptical vision of domination—the demand for identity, stasis—and the counter-pressure of the diachrony of history—change, difference," and in relation to this conflict mimicry "represents an *ironic* compromise" (Said, quoted in Bhabha, 86). In the context of the present study, this relationship can be usefully reconceptualized to describe the tension between a certain demand for identity in autobiography and the counterpressure of history and difference, and to similarly understand mimicry and repetition in autobiography as an ironic compromise—*almost the same but not quite.*

In *What Is Remembered*, Toklas says that Stein's voice is "like two voices" (26). Perhaps she is paying tribute to the way in which Stein spoke for both of them in *The Autobiography* (see Gilbert and Gubar, 255). However, the flow of (authorial) power between the two women cannot be easily determined. The source of the "I" in *The Autobiography* is forever deferred, impossible to pin down. In *What Is Remembered*, Toklas seems to echo Stein speaking as/for her in *The Autobiography*. When Toklas mimics Stein mimicking Toklas, the result is almost the same, but not quite. It could be argued that, by means of the slippage inherent in this figure, the latter text destabilizes the authority of the former and questions its originality. Stein may seem to "speak from beyond the grave" in the later Toklas autobiographies. On the other hand, at some level Toklas is clearly speaking from behind the authorial imprint "Stein" in *The Autobiography*: "We went to the bull-fights. At first they upset me and Gertrude Stein used to tell me, now look, now don't look, until finally I was able to look all the time" (160). It is impossible to ascertain whether Toklas in *What Is Remembered* is mimicking *The Autobiography* in the sense that she is imitating Stein's text or if she is just speaking in her "true" voice (assuming that such discursive transparency would be possible), which Stein then presumably "captured" accurately in *The Autobiography*: "Gertrude would say, Do not look, when a horse was being gored. She would say, Now you can look, when the horse had been led away" (*What Is Remembered*, 78).

There is widespread disagreement among critics and commentators over the way in which Stein's and Toklas's voices relate to each other. "I think Alice had a much surer feeling for painting than Gertrude," Bravig Imbs says, "but very few people knew that, for it was always Gertrude who had the word in public" (127). Harold Acton, on the other hand, indicates that Toklas was the official mouthpiece for the couple: "When [my friend] mentioned that Hemingway was in Paris, Alice Toklas, speaking for both of them as usual, said the only thing they liked about him was his good looks when they first knew him at the age of twenty-four" (114–15). Sylvia Beach suggests that each woman's speech supplemented the other one's: "[Stein's] remarks and those of Alice, which rounded them out, were inseparable" (52). Janet Flanner similarly emphasizes the way in which Stein and Toklas tended to speak, as it were, jointly (or in chorus) when she points out that their "good relations with modern paintings rather than with modern painters . . . best demonstrated the solidity of their jointly operating critical faculties. As they frequently chorused, painters were to be admired for their paintings, not for their characters" (280). Donald Sutherland claims that "Miss Toklas' conversational style . . . is . . . a variant of Miss Stein's conversational style, for she had about the same way with an anecdote or a sly observation in talking as Miss Toklas has," and thus Stein could "imitate" Toklas in such a way as to "put in writing something of her own beautiful conversation. . . . she re-created a figure of herself, established an identity, a twin" (quoted in Bloom, 83).[4]

Rejecting all these constructions of Stein and Toklas as speaking in the "same" voice, however, Bridgman considers them unlikely chorus girls and claims that Toklas's "voice constitutes the foremost problem of [*The Autobiography*]. Its ironic precision was utterly foreign to Gertrude Stein, and therefore it is natural to wonder if her companion was in any way responsible for the drastic stylistic metamorphosis" (209). Virgil Thomson similarly emphasizes the distance between Stein's and Toklas's styles: "Gertrude imitated [Toklas's voice] three times [in "Ada," *Miss Furr and Miss Skeene*, and *The Autobiography*] with striking success. She could not use it often, because its way was not hers" (176–77). In a very important recent study called *Gertrude Stein: The Language That Rises*, Ulla Dydo agrees that "Stein's [own] voice is inappropriate for the *Autobiography*" (496) and points out that after 1933, Stein "could not regain the Toklas voice. . . . [S]he was unable to repeat the successful impersonation. . . . [T]he gay voice would not speak again" (574).

It is true that Stein and Toklas seem to have spoken in very different voices, but it is also true that they frequently appropriated each other's styles, not only for *The Autobiography*. There is a document in the Yale collection that records Toklas's getting used to her new portable typewriter while Stein is asleep: "Hoé How do you do? Very well I thank you. It is quite surprising with what accuracy and speefsppef speef éi with what accuracy and speed I nowwi write on my little portable typewriter. Anf Anf And all ib And all in sicg si q sux sucg sy such a short time." It is interesting to note that Toklas in these typing exercises approaches, perhaps even imitates, Stein's repetitive experimental style: "Sweetest Sweetest Sweetest Sweetest happu happeir happier happier happier Sweetest happier congratulations in complete have alreadygive pleasure husband's loce love love love." In several more pages recording Toklas's practice at her typewriter, her style is distinctly and humorously Steinian: "BA bBaby is allwell. h b Baby is all well. b Baby is all well. b Baby is all well. N Baby is all well well. Baby is all well. That is vee vze v very b nicz b nice nicz nice nice nice nice, That is c very nice. That is c very nice. Thar Thar That is very nice. That is very no nice." There is a whole page of mistakes, corrections, and new beginnings on Mr. and Mrs. Cuddlewuddle and their "extraordinary devotion" to each other, and it ends (without mistakes): "I hear him ring his bell, I must fly."

It seems as though Toklas, practicing at her typewriter, is just writing whatever is on her mind, but the result looks like the repetitive language that can be found in Stein's published work. Toklas in these typing exercises also plays with proverbs in a way that brings to mind Stein's writings in, for instance, *A Birthday Book*: "Honesty is the best policy. A dyoycj stitch ib rime saves nine. stitxh qtitch in time stitch in rime saves nine. . . . Nothing quc seeds like success. success :othing succeeds li%e success. the best policy. stitch Nothing like. whrn in doubt count nine." (YCAL MSS 76, box 133, folder 2929). In this context, it is interesting to note also that other documents in the Yale collection indicate that Stein, in return, sometimes imitated not only Toklas's conversation (as she presumably did in *The Autobiography*), but also her *writing*, specifically the concrete appearance of her neat handwriting. There are notebooks where Stein's handwriting suddenly changes from being very large and characteristically difficult to read and instead approaches the eminently readable, extremely tidy, and much less space-consuming hand of Toklas. Perhaps these passages reflect Stein imitating the appearance of other notebooks, where she and Toklas actually take turns wielding the pen. These "mimicking" practices of writing indicate the impossibility of separating Stein's and Toklas's voices and styles.

Although Bhabha's theory is specific to a history of colonial contact and a tradition of postcolonial theory, I believe some of its basic properties can be retained as I appropriate it for my reading of three autobiographies written by white western bourgeois lesbians. Bhabha's construction "almost the same but 'not quite/not white,' on the margins of metropolitan desire" (92), a concept that presupposes a relation of asymmetrical power, access, and privilege in a specifically colonial situation, has to be recontextualized to serve my purposes here as "almost the same but 'not quite/not straight,' on the margins of heterosexual desire." It is not colonialism, then, but perhaps a normative heterosexuality—another regulator of power, access, and privilege—that produces mimicry and irony in this case. As Monique Wittig points out, "discourses of heterosexuality oppress us in the sense that they prevent us from speaking unless we speak in their terms" (quoted in de Lauretis, 18). It might be possible, however, to perform a certain transgressive act of doublespeak in relation to normative heterosexuality by means of mimicry, parody, repetition, and irony: almost the same but not quite/not straight.

Bhabha defines the discourse of mimicry as *necessarily* ambivalent. It must always produce "its slippage, its excess, its difference." Because of this element of difference, mimicry is also "the sign of the inappropriate," "at once resemblance and menace" (86). The latter function lies in "its double vision which in disclosing the ambivalence of colonial discourse also disrupts its authority" (88). Moreover, "Its threat . . . comes from the prodigious and strategic production of conflictual, fantastic, discriminatory 'identity effects' in the play of a power which is elusive because it hides no essence, no 'itself'" (90). Similarly, the threat of the Toklas autobiographies to the generic assumptions of "straight" autobiography comes from a double vision that disrupts the authority of the "original" text (on one level *The Autobiography*, but ultimately the "text" of "autobiographical truth") and *the production, through repetition, of identity effects that do not hide an essence*. At the same time, this is the saving grace of the Toklas autobiographies, taken together. In Stein's words, "by twice repeating you change the meaning you actually change the meaning. This makes it more interesting. If we attach it to a person we make for realization" (*Geography and Plays*, 260). Repetition, adding an element of difference to the stasis of identity, makes for an *other* form of "realization," one in which the distance between historical person and autobiographical persona is not eliminated in order to reinscribe the fantasy of autobiographical truth but instead, alongside the proliferation of many different personas, constitutes the (impossible) foundation for momentarily and provisionally understanding Toklas and making her "real."

In Bhabha's discussion, mimicry makes "problematic . . . the very notion of 'origins'" (89). Bhabha's principal example of this relation is the distinction between being English and being "Anglicized." A parallel tension between *being* Toklas and *mimicking* Toklas characterizes the Toklas autobiographies. "Mimicry *repeats* rather than *re-presents*," Bhabha says, and this repetition results in a certain form of impossible writing: "The desire to emerge as 'authentic' through mimicry—through a process of writing and repetition—is the final irony of partial representation" (88). If the Toklas autobiographies can be said to "represent" the historical person Toklas at all, it must be argued that they constitute, through repetition, a radically partial (in both senses of the word, "incomplete" and "biased") representation that unsettles the call for authenticity in the autobiographical contract. Indulgence in such impossible writing has been applauded as a stroke of genius (in the case of *The Autobiography*) and attacked as feeblemindedness and autobiographical failure (in the case of *What Is Remembered*). What matters here is the ambiguity of the original/copy dichotomy. It is impossible to prove that the *Cook Book* and *What Is Remembered* speak a "truer" version of Toklas, that these two latter texts represent essence or origin (*being* Toklas) whereas Stein's Toklas autobiography is removed from that immediate connection with "reality" (*mimicking* Toklas). Conversely, it is equally impossible to establish the greater truth of *The Autobiography* based, for instance, on certain literary qualities or on chronological priority.

The Toklas autobiographies are almost the same but not quite/not straight in relation to each other (despite the fact that they concern events in the "same" life and memories of the "same" historical person), to principles of autobiography and the fantasy of autobiographical truth (despite the fact that all three can be provisionally categorized as *recognizably autobiographical*), and to discourses of normative heterosexuality (despite the fact that the specifically lesbian nature of the relationship between Stein and Toklas is almost entirely unspoken in each one of these autobiographies). The Toklas autobiographies in limited but perceptible ways (they are *almost* the same but not quite) defy expectations of normative gender and sexuality (*be straight! straighten up!*), as well as the protocol of autobiographical discourse (*tell it to me straight!*). In other words, they disrupt rules of both gender and genre. While Toklas's sexuality does not "determine" the textuality of the Toklas autobiographies, and conversely the specific textual movements of these works cannot be used to "prove" that she is a lesbian, my reading actively connects aspects of sexuality and textuality by means of the "almost the same but not quite/not straight construction" in order to highlight certain chosen aspects of the primary material. Several critics have explored the connection between sex and text in Stein's work. One example, and a particularly sophisticated one, can be found in Carolyn Burke's "Getting Spliced," which recognizes the discursive and relational denotations of the word "splice" (among other things, a technique of writing related to modernist collage and a synonym for marriage).

In relation to my reconceptualization of Bhabha's concept "almost the same but not quite," it is important to note that his theory is fraught with multiple problems. First, his recourse to Foucault and Lacan to conceptualize colonial mimicry has been controversial. It would seem as though, in accordance with Foucauldian theory, the ambivalence of mimicry is "simply a more or less arbitrary conduit for the flow of power," and, following Lacan, the so-called *resistance* of mimicry "remains unconscious for the colonized" (Moore-Gilbert, 133). Either way, mimicry cannot serve as a basis for strategic counterdiscourse in an active sense—the category of agency is blanked out. Moreover, as Bart Moore-Gilbert points out, while Bhabha's version of colonial mimicry may seem revolutionary, historically speaking the type of "unconscious" resistance that he identifies does not seem to have harmed colonial authority appreciably (134). Gayatri Spivak more polemically and with an unmistakable nod to Bhabha speaks of "the upwardly class-mobile metropolitan ruse of recoding mimicry as resistance" (*A Critique of Postcolonial Reason*, 364).

While I would still like to emphasize that I am using Bhabha's concept of mimicry only in a limited and thoroughly recontextualized manner, the very weaknesses of his theory as a whole speak to the present subject in an intriguing way. As the Toklas autobiographies mimic reality, the autobiographical genre, and each other, the ensuing ambivalence (not quite/not straight) and subsequent threat to dominant discourse can indeed be seen as arbitrary and unconscious, even unwanted, in relation to Toklas the historical person. In other words, it is almost impossible to imagine these texts in terms of strategic counterdiscourse or as politically informed projects, and Toklas is certainly not a plausible insurgent. Stein and Toklas cannot be constructed as political activists in relation to any cause, and they remained closet lesbians in life and in writing (there are exceptions to this rule, such as Stein's "Sonatina Followed by Another"). In a striking image of the distance between Stein and Toklas, on the one hand, and the contemporary lesbian community in Paris, on the other, Gilbert and Gubar point to the contrast between Stein's salon, "with its collection of famous male painters," and Natalie Barney's Temple of Friendship, which constituted "a virtual no man's land." Stein visited Barney's salon only once, and regular visitors like Djuna Barnes "couldn't stand her" (238). In fact, the public facade maintained by Stein and Toklas was, if not *quite* straight, definitely more straight than queer. Moreover, the mimicry and irony of these not quite/not straight intertexts have hardly posed any real danger to (hetero)sexist discourse—so far. If, however, they are read and reread as part of a tradition of lesbian autobiography, there may come about a gradual change in the way that we read and interpret the life story of the "other woman." In this regard, I follow Gilmore's suggestion for a reorganization of the debate on Stein's writing as a site where Stein "persistently constructs a space where lesbian subjects can see and be seen. . . . In order to 'see' the lesbian in autobiography . . . we must widen our view . . . to see the other woman as the lesbian in this picture. . . . Whether she is behind or before the camera or the text, she requires a place in feminist criticism beyond invocation and hasty retreat" (*Autobiographics*, 223).

The figure of the other woman belongs to the feminist rearticulation of autobiographical mirroring and specularity, the best-known instance of which is Luce Irigaray's *Speculum of the Other Woman*. Elizabeth Grosz describes Irigaray's speculum as a mirror that "represents the 'other woman,' not woman as in man's other, but another woman, altogether different from man's other" (quoted in Marcus, 218). The Toklas autobiographies constitute an excellent example of two women mirroring each other, and past and present versions of each other, sexually and textually, without the primary counteridentification with a man. Following dominant practice in biographical and literary historical discourses, I define Stein and Toklas as lesbians, and talk about the way in which the Toklas autobiographies can be related to the subgenre of lesbian autobiography through the not quite/not straight formulation. In their way of life, Stein and Toklas engaged dominant discourses of heterosexual superiority through the register of parody or mockery as they performed an elaborate, almost the same but not quite/not straight, (sub)version of the patriarchal marriage. At the same time, the way in which "she/I" at least provisionally displaces the strong autobiographical "I" in the Toklas autobiographies makes the "one flesh" of the marriage sacrament take on a literal insistence, which is a way of actually claiming in writing married status for Stein and Toklas as a lesbian couple (for comments on Stein texts as textual enactments of a lesbian marriage, see Norris, 79, and Dydo, *Gertrude Stein*, 412, 498).

While trying to retain a keen awareness of the irreducible differences between the Toklas autobiographies (and between Stein and Toklas as writers), I define them as three instances of similarly liminal or renegade discourse in relation to protocols of both textuality and sexuality. These acts of defiance are not to be seen as separate. Instead, the assault upon principles of originality and unity in autobiography *overlaps* with a challenge to normative heterosexuality, in a way which brings to mind Judith Butler's influential problematization of the relationship between originality and sexuality: "The replication of heterosexual constructs in non-heterosexual frames brings into relief the utterly constructed status of the so-called heterosexual original. Thus, gay is to straight *not* as copy is to original, but, rather, as copy is to copy. The parodic repetition of 'the original' . . . reveals the original to be nothing other than a parody of the *idea* of the natural and the original." Butler's follow-up question is "What possibilities of recirculation exist?" (31). It is my argument that the Toklas autobiographies, taken together in the manner of the present study, perhaps do not answer but instead *enact* this very question. Butler's theory of a subjectivity constituted through repetition allows me to talk about Alice B. Toklas as a historical subject, her story as *a story of substance*, again without investing her with essence: "The subject is not *determined* by the rules through which it is generated because signification is *not a founding act, but rather a regulated process of repetition* that both conceals itself and enforces its rules precisely through the production of substantializing effects" (Butler, 145, emphases in original). Coupled with a reformulation of Bhabha's "almost the same but not quite" construction and his notion of repetition creating identity effects that do not hide an essence, Butler's concept of gender trouble, performed through repetition and parody, will inform the emphases of my investigation in its entirety and feed into my readings of the primary material.

Chapter 1

Genre/Textuality and Gender/Sexuality in the Toklas Autobiographies

The splice that joins separate elements edge to edge (as in the splicing of film) provided Stein with the means to imag[in]e a union that was simultaneously syntactical and erotic. Although such implicit punning lurks within many of her remarks about syntax, it has not often been noticed that Stein's formulation of modernist technique—for the splice makes possible one kind of juxtaposition—contains a poetics of gender hidden within its apparently formalist concerns.
CAROLYN BURKE, "Getting Spliced," 101

The sexual/textual relationship between Gertrude Stein and Alice B. Toklas began almost one hundred years ago. Among other things a lesbian marriage, an elaborate organization of public and domestic roles and practices, a strict division of labor, and a joint literary enterprise, this relationship was strong, intense, and enduring, lasting from Toklas's arrival in Paris in 1907 until Stein's death in 1946, and it has been analyzed in many ways over the years. The Stein–Toklas union presents itself to us in texts, images, and historical documents as gratifyingly theatrical, seemingly simple yet deeply enigmatic, open to the probing of curious minds yet irresistibly clandestine. Perhaps partly because of these alluring contradictions, Stein and Toklas have become the unlikely protagonists of popular myth. They are available to us today not only in Stein's entire oeuvre from 1907 onward, Toklas's writings, biographies, and critical works, but also in other media, for instance, famous paintings and portraits, well-known photographs, films, comics, Web sites, and even t-shirts. "Gertrude Stein and Alice B. Toklas are legends and icons now. They have achieved that cottony apotheosis of later capitalism, imprinting on a T-shirt" (Stimpson, "Gertrice," 124). These are sites where the Stein–Toklas legend is continually (re)created.

For instance, Gertrude, Alice, "Pabs" (Picasso), and Basket (the poodle) star in Tom Hachtman's comic book *Gertrude's Follies*, a collection of strips previously featured in the *Soho Weekly News*. Among many other extremely creative rearticulations of the Stein–Toklas legend, this work contains hot spots such as Stein exclaiming that Toklas is a "genius." This reaction is in response to Toklas's discovery that a copy center makes iron-ons, and her subsequent suggestion that they make Picasso t-shirts. "I'll bet you could fit a mural on one of mine!" Stein says. And then: "When we're in New York this summer we'll sell 'Guernica' shirts outside the modern! Pussy you're a genius!" (*Gertrude's Follies*, 1978). Other modern versions of the legend, for instance Truong's *Book of Salt*, redefine Toklas as the genius of the Stein–Toklas household as well. For the 1934 U.S. lecture tour, which makes Stein so nervous she would not have been able "to worry *and* to chew her food at the same time," Toklas makes sure that there will be oysters and honeydew melons for Stein to eat at every destination. In other words, she "devise[s] a menu composed of foods that are solid in form . . . and yet both courses can be consumed without the pesky need to chew. Miss Toklas is a genius after all" (253).

There is also a Web site, managed by Hans Gallas, which makes the case that "It is time for a new word—gertrudeandalice." The main purpose of the Web site is to "provide a site which recognizes the importance of this almost four-decade long partnership." It is declared that "Much of what Gertrude Stein accomplished could not have been done without Alice B. Toklas. Much of what Alice B. Toklas accomplished could not have been done without Gertrude Stein. Stein has received much deserved recognition and analysis over the years while Toklas has received some, but too little of either" (www.gertrudeandalice.com, accessed 17 November, 2002). Indeed. As I juxtapose works by Stein and Toklas, in defiance of critical convention and high-low literary hierarchies, I align my own study with projects of popular culture such as these. Like Hachtman's comic strip, my study could be seen as "an irreverent look at the life and times of Gertrude Stein and her faithful companion, Alice B. Toklas." Like Gallas's Web site, my engagement with Stein and Toklas posits a certain crucial doubleness or reciprocity that can be articulated as gertrudeandalice—or, in Stein's own words, "Gertrice/Altrude" (see Weiss, 66). In this chapter, I will map out the theoretical framework for my argument, specifically the question of "true stories" in autobiography and the troubled interplay of feminism and deconstruction in my own reading of the Toklas autobiographies as not quite straight in relation to both sexuality and textuality.

Each one of the texts under consideration in the present study can be provisionally described as a Toklas autobiography, an inscription of "the true story of Alice B. Toklas." Autobiography is an essentially hybrid genre, in itself a form of *bricolage* (Gilmore, *Autobiographics*, 125). Most critics agree that, as soon as the generic definition of autobiography—"a genre which rests, however unsteadily, on the fiction of Truth to Self" (Broughton, 84)—is invoked, a new dimension of complexity is added to the vexed relations between text and context, primary and secondary text, writer and critic. For instance, it has been claimed that "Autobiography meddles with academic knowledge in its desire for clear and detached understanding" (Robert Smith, 52). Gilmore points out that autobiography "threaten[s] to throw the inquiry off, or the inquirer" ("Anatomy," 224–25) and that it also involves an inescapable authorization complex, as "Critics/scholars of autobiography attempt to authorize their texts with introductions that contextualize their arguments within a comprehensible and already-authorized field of study" (*Autobiographics*, 125). Laura Marcus adds that the debate on autobiography has a tendency to split into extreme opposites: "Discussion of autobiography has tended to polarise between an impossible demand for representational accuracy or its abandonment in a fictionalist position" (245). Hinting at the same rift in autobiographical criticism, T. L. Broughton points out that "autobiography's theoretically fragile but politically tenacious relationship to 'real life' makes it especially ticklish to both humanist and poststructuralist generalizations" (92). Any engagement with autobiography necessitates critical self-reflection and exploration of the negotiations and decisions that have to be made in order to manage tricky dichotomies such as text/context, word/world, and person/persona. The provisional genre definition of the primary texts analyzed here seems to invite readings that move in a possibly flippant and simplistic way across the slash that separates these binaries.

Autobiography has its roots in the confession, which marks it as a necessarily truth-telling discourse, but, as Gilmore points out, "in telling the *truth*, autobiographers usually narrate, and thereby shift the emphasis to *telling* the truth" ("Policing Truth," *Autobiography and Postmodernism*, 68). Another way of saying the same thing is to define autobiography as the *telling of li(v)es*. Autobiographical truth and lies in autobiography then turn into aspects of the same impossibility of capturing life discursively. In the following, I shift the emphasis from the (supposedly "external") truth of the story to the story itself, the *writing* of autobiographical "truth," in the Toklas autobiographies and in commentary and criticism pertaining to them. Even as the subject matter of the present study makes it highly susceptible to the lure of autobiography as a discourse of *singular truth*, its obnoxious title, "the true story of Alice B. Toklas," is meant both to call upon the expectations for truth that adhere to the genre and to challenge them. This title—indicating both label and critical license or "entitlement"—is to be seen as a challenge, a paradox, and an ironic comment on the expectations and conventions of autobiography and literary critical engagements with autobiography. It will consequently be reformulated as a question in the Conclusion.

It is my conviction that "the true story of Alice B. Toklas," if there is one, resides in the textualization and multiplication or fragmentation of autobiographical truth and in the strategic (de)authorization of the author. These movements must be seen as a departure from the norm, since the concept of truth in autobiography is based on qualities such as unity, coherence, authenticity, and stability, and since, in Gilmore's words, "for both its writers and its critics, autobiography is driven by an authorization complex. Its writers attempt to situate themselves in relation to discourses of 'truth' and 'identity'" (*Autobiographies*, 124–25). Departures from the protocol, Gilmore says, will be scrutinized and possibly condemned, the perpetrator "deauthorized through [the] policing of . . . truth" (*Autobiographics*, 130). Again, the concept of license indicates the contradictory nature of this positioning. The autobiographical genre may seem to give carte blanche to the autobiographer to write whatever she wants (a form of self-authorization). At the same time, certain transgressions will be recognized as particularly provocative, acts of *intolerable* license, gestures of impossible excess. As Margot Norris points out in relation to *The Autobiography*, "The criticism of Stein for having herself called a genius in her memoir reflects a naive critical embrace of both the assumption and the convention of a disavowed egotism as *the proper gesture of autobiography* that makes little allowance for either generic play or gender play" (80, my emphasis). The enactment of a marriage license in writing can be seen as another "improper gesture" of autobiography in the context of a same-sex sexual/textual union.

This study explores how the concept of autobiography as a referential genre is transformed, and the expected semblance of transparency and truth in autobiography is jeopardized, in relation to several autobiographical texts written about the "same" person, the "same" life, but differently, by different writers, and at different points in time. Generally speaking, the most important effect of several texts telling the "same" story is the destabilization of the conception of an "original" text. As Richard Hardack puts it, "The central subtheme of [*The Autobiography*] is that posing, imitating, and copying are the primary components of autobiography." Because of this unsettling of conventional hierarchies of primary and secondary, "The copy . . . determines the original, not the reverse" (25–26). This turnaround brings to mind the *simulacrum* at the heart of postmodern theory, in Fredric Jameson's words the "identical copy for which no original has never existed" (quoted in Hilti, 37). *The Autobiography*, as the "first" Toklas autobiography chronologically speaking, may appear to be the original text upon which the *Cook Book* and *What Is Remembered* follow. Since *The Autobiography* can be seen as Stein's "imitation" of Toklas's conversational style, however, a copy rather than an original, and the two subsequent autobiographies presumably represent Toklas herself speaking (speaking her self), the question of originality turns into a critical impasse.

Moreover, *The Autobiography* is not the "first" Toklas autobiography in an absolute sense, since "Ada" preceded it. There is also the companion or shadow autobiography, *Stanzas in Meditation*, which puts in question which text is the authoritative version of the story. Similarly, *Three Lives* is highlighted in *The Autobiography* as Stein's first serious attempt at writing, but the idea of origin is challenged by there being always something before the beginning, in Stein's case the short novel with lesbian content later identified as *Q. E. D.* The riddle of originality also extends to Stein and Toklas themselves, their roles and discursive acts. One of Toklas's main responsibilities is to copy (decipher and transcribe) Stein's handwritten words. If copying is a primary component of autobiography, and the copy determines the original, her occupation at the typewriter is *primary insofar as it is secondary*. In other words, Toklas's processing of Stein's "original" text determines it and *establishes* its originality. At the same time, in *The Autobiography* Stein duplicates or copies Toklas's act of repetition in a third movement that possibly displaces Toklas once again: "The issue of transcribing someone else's voice is vital to Stein's project. Toklas is only an unreal copy, a simulacrum. Stein has to create a secretary, a copyist, for herself" (Hardack, 26, n. 18).

The complex issue of originality is not the only obstacle for interpretation in relation to the Toklas autobiographies. Moreover, the "I" in the text refs to a doubled, fictionalized persona (in *The Autobiography*), to the figure of a humble cook and recipe collector (in the *Cook Book*), or back to an earlier text (in *What Is Remembered*), never to a politically motivated real-life author. The lack of an accessible real-life referent to the autobiographical "I" is not unique to the Toklas autobiographies, of course, but rather the distinguishing impasse of autobiography as a genre, and perhaps modernist autobiography in particular. As Stephen Scobie points out, "Autobiography continually replays Rimbaud's famous aphorism, 'Je est un autre,' on which so many Modernist schemes of identity are based" (129). Nevertheless, the way in which, and the *extent* to which, the non-identity between historical person and textual persona is foregrounded and exploited in these three texts (in the *Cook Book* and *What Is Remembered* no less than in *The Autobiography*) matters, and it enables me as a critic to pursue the question of a troubled and troubling world–word connection. Still today, it seems, a common assumption is that there is one potential autobiography for each person. In other words, historical person and autobiographical persona are expected to "match" as world and word meet. Multiple autobiographical accounts of the "same" person will therefore cause a certain discord with generic norms and readerly expectations, and thus the Toklas autobiographies can be seen as particularly problematic instances of the genre.

In and between the Toklas autobiographies, a textual persona, seemingly more or less directly linked to the historical person Toklas, is written and rewritten until the immediate person/persona relation (which we *expect* from autobiography) becomes a matter of contention rather than a matter of course. According to Philippe Lejeune, autobiography "supposes that there is *identity of name* between the author (such as he figures, by his name, on the cover), the narrator of the story, and the character who is being talked about" (quoted in Marcus, 254). This fantasy of identity constitutes the foundation for the autobiographical contract. An intriguing slippage of meaning occurs as the "I" of autobiography, the authorial presence that is supposedly guaranteed in the autobiographical contract, and secured in its presumed "identity" with the proper name on the book cover and the flesh-and-blood person behind that name, multiplies. Even though the Toklas autobiographies resist readings that would try to make person and persona correspond, however, taking the easy way out and equating autobiography and fiction is not an option. The fact that there *was* a historical person Alice B. Toklas is an irreducible aspect of the text, however far removed from its operations. It would be simplistic and irresponsible in this case to uncritically reinscribe Paul de Man's claim that "any book with a readable title-page is . . . autobiographical" (922). Instead, it might be more useful to consider Derrida's conceptualization of the signature as particularly pertinent for autobiography: "By definition, a written signature implies the actual or empirical nonpresence of the signer. But . . . it also marks and retains his having-been present in a past now" ("Signature Event Context," 328). The Toklas autobiographies may not embody the *essence* of Toklas the historical person but perhaps rather harbor the elusive trace of her "having-been present" in their production in a "past now." At the same time, signatures are not always to be trusted. Stein originally finished *The Autobiography* as Mark Twain finished *The Adventures of Huckleberry Finn* (creating another link to male canonical writing, apart from *Robinson Crusoe*)—"Sincerely Yours, Alice B. Toklas"—but subsequently crossed it out (see Dydo, *Gertrude Stein*, 537–38).

Reading the Toklas autobiographies alongside one another opens up new critical perspectives. Even considered separately, none of the three texts meets the minimal requirement of a traditional autobiography, which is to present a history of a person's life and character in which there is never a doubt about (some sort of) referentiality—no matter how fragmented the text/life. Again, according to Lejeune, autobiography is a "Retrospective prose narrative written by a real person concerning his own existence, where the focus is his individual life, in particular the story of his personality" (*On Autobiography*, 4). (It is very important, however, to recognize the distance between actual autobiographies and theoretical descriptions of—or prescriptions for—the genre. As has been pointed out by several critics, theories of autobiography have been formalized and sedimented to a point where the theoretical framework frequently loses sight of the autobiographical material.) If the three Toklas autobiographies are considered in relation to each other, with an awareness of the foregrounded position of the "real" subject in autobiography, we are faced with an almost intolerable possibility of a breach in representation, a *failure* of referentiality. The very occurrence of repetition in autobiography, even when it takes the form of seemingly loyal mimicry (*What Is Remembered*), creates a fundamental ambivalence, the possibility of a crucial split between historical person and autobiographical persona, between world and word. Therefore, the fact that there are three

Toklas autobiographies, seemingly all testifying to the truth of the "same" story, complicates rather than strengthens the direct connection between text and reality.[1] This abyss between text and *hors-texte* troubles discourse in general. Autobiography is a special case, however, often considered particularly problematic in this regard. Moreover, the Toklas autobiographies operate to make the text/life rift visible to an extent that is not typical of the genre.

As I see it, giving in to biography to some degree when analyzing autobiography is not only tempting but also potentially productive of bolder and more exciting readings. Many crucial aspects of the Toklas autobiographies are in a sense unreadable, or perhaps simply less significant, if the biographical context is overlooked. At the same time, biography must be understood as just another form of writing. Derrida's *Of Grammatology* helpfully establishes "the psychobiographical" as "one form of writing or signification amongst others," so that "when we read biography or autobiography we are reading, as everywhere we must, nothing other than writing." As Seán Burke points out in quoting this Derrida passage, this perspective "provides the most direct route of return for the author as a biographical figure in criticism. The writer's *(auto)biography is writing*. . . . Thus we can re-mobilise the autobiographical without lapsing once more into positivist or geneticist assumptions" (126, my emphasis). In the present study, my ambition is precisely to reconsider the Toklas autobiographies as *writing*, in relation to other forms of writing contributing to the "same" story, and without recourse to the fantasy of autobiographical truth as primary or unitary.

In relation to points of resistance in categorizing the Toklas autobiographies precisely as "autobiography," my study has been greatly influenced by Gilmore's *Autobiographics*. The term *autobiographics* is used by Gilmore to describe "those elements of self-representation which are not bound by a philosophical definition of the self derived from Augustine, not content with the literary history of autobiography," and to denote a reading that centers on "interruptions and eruptions, . . . resistance and contradiction as strategies of self-representation." It is my opinion that the Toklas autobiographies, especially when taken together, can be usefully conceptualized, and aspects of politics and agency retained and reformulated, along the lines of Gilmore's definition: "A text's autobiographics consist in . . . an emphasis on *writing itself as constitutive of autobiographical identity*, discursive contradictions in the representation of identity (rather than unity), the name as a potential site of experimentation rather than a contractual sign of identity, and the effects of the gendered connection of word and body" (42, my emphasis). The theory of autobiographics provides a tool for bridging the gap between the two positions that may provisionally be termed person and persona in the Toklas autobiographies, where the historical person matters but where her name in the text is a function of writing rather than a seal of identity.

Again, the Toklas autobiographies hardly break new ground in the act of destabilizing the autobiographical subject. As Hardack points out in "The Franklin-Stein Monster," there is a long and clearly discernible tradition of "missing persons" in American autobiographical writing: "In one sense, these autobiographies are structured around the pretense of biography, or perhaps the biographies of missing persons" (16). Hardack argues that, because of these tendencies, American autobiography "veers into the fictional genre," and the questions that conclude his article indicate that he is not completely happy about this development: "Why is the American autobiographical self under such siege that it needs this artifice to protect itself? Why is the autobiographical participant sacrificed to the observer? And why has that autobiographical self become purely fictional?" (27–28). The traditional model for autobiography, which presumably precedes the "monstrous" deviation that Hardack describes, has been thoroughly theorized by, for instance, Lejeune, Gusdorf, Spengemann, and Olney and then deconstructed in an equally thorough fashion by Derrida, Barthes, Foucault, de Man, and others. All these formulations and reformulations of the genre are thoroughly androcentric. Gilmore remarks on the curious fact that *The Autobiography* has not generally informed the poststructuralist reformulation of autobiography, despite Stein's "enactment of Foucault's notion of writing as a game in which the author constantly disappears, [which] makes her an obvious candidate for such studies" ("Signature," 61).

Hardack's autobiography of missing persons and the three Toklas autobiographies create confusion not because they refuse to deliver truth claims, but precisely because the *holder* of this particular truth-telling "rhetorical position," the author, has been turned into a site of ambivalence. The categories of autobiographical truth and authorial identity are inextricably intertwined. As Gilmore points out, "Whether and when autobiography emerges as an authoritative discourse of reality and identity, and any particular text appears to tell the truth, have less to do with that text's presumed accuracy about what really happened than with its apprehended fit into culturally prevalent discourses of truth and identity" (*Autobiographics*, ix). What is particularly interesting about the Toklas autobiographies is their *partial* fit into dominant categories of truth and identity—almost the same but not quite/not straight. I am interested in the way in which the Toklas autobiographies both invoke and revoke the generic markers of autobiography, simultaneously establish and cancel truth effects, and alternately launch and puncture the autobiographical "I." My focus is the troubled connection between person and persona, world and word, as implied in articulations and disruptions of genre and in the tricks of a foregrounded textuality. In relation to this perspective, the historical person Toklas, endowed with agency and intention, becomes the impossible ever-escaping referent or signified in relation to the text. In the simplest terms, the "real" Alice B. Toklas seems to grow more and more distant the more we try to decode her autobiographies to find her.

It must be emphasized once again that the very terms of selection at the center of my study are dubious. The *Toklas* autobiographies? The Toklas *autobiographies*? The texts, by themselves and taken together, fail (refuse) to create the effects of referentiality, directness, transparency, and authenticity that are historically part of Lejeune's *pacte autobiographique*: the combination of contextual elements such as names, title page, preface, and library classification that marks texts for a certain category, calls upon and creates a particular authorial figure, and shapes readerly expectations. The Toklas autobiographies in different ways defy the protocol for autobiographical writing and thus participate in the ongoing destabilization of the autobiographical "I" as well as the very *connection* between the authorial figure, the proper name on the cover of the book, and the elusive "real" writer outside the text. As I see it, however, the fact that all three Toklas autobiographies to a greater or lesser extent operate to exceed their placement within the category of autobiography, and indeed unsettle the very definition of this genre, only strengthens my argument that they can and should be read precisely as autobiographies. It can be argued that experiments in autobiography, even to the point of generic breakdown, still warrant an approach that retains the analytical scaffolding of autobiography as a provisional tactic to be able to engage with the text at all. Indeed, such an inclusive critical approach may be necessary, since in the final analysis there are no pure autobiographies, but only a wide range of ways to relate to the genre and its conventions. As regards the Toklas autobiographies, it is certainly possible to say that each text to a greater or lesser extent "remain[s] a recognizably autobiographical venture" (Gilmore, "Anatomy," 226). They can also, however, be seen as resistant texts, and their relationship to autobiography is not so much one of belonging but rather one of dialogue. Precisely *because* of this relation of ambivalence and resistance, autobiography serves as a productive integrating category for my study.

One of the most important questions in relation to the Toklas autobiographies concerns the relationship between genre/textuality and gender/sexuality and the way in which these texts can be seen as experiments and challenges in relation to both. Derrida's "Law of Genre" provides a useful theoretical framework for this discussion. The famous ending of *The Autobiography* designates the text as a whole as a "mock" autobiography. It reveals the author of the text to be someone else than the person whose name appears in the title and who ostensibly serves as a reference for the autobiographical "I" in the text, thus overturning the very foundation for autobiographical writing. The final disclosure of the writing relationship between Stein, as (auto)biographer, and Toklas, as autobiographee, constitutes a "genre-clause" within the text, Derrida's "remark of belonging" (60). This is interesting in relation to the claim that "this supplementary and distinctive trait, a mark of belonging or inclusion, does not properly pertain to any genre or class. The re-mark of belonging does not belong. . . . [G]enre-designations cannot be simply part of the corpus" (61). Derrida's example is the novel, which may or may not be classified as such in a subtitle, and he points out that this designation itself is "not novelistic; it does not, in whole or in part, take part in the corpus whose denomination it nonetheless imparts." Instead, its function is to "keep [the corpus] from closing, from identifying itself with itself" (61).

The designation "autobiography" in the title of *The Autobiography*, the "generic mark" that signals "the *trait* of participation itself," obviously remains outside, but what about the proclamation of genre, namely "mock" autobiography, that concludes the text itself? And similarly, what about the way in which the text of the *Cook Book* exceeds its title through the inclusion of autobiographical material? And again, what about the way in which the title *What Is Remembered* seems to constitute a challenge or ironic comment in relation to the content of this memoir? I suggest that this discord between title (outside) and text (inside), brought to an extreme level in the ending of *The Autobiography* (and mimicked in the present study), not only qualifies Derrida's argument that the generic designation of a text cannot be part of the text but also provides a useful way of thinking about a text that unsettles and questions its own frame.

Not only are Derrida's comments on the genre-clause interesting in relation to the Toklas autobiographies. Moreover, the inclusion of the handwritten first page of the manuscript after the ending in the first edition of *The Autobiography* corresponds to the paradoxically open-ended ending (connecting back to the opening) of Maurice Blanchot's *Folie du jour*, which Derrida analyzes in his lecture on genre. He famously theorizes the effect of such citationality and circularity as a "pocket" or "invagination," something that thwarts our desire for order and knowledge and shows that "there is no 'entire' story except for the one that interrupts itself in this way" ("Law of Genre," 66). In the same way, the Toklas autobiographies, taken together, deconstruct the idea of an "entire" story or a full account by way of repetition and circularity. What is different and interesting about the Toklas autobiographies in relation to Derrida's account of the law of genre, however, is the way in which the question of "feminine and masculine genre/gender" and "the hymen between the two," in short, the "relationship between genre . . . and marriage" becomes reorganized—performed otherwise—in a specifically *lesbian* marriage, and in three texts written by two women who are not defined primarily in relation to men (see de Lauretis, 14).

Without going into the question of same-sex relationships, Derrida indicates the possibility of a different concept of gender: "What about a neutral genre/gender? Or one whose neutrality would not be *negative* (neither–nor), nor dialectical, but affirmative, and doubly affirmative (or–or)?" (70). "It is 'usually' women who say yes, yes," Derrida adds. "To life to death" (71). In his account of Blanchot's text, the law is "in the feminine," beautiful but faceless, and rearticulated as "madness" (rather than order). The authorial "I" is a man (Blanchot) who may, by mimicking *yes, yes*, engender the following probability: "*I am a woman, and beautiful.*" It appears that authorship in itself makes possible this "random drift," confers this ability: "'I,' then, can keep alive the chance of being a fe-male or of changing sex. His transsexuality permits him, in a more than metaphorical and transferential way, to engender. He can give birth" (72). The androcentrism of this account, or, rather, these accounts (Blanchot's and Derrida's), should be immediately obvious. Derrida's lecture, however, also presents certain intriguing possibilities for my reading of the Toklas autobiographies in relation to the issue of genre and gender. Summing up his argument, Derrida says, "Let us be attentive to this syntax of truth. . . . One cannot conceive truth without the madness of the law" (76). The "truth" of his own reading of Blanchot is that the law, which conventionally signifies order, can be exposed instead as madness, *madness in the feminine*. The Toklas autobiographies, however, create genders and genres that can be constructed as "doubly affirmative" in an even more radical sense. Here, the authorial "I" is a woman who is able to not only "engender" text but also *actually* give birth. Moreover, this locus of authorial dissemination is split or doubled, shared by two women, so that there is a expansion of *yes, yes, yes, yes* even beyond Derrida's notion of "excessiveness" (73). At the same time, the very proliferation of affirmation destabilizes the idea of binary man and woman, masculine and feminine—in terms of both gender and genre—that can be momentarily grasped and refracted through the figure of woman as law and order *or* madness.

Derridean theory is crucial for any understanding of autobiography today and has influenced my own thinking and critical practice greatly. The present study opens with the staging of a dialogue between Stein and Derrida, and I will return to Derrida and to deconstruction generally throughout. At the same time, I have found it necessary to make use of Derrida only in very limited and careful ways. His conceptualization of gender/genre is not flexible enough to be unproblematically appropriated for readings of women-authored works, analyses of the "I" that refers to a proper name "in the feminine," or investigations into lesbian writings. As Franziska Gygax points out, Derrida's lecture on genre "does not elaborate how *sexual* difference relates to genre and on the impact gender can have on the formation of a genre" (3, emphasis in original). Moreover, Richard Dellamora identifies the way in which Derrida, in conversation with North American feminists (an interaction published as "Choreographies"), "characterizes his addressee in contrast to 'feminine homosexuality,' a move that is violently exclusionary" (221).

In general terms, as many feminist critics have argued, deconstruction and feminism do not mix easily. Subjectivity and agency, thrown out with the rest of the humanist baggage by some critics influenced by deconstruction, cannot be simply discarded in a discourse that historically based its political agenda on the recognition that women have been denied access to either one. At the same time, deconstruction and feminism share a number of key concerns, such as autobiography, authority, and authorship. A great deal of recent feminist criticism has been focused on women's autobiography, and some of it on lesbian autobiography. This work seems to represent a sudden surge of interest in issues of gender and autobiography, a departure from the tradition of autobiographical criticism: "In fact, until the last few years, the impact of gender on the autobiographical project has not been a serious focus of critical or theoretical inquiry" (Sidonie Smith, *Poetics*, 7). Feminists like Domna Stanton and Estelle Jelinek "address the puzzling irony that historically, female autobiographers have been excluded from studies of autobiography, while at the same time, much women's writing has been dismissed as 'autobiographical'" (Davis, 39, n. 3). In "Autogynography: Is the Subject Different?" Stanton observes that "'autobiographical' constituted a positive term when applied to Augustine and Montaigne, Rousseau and Goethe, Henry Adams and Henry Miller, but . . . it had negative connotations when imposed on women's texts" (132) Sidonie Smith points out that important male critics of autobiography, such as Spengemann and Olney, "note the importance of autobiography in gaining information about woman's *bios*, [but] neither goes beyond that acknowledgement to comment on the larger and more complex issues of woman's *aute*, woman's *graphia*, and woman's reading" (*Poetics*, 7). One of the primary objectives of the present study is precisely to rethink the Toklas autobiographies as practices of writing, as *graphia*. As I articulate the possibilities for this reorganization of the discussion, it becomes necessary to talk not only about the idea of autobiographical truth and the relationships between true stories, lesbian lies, and lived realities, or the multiple definitions of autobiography as a genre, but also about the complicated interplay of feminism, poststructuralism, and deconstruction in my own discourse.

Feminist critics have generally been oblivious of Toklas and ambivalent about the "worth" of what has been seen as Stein's insufficiently political or sometimes even antifeminist work. Shirley Neuman argues that "the question is how . . . woman can achieve agency, rather than self-silencing, through autobiography" (*Autobiography and Questions of Gender*, 3). I find it difficult, in relation to the Toklas autobiographies, to speak of agency as the opposite of self-silencing, and this is where the Toklas autobiographies very clearly refuse to be claimed unproblematically for a traditionally feminist reading. Stimpson points out that *The Autobiography* "cuts against strongly felt feminist notions of a female identity that an author can present and valorize" ("Gertrude Stein and the Lesbian Lie," 164, n. 10). The dominant critical conception is that Stein is as conservative in politics as she is revolutionary in language, and *The Autobiography* has been one of the works in Stein's oeuvre most difficult to claim for feminism, primarily because of the role of Toklas in the text. Stein's and Toklas's enactment and display of a hierarchical relation in various texts is a thoroughly gendered enterprise, the public reflection of their private butch/femme performance. Although both Stein and Toklas are women, the gender inflection of these structures often seems misogynist, or at the very least androcentric. Stimpson explains that the Stein–Toklas marriage "continually meets with skepticism now" because "To egalitarians, its outward patterns—that hierarchy of 'male' domination and 'female' submission, that solar system in which nurturers orbit around a shining, central male genius—seem obsolete, even cannibalistic" ("Gertrice," 135).

Until recently, *The Autobiography* figured as the token woman's autobiography in overviews of autobiographical writing. When Jelinek in 1976 started writing her dissertation on the tradition of women's autobiography, the *only* female autobiographer that had received extensive critical attention up until that point was Stein (ix). Julia Watson comments upon this fact in such a way as to underline the perceived uselessness of *The Autobiography* for feminist and queer criticism: "Although canonical lesbian texts such as Gertrude Stein's *The Autobiography of Alice B. Toklas* had long been in print [by the late 1970s], they remained texts of privileged white women whose major identification was with male expatriate writers and the cult of genius. (In fact, in the 70s Stein's writings were not yet being read as lesbian texts—not surprisingly, given Stein's own equivocation about homophobia and her 'ventriloquist' silencing of Alice in the text.)" ("Unspeakable Differences," 400). In the past couple of decades, however, Stein's work has been subject to a critical renaissance and a feminist project of recovery. Beyond its generic innovation, *The Autobiography* has been recovered as an experiment in (the writing of) gender: "Recently, feminist critics have begun to 'bring out' Gertrude Stein—beyond the conventional nod to her 'longtime companion, Alice Toklas'—by focusing on the 'encoding' of a lesbian autobiography within Stein's asyntactic poetics" (Gilmore, "Signature," 58). Norris describes the importance of *The Autobiography* for feminism as follows: "As arguably the most important female memoir of the period, Gertrude Stein's *Autobiography of Alice B. Toklas* has reaped a harvest of gender trouble that makes it highly useful for delineating the relationship between modernism and the memoir as a 'technology of gender'" (79).[2]

Nevertheless, the long-standing conceptualization of Stein's work as incompatible with feminism remains. Karin Cope recalls an MLA special session dedicated to the question of "what to do" with certain "problematic early twentieth century women writers . . . who might have been, but for fatal moral or political flaws, appropriate 'foremothers' to contemporary feminism." The problem, it seems, is that Stein, along with H. D. and others, "exoticized and appropriated 'the other'" (155). In short, as Cope very succinctly puts it, Stein "was never as feminist as feminists would like" (159). How is it possible, from a certain standpoint and at a certain moment, to make sense of this ambivalence in critical conceptions of the political worth of Stein's work in general and *The Autobiography* in particular? Davis, in her problematization of the critical tendency to overlook ideological complications in Stein's literary experiment and to "imbue her innovative aesthetics with a politics of resistance" (21), turns to Rita Felski, arguing that "Such a reclamation of a female avant-garde tradition undoubtedly forms an important part of the feminist rewriting of literary history through its creation of a pantheon of major, inspiratory women artists. Yet it also often perpetuates an unfortunate dichotomy of literary and political value which identifies formal experimentation as the most authentic resistive practice, with a consequent stigma attached both to representational art forms and to the regressive, sentimental texts of mass culture" (Felski, quoted in Davis, 22). This is precisely where I locate my own feminist intervention, by proposing a different way of approximating Stein's *Autobiography* to feminism. By following Sara Blair's lead in reading domestic and avant-garde spaces as overlapping and cross-referential, and by reading *The Autobiography* alongside the *Cook Book* and *What Is Remembered*, rather than alongside other Stein texts, I want to displace the dichotomy that Felski identifies and imagine a far more wide-reaching sense of "literary and political value."

The Toklas autobiographies will thwart any critical attempt to claim them fully or easily for political discourses based on a sense of oppression or injustice that is opposed, or at least *registered*, by the oppressed party. The legend of Stein and Toklas represents both women as thoroughly indifferent to the "cause" of (lesbian) women. A concept of subjectivity that involves a feminist consciousness or agenda is not applicable to the Toklas autobiographies, nor is a concept of lesbian subjectivity that entails a desire for recognition or acceptance. Indeed, in the Toklas autobiographies there is no unitary autobiographical subject that would be the locus for such consciousness and such desire. Even so, my project participates in a feminist tradition. The recovery of an obscure woman writer must be seen as a feminist project, even though the definition of feminism will necessarily be problematized in relation to this particular woman writer and this particular reading. Simply put, the feminist agenda of my study is inflected by an emphasis on ideological aspects of the Toklas autobiographies other than the notion of a political "content" of the texts themselves that can be identified and theorized by the feminist critic. Marcus argues that autobiographies written by people who do not conform to the traditional model of the autobiographer as a straight white male from the upper classes of society will make "the battles between humanists and deconstructionists over the ideal subject appear irrelevant compared to the theoretical innovations and changes in cultural awareness required to accommodate all these real writing subjects" (223). After the death of the author, it is tricky to talk about two women supposedly sharing the authorial "I." But a provisional recovery of Toklas must necessarily retain a commitment to "real life" writers, and to some extent a commitment to their agency and intentions, no matter how thoroughly redefined and conditional these categories will have to become in order to make sense within a generally poststructuralist framework. In other words, I strive to accommodate both Stein and Toklas as real writing subjects—by theoretical innovation, if necessary.

Although it may cohabit uneasily with deconstruction, feminist study of women's/lesbian autobiography has been one of the most prolific areas of literary criticism over the past couple of decades, perhaps because it in many ways enjoys a productive relationship with important recent interventions in literary theory. In my own work, I have been inspired by Gilmore's theory of autobiographics as well as Sidonie Smith's and other critics' appropriation, specifically for the study of autobiography, of Butler's theory of (gender) performativity.[3] Most critics dealing with women's autobiography today, however, focus on recent publications that in some way further a feminist cause: either at the micro level, as the individual protest and intimate self-realization of an individual woman, or at the macro level, as a feminist intervention or manifesto that takes the form of an autobiography. The same thing is true with regard to lesbian autobiography. Gilmore's overview of the history of lesbian autobiographical criticism indicates that the Toklas autobiographies belong to its prehistory to such an extreme degree as to fall outside the picture altogether: "The recent history [of lesbian self-representation] may be said to begin in the mid-1970s. . . . The lesbian coming-out story as a narrative with a specific act at its center initiated a narrative tradition informed by a desire for representation" (*Autobiographics*, 228–29). Most lesbian autobiographies receiving critical attention today, with the possible exception of Stein's *Autobiography*, are read for their political objectives. As Biddy Martin points out, "the centrality of autobiography in lesbian writing is fundamentally connected with the emergence of a lesbian-feminist politics of experience and identity" (384).

Lynda Hall's "Lorde, Anzaldúa, and Tropicana Performatively Embody the Written Self" may serve as an example of a reading based on this particular intersection of (autobiographical) text and (lesbian-feminist) ideology: "Writing is a conscious strategy to resist oppressive silences surrounding women's sexuality and the marginality that circumscribes lesbian lives. . . . [C]ontestatory autobiographical practices form bridges between the self and the self, and between the self and others" (96–97). Hall goes on to talk about the "autobiographical gesture" and autobiography as performance, but her emphasis is still on autobiography as "contribut[ing] to understanding and community," and her conclusion is that the texts of Lorde, Anzaldúa, and Tropicana perform "courageous acts of self-authorization that empower others as well" (121). As I see it, the Toklas autobiographies cannot be read in this way, even if the historical context and the discursive conventions that ruled when they were written are taken into account. There is no indication in the Toklas autobiographies, or other texts by Stein and Toklas, that these two women were concerned with recognition, community, lesbian sisterhood (or any kind of sisterhood), or even the political empowerment of themselves or other lesbians. The Toklas autobiographies are very far removed from the lesbian coming-out narrative and autobiographical "manifestoes" from the margins, in Sidonie Smith's sense of the term "self-consciously political autobiographical [acts]" (examples of such autobiographical manifestoes are texts written by Gloria Anzaldúa, Donna Haraway, and others) ("The Autobiographical Manifesto," 189).

It is clear that the Toklas autobiographies cannot be easily claimed (even as precursors) for recent critical categories of lesbian autobiography. The theoretical framework in a certain sense excludes them prior to even recognizing them. Even as I applaud the ongoing reformulation of autobiographical theory and criticism, then, I also place pressure on the new emerging standards of lesbian autobiography by promoting a sustained consideration of the Toklas autobiographies as not quite/not straight autobiographies, which do not fit into traditional models for autobiography *or* the dominant protocol for lesbian life-writing. James Breslin points out that "readers who approach [*The Autobiography*] with expectations shaped by the revival of confessional writing in the 1960s are apt to reject it as too reserved" (149). This is particularly true in relation to the issue of a lesbian sexuality. It has been pointed out that perhaps the complete reticence on this subject is meant to protect the reader: "It is . . . hard to imagine a reader who would even mentally venture to put him or herself in Gertrude's bed" (Alkon, 863). At the same time, however, issues of gender and sexuality are absolutely crucial for an analysis of the Toklas autobiographies. Even though they are not explicitly political texts, the silencing or marginalizing of lesbian sexuality is evident in the blanking out of the name "Alice B. Toklas" in critical and literary historical discourses, a move that reinforces dominant (hetero)sexist conceptions of the nature of autobiography, authorship, and authority. As Stein is constructed and reconstructed as one of the great modernist writers, and Toklas's labor is largely left out of literary history, the profound challenges of the lesbian couple as text are effectively neutralized. My argument is that the framework for discussing these issues, and their political implications, should not only be authorial intention and agency, but also (inter)textuality, mimicry, and repetition. Moreover, the subversive *effect* of certain seemingly apolitical discursive movements must be taken into account. For instance, consider Toklas's contributions to magazines such as *Vogue* and the subtly but manifestly ironic effect of excerpts from the *Cook Book* squeezed in among an abundance of glamorous advertisements that tell women how to achieve a perfectly straight femininity.

While issues of gender and sexuality are hidden in the Toklas autobiographies, they are paramount in the legend of Stein and Toklas as it has developed after Toklas's death in 1967. The scandal of lesbianism seems to haunt (readings of) the Toklas autobiographies, partly because today's readers and critics are inevitably aware of the legend of Stein and Toklas, which persistently and compellingly centers the issue of sexuality. The legend of Stein and Toklas is characterized today by a great emphasis on the lesbian marriage, typically conceptualized as a strictly hierarchical relationship between the two women as husband and wife, taking on gender roles that seem thoroughly conventional *except for the fact that Stein too is a woman*. Stimpson points out that "As they violated the rules of sex, they obeyed those of gender. As they discarded heterosexuality, they enforced the codes of marriage. They were at once defiant and submissive, traditional and modern" ("Gertrice," 126). The Toklas autobiographies, on the other hand, offer only an inkling of this relationship, faint echoes of the conspicuously absent, indeed impossible, lesbian subplot. In Stimpson's terms, Stein and Toklas apparently favored obedience, submission, and tradition in their autobiographical writings.

In the past few decades, however, a wide range of possibilities for creative reassessment of the Stein–Toklas legend has followed upon the heels of interventions in literary criticism. Today, the lesbian marriage between "Pussy" and "Lovey" is conceptualized in terms radically different from the polite contemporary constructions of the avant-garde writer and her secretary, or the eccentric expatriate lady and her companion. One example is the now common reading of Stein and Toklas as involved in elaborate butch-femme role play (see Gilbert and Gubar, 243; see also Sally Munt's *Butch/Femme: Inside Lesbian Gender*). The Victorian role play of Stein and Toklas, mimicking patriarchal models of gendered behavior and interaction, may seem old-fashioned today. But such patterns of theatricality are no longer seen as false consciousness or an unfortunate (passive) imitation of heterosexuality, as they might have been in the 1970s, when there were supposedly no butches, no femmes, but only dykes (see Judith Roof's "1970s Lesbian Feminism Meets 1990s Butch-Femme" and JoAnn Loulan's *Lesbian Erotic Dance: Butch Femme Androgyny and Other Rhythms*). Because of the relative validity of butch-femme roles in lesbian communities today, Stein and Toklas appear strangely dated and up-to-date at the same time.

Sometimes previously unknown records of the Stein-Toklas union are discovered and typically feed into the reconstruction of a certain belated narrative of homosexuality, which was suppressed until Toklas died in the late 1960s. The publication of selected private love notes in 1999 is one example of the accumulative, ever-changing nature of the story of Stein and Toklas and their relationship. The notes, published as *Baby Precious Always Shines* and edited by Kay Turner, provide scholars interested in the biographical and autobiographical aspects of the Stein–Toklas legend with new fodder for the ongoing narrative. Certain Stein pieces, for instance, "A Sonatina Followed by Another," can be neatly placed in the stylistic context of these intimate daily notes: "You are my honey honey suckle. / I am your bee" (291). Even as *Baby Precious* adds to the legend, however, it also radically modifies and amends it. For instance, the introduction presents a scatological reading of Stein's writing and the Stein–Toklas relationship, as Turner without hesitation redefines "cows" in Stein's writing to be Toklas's stools (rather than her orgasms, one of the most persistent critical "truths" in Stein scholarship), and emphasizes the element of "fecal infatuation" in Stein's relation to her wife and her work: "I would suggest that in its unpunctuated, uninterrupted rhythms Stein's writing approaches the mechanics of excretion. Even in content, certain of Stein's works are illumined by the excretory point of view." Further rocking the boat of long-standing critical truths about Stein's work, Turner unflinchingly goes on to suggest that "Lifting Belly" is perhaps not about lesbian vaginal love-making at all but rather about "the erotic delights and effects of giving . . . an enema" (33). Turner's reading is somewhat startling, but undeniably supported by the primary material: "And / what is a stool. That was / the elegant name for a cow" (79).

The love notes published in *Baby Precious* are interesting even apart from "the excretory point of view," however. In several notes, Stein returns to the fact that she uses *Toklas's pen*: "My dearest wife, / This little pen which / belongs to you loves to be / written by me for you" (77). Turner spells out the way in which this appropriation of the phallic pen, and the additional twist of defining the owner of the pen as "wifie," is a specifically lesbian gesture of (pro)creativity: "There is something lustily contradictory and compelling, something really quite revolutionary, in the notion of this symbolic phallus being controlled by two women. Between them, they used the propagating potential of the pen to affirm their union and, as married couples do, to make babies—in the form of Stein's literary productions" (17). In the same way, in direct relation to *The Autobiography*, it could be argued that Toklas's autobiographical raw material and characteristic conversation fertilizes (makes possible) Stein's text. Generally speaking, the Stein–Toklas sexual/textual relationship problematizes the issue of (pro)creation. In their own private realm of imagination, Stein is "Baby Woojums" in relation to Toklas ("Mama Woojums") and Carl Van Vechten ("Papa Woojums"). At the same time, Stein's literary *works* are her and Toklas's "babies." In relation to these texts, despite Turner's problematization of the relationship between Stein and Toklas, and despite Stein's famous declaration in *Everybody's Autobiography* that "there is no doubt about it fathers are depressing" (133), Stein is most likely as their "father." In yet another twist, the characterization of Stein as a *maternal* figure has caused some critical controversy: "To avoid recognizing [Stein and Toklas as lesbians], some even try to womanize Stein, to call her the mother or 'the grandmother' of experimentation and nonconformity" (Stimpson, "Gertrice," 135, referring to Steward's *Dear Sammy*). The pun on the verb *womanize* is relevant here, especially in relation to Hemingway's attempt in *A Moveable Feast* to manage his inferiority complex in relation to Stein by "womanizing" her, that is, making her a (less threatening) *woman* through imagining her as one of "his women."

Similarly intriguing to anyone interested in the dynamics of a butch-femme lesbian marriage that apparently thrived on strictly enforced hierarchical patterns of labor, behavior, and interaction is the self-confident tone in Toklas's notes, which seems to confirm the alternative view of her as a powerful and independent wife, even as she herself plays with the idea of being submissive and dominated by her husband: "Baby boy / You're no toy / But a strong-strong husband," Toklas twitters coyly, but then: "*I dont obey* / Do this you say / Well do it together and / Thats the way we obey" (Turner, 158, my emphasis). In another note, Toklas says, "Husband is an instantaneous obediencer / He likes to be well / And be hers Mrs. speaks he ups & obeys her" (160). In this way, Toklas contributes to the gender-bending reconfiguration of patriarchal marriage structures in a specifically lesbian relationship and invests her own position, which to an outward observer seems inferior and submissive, with considerable power. Stein seems to answer her in "A Command Poem, / Commanded by wifie, written by hubbie, / who is always commanded by wifie to be wifey's / hubby and he is, would be even if he wasn't / commanded cause he just is but loves to be commanded" (109). Outside the private notes, in "Lifting Belly," Stein again confirms Toklas's power in the relationship: "Husband obey your wife" (47). In the *Cook Book*, Toklas effects a similar reversal of married roles in a juxtaposition of two anecdotes, one about Stein and herself and their relation to bugs, and the other about a straight married couple and the way in which they deal with spiders:

> Every year hornets would make a nest in the trunk of one of the bushes and with a sharp knife I would have to cut it out. Wasps, hornets and bees

rarely sting me, though my work with them has always been aggressive. Gertrude Stein did not care for them, nor for spiders, centipedes, and bats. . . . she would call for aid. . . .

A charming story of wifely and husbandly devotion was that of two of our friends. She did not wish her husband to be bored, annoyed or worried. When they were first married she allowed him to believe that she was very much afraid of spiders. Whenever she saw him disturbed she would call him with a wail, Darling, a spider; there, darling—don't you see it. He would come flying with a handkerchief, put it on the spot indicated, and, gathering up the imaginary spider, would throw it into the garden. The wife would uncover her face and with a sigh say, How good and patient you are, dearest. (*Cook Book*, 278)

Stein's and Toklas's subversion of the straight model of devotion involves a husband calling for aid and a wife providing it. The juxtaposition of these two anecdotes in the text allow for the interpretation that Stein, too, fakes her fear of bugs in order for Toklas to "rescue" her, and butch-femme categories are radically destabilized at this point. The Toklas autobiographies and the notes in *Baby Precious* allow for an image of the butch-femme role play of Stein and Toklas as an elaborate ironic performance of gender where Toklas "commands" Stein to be a "strong-strong husband"—in other words, to command *her* to "do this"—only to be able to revolt: "I dont obey." In the same way, it is possible to imagine that Toklas "commanded" Stein to write *The Autobiography* in such a way as to partly disguise her story behind the story of Stein's genius. The theatricality and gender-bending performativity of the Stein–Toklas marriage serves as an enabling modus operandi for my study, which seeks to explore this relationship in text and context without necessarily positing *one* "true story" of Stein and Toklas as its end objective.

The intimate notes in *Baby Precious*, finally made public like an awe-inspiring archeological discovery, obviously constitute a significant part of the ongoing legend of Stein and Toklas. But are they more valuable in terms of autobiographical truth than previously published material, particularly the texts that Stein and Toklas themselves intended to have published? Toklas apparently included the love notes in one of her dispatches of documents to Yale by mistake and when told they would be available to the public in the future at first refused to accept it. In an era of extreme fascination with the public disclosure of private lives and an exaggerated celebration of voyeurism, can this anecdote be read as a guarantee that *this is the real thing*? This question, a trick question of sorts, extends to all the texts that deal with the true story of Alice B. Toklas. We have seen that all the biographical "evidence" suggests that Toklas was and wanted to remain an extremely private person. With this predilection for reticence in mind, can the *Cook Book* and *What Is Remembered* really be thought to express Toklas's views more directly or reliably than Stein's "I" in *The Autobiography*? Some critics have suggested that Stein in *The Autobiography* sometimes "makes" Toklas say things by twisting her arm. It is also possible, however, that *The Autobiography*, "ghostwritten" by Stein, is more autobiographically "truthful," or in any case more outspoken, than it would have been had Toklas composed her own autobiography in 1932. At the same time, if the *Cook Book* and *What Is Remembered* reveal less about the author because it is her *desire* to remain hidden, is it not possible to reformulate this very absence as "truer" and more "authentic"? This move would of course require provisional recourse to the problematic category of authorial intention.

Again, the relationship between autobiographical discourse and reality proves vexed and precarious. Some critics have voiced concern about the recent "biographical turn" in debates on Stein and Toklas. Stimpson, for instance, suggests that "Perhaps the danger now is not that we will avoid their wedding and their bedding, but that we will linger there too long" and thereby run the risk of "Confusing attention and voyeurism" ("Gertrice," 128). Indeed, Stimpson seems to be confused herself and linger a little too long, because in the very same article she says, "Some of the interpretations [of Stein's erotic poetry] might be even better if they were more aware of the technicalities of lesbian sexuality. For example, hands, fingers, and the tongue, as well as things, can be vaginally inserted" (138, n. 40). This comment can be seen as an example of the type of treatment of homosexuality that is not possible to imagine transposed to a heterosexual context—first, because of its construction of lesbian lovemaking practices as *aberrations* that require *special knowledge*, and second, in conjunction with this gesture, the implicit but apparent reduction of (heterosexual) lovemaking to being synonymous with vaginal penetration by the male sexual organ (see de Lauretis, 14). Readings of straight *and* lesbian discourses alike are defined by the law of normative heterosexuality, "straightjacketed by the pervasiveness of what Wittig has called 'the straight mind.'" (Gilmore, *Autobiographics*, 206). In my own work, I am trying to shift the emphasis slightly from the scandal of a lesbian sexuality to the challenge of a not-quite-straight textuality, from the space of the bedroom to spaces such as the kitchen and the garden, from Toklas as a good lay to Toklas as a good cook, a writer, and a cultural laborer, indispensable to Stein's work and literary reputation. Nevertheless, I think it would be unfortunate to retreat prematurely from a focus on the "wedding and bedding" of Stein and Toklas without having first acknowledged and explored the doubly sexual/textual nature of their union and the way in which neither is quite straight.

Why and how is it appropriate, or even possible, for me to define the Toklas autobiographies as *specifically lesbian* in a reading that calls itself both (inter)textual and historical, if the primary texts themselves evade the issue of sexuality, and if it is kept in mind that "Few, if any, printed references to Stein and Toklas' sexuality appeared until the end of World War II, when Stein died" (Stimpson, "Gertrice," 128)? First, the concept of intertextuality that I employ for my study exceeds the limits of the three Toklas autobiographies under investigation, to include other primary and secondary materials (such as private love notes, various biographies, and instances of current Stein scholarship). Moreover, aspects of gender trouble and a scandalous sexuality can be seen as a key to the disruptions of genre and the foregrounding of textuality that characterize the Toklas autobiographies and thwart readerly and critical expectations for straight (in both senses of the word) autobiography. My perspective entails an emphasis on the inscription of almost the same but not quite/not straight challenges to rules of genre and gender, rather than a focus on biographical evidence on Stein's and Toklas's real-life sexuality. I do not mean to suggest that a certain autobiographical form follows automatically from the sexuality of the autobiographer. Obviously a great number of *straight* people have written autobiographies that thwart readerly and critical expectations in similar ways. In the present study, I am trying to envision ways of talking about texts as "not quite straight" without making the real-life sexuality of the writer and her partner the foundation for analysis.

Martin's "Lesbian Identity and Autobiographical Difference(s)" helpfully points to the difficulties inherent in any attempt to define lesbian autobiography: "the *lesbian* in front of *autobiography* reinforces conventional assumptions of the transparency of autobiographical writings. And the *autobiography* that follows *lesbian* suggests that sexual identity not only modifies but essentially defines a life, providing it with predictable content and an identity possessing continuity and universality" (380–81). Martin's problematization of "lesbian autobiography" is extremely relevant to the concerns of the present study. Her article, however, concerns "recent autobiographical writings . . . in which lesbianism comes to figure as something other than a 'totalizing self-identification'" (383). What about so-called lesbian autobiographies where lesbianism does not figure at all, except perhaps as an absence unaccounted for, a few mysterious contradictions in the text, or in the critical leap of faith that can perhaps be described provisionally as extratextual conjecture? My own reading of the Toklas autobiographies depends on a definition of "lesbian autobiography" that, without recourse to a "primary" coming-out narrative, actively and strategically connects aspects of textuality and sexuality. A similar gesture toward using textuality and genre to articulate the issue of (homo)sexuality is evident in Stimpson's provocative article "Gertrude Stein and the Lesbian Lie," where she defines *The Autobiography* as an instance of "a sub-genre we insufficiently understand: the lesbian lie" (152–53). "Like language, the lesbian lies," Stimpson says (163). Stimpson's term is problematic and somewhat unfortunate. Other critics, such as Gilmore, have argued the need to question "the attachment of 'lying' to women's cultural productions" and "break the link between 'women' and 'lying'" (*Autobiographics*, ix–x).

At the same time, if read with Gilmore's proviso that truth and lying are "constructs with histories" in mind, Stimpson's argument about the lesbian lie seems largely valid. It is true that, historically, the gap between lesbian realities and the protocol of normative heterosexuality has often entailed a discursive rift where the (re)writing of a licentious sexuality has matched the culturally determined definition of a lie. Stimpson envisions the lesbian couple speaking together, in chorus, in texts that enact this particular sub-genre: "the lesbian lie ('No lesbians here') has . . . been a source of a courageous, jaunty, often outrageous style. . . . The liars, when they speak together, as Stein and Toklas do in Stein's more radical texts, can create a ritualistic theater. This theater's purpose is to strengthen the community of liars. . . . [The] purpose is to deceive a public that is both vigilant and unwary as it patrols the borders of permissible speech and behavior" (163). Elsewhere, Stimpson suggests that the foregrounded theme of Stein's genius in *The Autobiography* helps mask her lesbian relationship with Toklas: "The focus on Stein's genius is as crucial to the packaging of lesbianism as it was to the Stein/Toklas 'marriage.' As Stein's genius justi-

fies Toklas' devotion, so it defuses the erotic threat of that marriage. . . .
[B]ecause the genius transcends ordinary intellectual and artistic categories, she or he can rationalize an escape from ordinary social and moral
judgments" ("Gertrice," 134).

Obviously, in a historical context the way in which a transgressive sexuality is unspoken in the Toklas autobiographies is not unique to these
particular texts or writers. Gilmore describes the impossible position of
lesbian autobiography within the tradition of a genre that has contributed
to the establishment of norms for living and writing in relation to which
lesbian is a noncategory. Autobiography not only "underwrite[s] the nor-
malcy of gender hierarchy as either an inevitability . . . or an achievement"
but is also "saturated in a presumptive heterosexism that construes heterosexuality as the unmarked category of sexuality, that is, as a synonym
for sexuality" ("Anatomy," 228). Consequently, as Watson points out, since
heterosexuality is an "unmarked" category, homosexuality when spoken
out loud means outrage: "In autobiography, which as a genre has func-
tioned as the keeper of the 'law' of patriarchal identity, women's sexuality
has usually been presumed heterosexual except when spoken otherwise.
When it is spoken as lesbian in autobiography, it has been read as voicing
a transgressive sexuality—as the naming of an unspeakable—whose difference is read as deviance" (394).

In relation to an autobiographical tradition that presupposes heterosexuality, the Toklas autobiographies simultaneously conform to and
undermine generic conventions and expectations on the level of content.
What we get is, on the one hand, a neutral account of the genius and "his"
secretary (a highly conventional gender hierarchy), and on the other, a
few mysterious evasions where the scandalous lesbian undercurrent
threatens to break through the orderly (seemingly straight but not quite)
chit-chat about people, art, food, and travel that constitutes the textual
surface. A specifically lesbian sexuality *is* to a certain extent "spoken otherwise" in the Toklas autobiographies, then, but primarily through the
paradoxical noncategory of absence, which may be translated into frus-
trated readerly questions: Where is the male main character in the story
(who is not a brother, a friend, or a protégé, but a love interest who confirms the heterosexual framework)? And what really *is* the relationship
between these two women? Perhaps the need to camouflage and reformulate, or in a certain sense articulate more freely, a lesbian relationship
is indeed the reason for the evasive maneuvers that can be surmised from

reading the text. It may not have been possible or even particularly tempting, given the sentiments not only of the public and the critics but also (and not insignificantly) of the two women themselves, who seem outwardly almost prudish despite their unconventionality and avant-garde lifestyle, to write in a less textualized, more transparent way the story of this relationship. It is possible, as Stimpson suggests, that the accessible style of *The Autobiography*, supposedly borrowed from Toklas's conversation, functions much like Stein's experimental technique elsewhere in terms of disguising a transgressive sexual reality: "a gap does exist between style's apparent promise of full disclosure and the actuality of partial disclosures. . . . [*The Autobiography* and *Everybody's Autobiography*] dramatize an actuality, . . . homosexual dissimulation. . . . Dissimulation is a tax that homosexuals pay in order to go on being members of a society that would abhor their honesty" ("Gertrude Stein," 161).

The question of unspeakable content and inescapable "dishonesty" is highly significant in relation to the Toklas autobiographies as examples of "lesbian" autobiography. Gilmore reads Jeanette Winterson for a consideration of the (impossible) connection between lesbian sexuality and autobiography. "What do Lesbians do in bed?" Winterson asks. "'Tell them,' said Sophia, the Ninth Muse. / Tell them?/ There's no such thing as autobiography, there's only art and lies" (quoted in Gilmore, "Anatomy," 224). Gilmore's analysis of this question-and-(non)answer highlights the complicated relationship of autobiography to categories of truth and lying: "The circuit from sexuality to autobiography is made with dazzling brevity on the way to 'art and lies,' and in this moment autobiography is negated and absented in the place where one is most likely to look for it. The autobiographical trace is significant here, for it indicates the way autobiography is embedded in both sexuality and artifice" ("Anatomy," 224). It seems as though the category of autobiography is threatened by the (im)possibility of "lesbian content" to such an extent that its existence must be denied as a means to deny the existence of homosexuality. In the Toklas autobiographies, the category of autobiography is largely retained but voided, as far as it is possible, of its scandalous content. But the complete dissociation of autobiography and sexuality is not possible (there is a marriage here, but no biological male in sight) and therefore these texts create the unsettling impression that the category of autobiography is canceled or abandoned even as it is invoked.

In her discussion of the lesbian lie, Stimpson points out that *The Autobiography* in fact "leaves a paper trail about homosexual realities" (159). These clues reside, for instance, in the spatial setting of the story, "the water in which the fish of anecdotes swim" (159), and in references to Stein's more openly lesbian writings. She also suggests that the authorial ruse of *The Autobiography* serves to draw attention away from the reality of homosexuality: "Getting to play 'Author, author, who's got the author,' [Stein's] readers swing their attention away from the lesbian couple and onto the game the couple is offering them, rather as if the coda were a party treat or tea cake" (158). Stimpson goes on to say that Stein's sexuality is "acceptable because she either evades it or stylizes it as a joke about authorship" ("Gertrude Stein," 160). Even as I agree in principle with this reading, which has influenced my own thinking about the connections between textual and sexual license, I would also like to point out that the emphasis in critical commentary of the last few decades on Stein's and Toklas's lesbian sexuality as something supposedly missing from the auto-biographical texts can be seen as a ruse *in itself*, a smokescreen that effectively prevents us from looking directly at the *real* scandal of the Toklas autobiographies—the inscription on the *textual* level of the lesbian couple and the concomitant challenge to "straight" textual and authorial structures and expectations of autobiographical truth. I think it is possible and desirable to both recognize the paper trail of homosexual reality in the Toklas autobiographies *and* to refrain from making the "true story" of the lesbian marriage the be-all and end-all of analysis, especially since these texts contain other forms of scandalous (non)content. Just like the notion that Toklas is strangely absent in her own autobiographies, the common assumption that her sexuality is conspicuously missing from these texts is ultimately based on a certain conventional model of autobiography as the *full account* of someone's life, a *realist* discourse where person and persona seem to merge, and the textual level is transparent in favor of full disclosure of the content. As I see it, the Toklas autobiographies can be read otherwise and the critical focus shifted to instead foreground certain patterns and structures on the level of (inter)textuality.

Any critical practice that operates by linking registers of textuality and sexuality must necessarily acknowledge the contested status of this correlation in literary critical debates. Some critics, for instance Stimpson, have issued warnings against excessive attention to Stein's (sexual) relationship with Toklas (see "Gertrice," 128). In the very same article, however, Stimpson emphasizes the extreme mutuality of the Stein–Toklas relationship, the way in which "they were symbiotic . . . they saved each other—Stein from a far less productive career, Toklas from a far greater marginality" ("Gertrice," 134). This type of ambivalence is typical of the critical conversation in question and can perhaps be related to the difficulty inherent in theorizing an irreducibly double relationship—a sexual/textual union. Shari Benstock's *Textualizing the Feminine* concerns itself precisely with "the textual ordering of sexual difference," but Stein's work is discussed in the introduction in order to critique the critical tendency to simplify it according to the following formula: "for 'textuality' read (lesbian) 'sexuality.'" Benstock cautions that this reading may cause us to "bump our noses against the gynocritical reading method that sees language as a tool, a window onto reality, transparent in itself but framing a scene that gives itself to representation" (xxiv–ix). My own engagement with the Toklas autobiographies is based upon the assumption that, whereas these texts do *not* provide a window onto the reality of the author's sexuality, aspects of textuality and aspects of sexuality in "the true story of Alice B. Toklas" can be strategically and provisionally connected in a critical practice that at each turn remembers not only the pleasures but also the perils of such licentious intercourse.

Chapter 2

Authorship and Authority in
The Autobiography of Alice B. Toklas

I double you, of course you do. You double me, very likely to be.
You double I double I double you double. I double you double me
I double you you double me.
GERTRUDE STEIN, "Patriarchal Poetry," 115

The Autobiography, "a book which brilliantly analyzes both the liabilities and the benefits of being a female man" (Gilbert and Gubar, 250), occupies a remarkable position in Stein's oeuvre. It is one of the most widely known and read Stein works, but it can also be described as thoroughly uncharacteristic of Stein's literary production as a whole, especially in relation to the reputation of Stein as a great modernist writer of avantgarde experiment. The challenges of *The Autobiography*, above all the play upon conventions of authorship, are quite distinct from the challenges of other Stein works, where literary experiment interferes with the reader's construction of meaning in more intrusive and extensive ways throughout the text, while leaving intact the impression of a solitary author (indispensable for the kind of literary reputation just mentioned). Even other autobiographical works written in Stein's "money-making style," for instance, *Everybody's Autobiography* (1937) and *Wars I Have Seen* (1945), differ distinctly from the gossipy informality of *The Autobiography*.

In the early 1930s, Stein was well known in Parisian Left Bank circles as an art collector and the eccentric hostess of an illustrious salon. She was not, however, generally known as a writer, had gone through decades of more or less unrefined rejection letters from publishers, and had not yet acquired a substantial American readership. As Stimpson puts it, "Until 1933 and the appearance of *The Autobiography of Alice B. Toklas*, only a few supporters knew that [Stein] was more than a bohemian character, an art collector, a language freak, or a joke" ("Gertrice," 132). It is obvious that *The Autobiography* represents a turning point in Stein's career, and as such it both alleviates and creates a crisis in her writing. Although it landed Stein her very first book contract at the age of 58, brought in some money, took her and Toklas to the United States on a lecture tour, and above all made possible the publication of her less accessible works, *The Autobiography* undermines itself as a worthwhile literary venture in the eyes of its author, since "the autobiographical act is one at odds with, even a betrayal of, Gertrude Stein's aesthetic principles" (Breslin, 149). Since Stein was "obsessed with the question of her own identity" but "became famous for writing in someone else's voice," the success of *The Autobiography* was not compatible with her conception of herself as a genius (Weiss, 94). One crisis was replaced by another.

Davis describes the stakes of publishing *The Autobiography* as follows: "Stein faced a dilemma: how could she, a Jew, a lesbian, publish a private 'love letter' to Alice as a best-selling book in America? After all, the reception of Stein's work was plagued by accusations that she was an illegitimate 'alien' whose experimental aesthetics called into question her claims to American citizenship" (37). In this context, both the accessibility and the narrative gimmicks of *The Autobiography* have been interpreted as strategic moves contrived by Stein to woo potential readers, "more decorous than she," into acceptance: "In a complex act of deception, confession, and assertion, a misunderstood, underpublished author is giving the public what she calculates it can take" (Stimpson, "Gertrude Stein," 152). This reading is supported by *Stanzas in Meditation*, the obscure companion text of *The Autobiography*: "I have tried earnestly to express / Just what I guess will not distress" (Part V, Stanza X, 583). Perhaps because of the need to court readers and critics, *The Autobiography* is a literary balancing act. It has been described as a modernist innovation, but it has also been recognized as part of a long tradition of American writing, "an elaborate tall tale in which Gertrude Stein creates herself as a legendary figure, given to outrageous bragging and superhuman abilities." The subgenre "mock autobiography" is said by Timothy Dow Adams to be invented by Stein for *The Autobiography*, but the device of "pretending to be someone else writing about [one's own] exploits" is typical of the tall tale.[1] Perhaps partly because of its affinity with a recognizable literary tradition, *The Autobiography* when published was eminently readable (a relief to readers wary of Stein's incomprehensible style, who could now feel initiated) and quickly became a bestseller.

At first glance, *The Autobiography* may seem coherent and unitary compared to Stein's more experimental works, but its dominant narrative, foregrounding Stein the genius at the expense of Toklas the wife, coexists with an alternative and very different version of the "same" structure. Like the other two Toklas autobiographies, *The Autobiography* is dominated in its entirety by the story of Toklas and her role in Stein's life and work, even as the text seems to preoccupy itself with the proclamation of Stein's genius, and this preoccupation or obsession follows very closely upon Toklas's proclamation of her own "genius" at the end of the first chapter, namely her aptitude for recognizing (and thus enabling) genius in others. My argument is that the text in fact invites critical engagement with a "true story" of Alice B. Toklas, but that this is the story of her being *indispensable* in very particular domestic and literary contexts rather than the seemingly transparent record of a straight autobiography. Moreover, the authorial ruse is not just a joke contained by Stein's "own" text but also pertains to the production of this text in the specific context of the domestic, sexual, and literary coupling of Stein and Toklas. Therefore, a reading of *The Autobiography* that returns to the question of authorship and expands the area for critical engagement to include this particular context (in other words, to include Toklas) is urgently called for. In this chapter I will talk about the irreducible doubleness of the authorial function in *The Autobiography*, the centrality of Toklas's enabling labor, and my conception of this text as a gift from Toklas to Stein (rather than the other way around).

There has been extensive speculation over the extent and defining importance of Toklas's influence on all the canonized modernist classics authored by her partner (see especially Bridgman, 209–17). *The Autobiography*, however, is a special case. The heretically doubled or split authorial signature of Stein's bestseller has puzzled critics and thwarted straightforward interpretations of it as one experiment among many Stein experiments. Most critics—myself included—have accepted the "obvious" premise that Stein *did* write *The Autobiography*, at least for the purposes of literary history and criticism. But the text itself refuses to offer a simple solution to the problem. At the time of publication, Stein requested that her name, her authorial signature, not be printed on the binding, the dust jacket, or the title page of *The Autobiography*. Instead, a Man Ray photograph captioned "Alice B. Toklas at the door" faces the title page, so that the splitting of the authorial function and the provisional merger of "she" and "I" characterize the text in its entirety, both inside and "outside." Breslin helpfully points out that "perhaps the most important point about this debate [concerning the true authorship of the *Autobiography*] is that it seems to have been generated not just by an extraliterary curiosity about the book's composition, but by an actual literary effect the book has on readers—namely, the effect of raising questions about just whose book it is" (151). In other words, the point of *The Autobiography* as text is to invite and provoke these questions—*and* to withhold the answers.

The Autobiography seems to epitomize the special case of autobiographical discourse treated by Lejeune in a chapter of *On Autobiography* entitled "The Autobiography of Those Who Do Not Write." During Stein's lifetime, while the elaborate division of labor structuring their marriage was in place, Toklas seemed unable (or at least unwilling) to write. Dydo points out that "Toklas always presented herself as amateur—secretary, typist, housekeeper—but never as writer, as if that was why Stein had to write her autobiography for her" (574). A possible context for this modesty is indicated in a letter from Carl Van Vechten to Donald Gallup: "Gertrude invariably told Alice she could not write. Even a cookbook. When Alice suggested this [Gertrude] ridiculed and tortured her, to such an extent that Alice never even wrote a long letter during Stein's lifetime. . . . On one occasion Alice was so upset and hurt that she did not speak to GS for a couple of days" (quoted in Dydo, *Gertrude Stein*, 574–75). Van Vechten's remark is truly remarkable, considering the amazing wealth of Toklas's later correspondence, starting with this telegram from Toklas to W. G. Rogers on the day of Stein's death: "Gertrude died this afternoon. *I am writing*" (*Staying On Alone*, 3, my emphasis). Toklas's picking up the pen only after Stein's death has caused some commentators to suggest that, at this moment of great sorrow and possibly great liberation, "her strong and vital personality emerged from the shadow in which she had deliberately kept it during Gertrude's lifetime" (Steward, *Dear Sammy*, 86).

In the early 1930s, Stein refuses to produce a "straight" autobiography, perhaps because venturing into the "low" genre of autobiography would destabilize the hierarchical structure that elevates her as genius in relation to lesser writers and, ultimately, in relation to Toklas. In the autobiography that she *does* write, she deflects this danger through an ingenious twist: fictionalization. This strategy is brought to the fore with a vengeance at the very end of *The Autobiography*: "About six weeks ago Gertrude Stein said, it does not look to me as if you were ever going to write that autobiography. You know what I am going to do. I am going to write it for you. I am going to write it as simply as Defoe did the autobiography of Robinson Crusoe. And she has and this is it" (342). The dynamics of this passage are quite remarkable. Stein, in a move of intricate substitution, slips into the (only) authorial place that is open to Toklas as the wife of a genius, turns Toklas into a fictional character (Crusoe), and fashions herself as the (male) creative artist (Defoe), thus evading the strictures that make it "impossible" for her to write *her* autobiography while, in a sense, blocking the passage to self-representation for Toklas. This move allows Stein to say everything she wants about her own greatness and other people's flaws and failures, but in Toklas's name, so that she is somehow removed from the swaggering and the gossip. At the same time, she closes the text by naming herself the author of a clever literary experiment. This is the brilliant move that has elevated *The Autobiography* to a remarkable position in literary history. As Dydo puts it: "This puts the best possible light on the affair and allows Stein, against all her earlier refusals, to get away with a book of memoirs, not her kind of writing, as a favor to Toklas" (*Gertrude Stein*, 536).

Several critics have pointed out that the ending of *The Autobiography* is radically ambiguous in its political implications. Stimpson argues that the "joke" about authorship has three principal consequences. First, the ending of *The Autobiography* "demonstrates Stein's theory about the impossibility of autobiography"; second, it turns the text into "a cautionary tale about the ease with which 'fact' can slip into 'fiction,' 'fiction' into 'fact'"; and third, the twist that ends *The Autobiography* "reveal[s] a contradiction in Stein's packaging of lesbianism. On the one hand, the coda is a tribute to the lesbian couple. . . . On the other hand, the coda maintains heterosexual roles. The husband, male-identified woman, has actually done the work of writing. The wife, the lady, merely speaks" ("Gertrude Stein," 157–58).

Stimpson's observation that the ending of *The Autobiography* is fundamentally self-contradictory is compelling. On the one hand, it is possible to read into it a challenge to the superior status of writing and writers in relation to, say, housekeeping and domestic laborers. If only there is time, and someone else takes care of all the practical aspects of life, *anybody* could be "a pretty good author." This reading would concur with the argument, forwarded by Norris and others, that Stein in her work wanted to envision equality, and even *equivalence*, among all people, men and women, and all professions, high and low. On the other hand, the potential challenge to the elevation of literary creation at the very end of *The Autobiography* is tempered by the fact that, as Weiss remarks: "Like the rest of the world, Gertrude Stein believed genius to be male" (63). Therefore, the impression we get from the ending of *The Autobiography* is the unblinking exposure of a strictly organized and vastly asymmetrical division of labor in the Stein–Toklas marriage, on the one hand, and, on the other, the power of Stein's words over Toklas's (textual) existence from "Ada" onward: "I am going to write it for you."

It is not surprising, because of the mock-autobiographical framework of the first Toklas autobiography, that Stein has sometimes been accused of treating her partner like a ventriloquist's dummy in the text. For instance, Hardack critiques Stein's strategy as follows: "Such unctuous ventriloquism reveals that third-person narration always creates monstrous dissonance and self-fissuring of some kind, a kind of autobiographical crash test dummy which takes the blows meant for the real driver who has long ago abandoned the vehicle" (27). Gilbert and Gubar claim that "although she satirizes great men by demonstrating their dependence on 'little women,'" Stein's "collaboration" with Toklas "becomes an appropriation that further effaces such women." They argue that the way in which Stein "Usurp[s] Alice's persona, appropriat[es] Alice's voice" is "a kind of cannibalism" that "demonstrates how lesbian collaboration can degenerate into collusion," and point out that "To 'have' Alice is to be a genius; but to 'be' Alice is to be fictionalized as a creature who functions like a rubber stamp" (251). In other words, Stein remains in charge, and Stimpson talks about the partial destabilization of authorship in *The Autobiography* as follows: "Playfully, *The Autobiography* might seem to foreshadow postmodern theories of the death of the author, but, in another contradiction, it at once defends and defeats them. Toklas can be Stein, but only if Stein dictates that. So doing, *The Autobiography* balances an unstable subject, i.e., a Stein who can seem to be Toklas for nearly an entire book, against a stable self, a Stein who can reassert her Steinishness at will" ("Gertrude Stein," 160).

In the final analysis, it is true that *The Autobiography*—despite the doubling of the autobiographical "I"—does not seem to radically threaten

Stein's claim to the superior role of author in relation to Toklas as mere "material" for her text. As Dydo points out, "Even once [Stein] mastered [Toklas's] voice, she retained authorship. In the *cahiers* for the final text, after notebook number and title . . . she often adds, as elsewhere, 'written by Gertrude Stein'" (*Gertrude Stein*, 542). At the same time, blaming Stein for appropriating Toklas's name and story and remaining in charge of the text will not bring us any closer to a productive reassessment of the text. Instead, recognition of the way in which Stein speaks for Toklas in *The Autobiography* can be coupled with a consideration of the way in which Toklas sometimes slips into Stein's place and speaks for *her*: "Gertrude Stein did not like going to offices—she said they, army or civilian, were obnoxious. To replace her, I had introduced myself with her official papers and had allowed the major to call me Miss Stein. What difference could it make to him. We were just two Americans working for French wounded" (*Cook Book*, 60). According to Adams, this incident, where Toklas substitutes for Stein in dealing with the French major in charge of gasoline, strengthens his theory of "Alice's natural predilection for mistaken identity." The major, when told about the ruse, is shaken: "He drew back in his chair and with a violence that alarmed me said, Madame, there is something sinister in this affair" (61). Another version of the "same" anecdote can be found in *The Autobiography*, where the major "almost jumped out of his chair. What, he shouted, not Mademoiselle Stein. Then who are you." He asks Toklas what she would have done if she had had to "sign something" (241–42). Adams claims that "this episode is representative of Alice's metaphor of self. For not only did she delight in pretending to be Stein in a story (told by Stein pretending to be her), but she also allowed Stein to 'sign something' in real life that she had actually written." He goes on to mention Robert Wilson's discovery that "although published as Gertrude Stein's work, the English translation of *Picasso* was actually done by Miss Toklas, with some slight revision by Miss Stein" (6–7).

It is interesting to note that Toklas lends her name, her signature, to other people as well. Stein recalls an anecdote about Janet Scudder, who wanted to exhibit a painting at the spring salon but was unable to do so a second time because of salon regulations. Therefore, "she suggested to Alice B. Toklas that she Janet would exhibit under her name," and Toklas said yes. The artwork attributed to Toklas is a female nude (YCAL MSS 76, Folder 4289), which intriguingly looks a little bit like Stein. Pablo Picasso is shattered when told that Toklas painted only this one picture and was accepted: "He was so upset that I began to laugh. What is the story he demanded. I told him and he was so relieved. I knew he said that it was not possible. It just could not be possible otherwise nothing would have any meaning" ("And now: And so the time comes when I can tell the story of my life," *Vanity Fair*, Sept. 1934, 33).[2] Picasso's reaction indicates how controversial it would be to imagine that Toklas actually *did* everything signed "Alice B. Toklas" and parallels the response of certain critics to the provocative suggestion that Toklas may have composed her own autobiography. This is not to say that I think she did—not in 1932, anyway. But I consider the ambiguity of authorship that characterizes *The Autobiography* as *text* to be an urgent invitation for the critic to fully engage with Toklas and her role in Stein's life and work.

The fact that Stein is the official author of the only text on Toklas that is actually labeled "autobiography" has been widely recognized and debated by critics. Stewart speaks of *The Autobiography* as "Alice Toklas' first 'dictated' book" and argues that "Toklas was not a puppet but a vital person of confirmed ideas—and those ideas were not always those of her biographer" (120–21). Other critics have contested rumors that Toklas wrote, or cowrote, *The Autobiography*. Stimpson, for instance, prefers to leave the traditional rendition of the Stein–Toklas writing pact intact and position Toklas as essentially and primarily liminal: "I believe that Toklas' typing, appraising, and editing often became a mild rewriting, but to call Toklas the writer, rather than the frame that kept the writer within bounds, would be excessive" ("Gertrice," 137, n. 25). The debate over authorship goes on, seven decades after the publication of *The Autobiography,* as critics seem adamant still in the twenty-first century to avoid a thorough reconsideration of the text as the inscription of a radically nonunitary lesbian autobiographical subject.

The scandal of collaborative autobiographies resides in the act of disregarding, twisting, or exceeding the autobiographical contract, defined by Lejeune as follows: "The device of the autobiographical contract results in facilitating a confusion between the author, the narrator, and the 'model' and in neutralizing the perception of the writing, in rendering it transparent. This fusion takes place in the autobiographical signature, at the level of the name on the title page of the book." Lejeune goes on to explain that "the autobiography composed in collaboration . . . introduces a flaw into this system. It calls to mind that the 'true' is itself an artifact and that the 'author' is a result of the contract. The *division of labor* between two people (at least) reveals the multiplicity of authorities implied in the work of autobiographical writing, as in all writing" (187–88). In accordance with Lejeune's theory of the scandalous effects of cheating the system, the question of authorship was raised in relation to *The Autobiography* even before publication: "I did a tour de force with *The Autobiography of Alice B. Toklas* and when I sent the first half to the agent they sent back a telegram to see which one of us had written it" (Stein, *Transatlantic Interview*, quoted in Johnston, 603, n. 16). This reaction is only to be expected, since the agent was still unaware of the reversal of the ending, where the authorial ruse is revealed. The same effect on readers was presumably repeated in the serialization of *The Autobiography* in the *Atlantic Monthly*, which began in May 1933.

When *The Autobiography* was published as a book in the fall of 1933, it was a huge immediate success and received a massive amount of positive attention, but it also sparked controversy. A supplement to *transition* magazine, aptly called "Testimony against Gertrude Stein," treats Stein "as if she were a criminal on trial" (Adams, 9). Eugene Jolas, one of the magazine's editors, immediately raises questions of history and truth in an introductory note: "*Transition* has opened its pages to several of those who, like ourselves, find that [*The Autobiography*] often lacks accuracy. This fact and the regrettable possibility that many less informed readers might accept Miss Stein's testimony about her contemporaries, make it seem wiser to straighten out those points with which we are familiar before the book has had time to assume the character of historic authenticity" (2). Jolas's justification for the "trial" of Stein and her book pinpoints the complicated relationship between word and world in Stein's work. In this case, the distance between the two is considered unacceptable, and those with a vested interest in another version of the "same" story gather to close the gap. Adams rightly remarks that the *transition* attacks on *The Autobiography*—like Leo Stein's embittered response to the same text—"are marked by a curious tone of malice and anger out of proportion to the inconsequential nature of the errors objected to" (8).

Tristan Tzara's contribution to "Testimony against Gertrude Stein" is particularly fierce. He calls the double-voicing tactic of *The Autobiography* a "childish subterfuge" of "two maiden ladies greedy for fame and publicity," deplores "a considerable display of sordid anecdotes," argues that Stein "understood nothing" about "humanly important enterprises," and ends with such phrases as "the exploitation of ideas," "'baby' style . . .

simpering at the interstices of envy," "a really coarse spirit, accustomed to the artifices of the lowest literary prostitution," "a clinical case of megalomania," and "the realm where lie and pretention meet the depraved morals of bourgeois society," all of which produce in him a feeling of "strong loathing" (12–13). This critical reaction to *The Autobiography* is similar to the reaction to modern art, specifically Henri Matisse's *Femme au Chapeau*, described in it (see Adams, 9).[3] The critical reception of Stein has changed since *The Autobiography* became an immediate bestseller and caused Tzara to condemn it, but it has remained split: "Since the 1970s, a mélange of audiences has inverted Stein's reputations. The Old Good Stein is the New Bad Stein. She is too obedient to convention. The Old Bad Stein is the New Good Stein. Her transgressions are exemplary deeds" (Stimpson, "Gertrude Stein," 152). From another perspective than the *transition* crowd and early Stein criticism, then, some latter-day feminists have also regarded *The Autobiography* with suspicion, not only in terms of its conventionality, as Stimpson suggests, but also by equating its scandalous authorial ruse with Stein's violent appropriation of her partner. It can be argued that Toklas's influence on Stein's work, her *indispensability* for it, bothers discourses of literary criticism much like it bothered contemporaries of Stein such as her brother Leo, her friend Luhan, and her protégé Hemingway and therefore triggers certain protective measures.

In my mind, the revolutionary thrust of *The Autobiography* does not reside in inconsequential errors or more or less disguised taunts, the covert representation of a lesbian marriage, or even an oppressive ventriloquist literary practice, but, what is more interesting, in the destabilizing effects of a doubled or split authorial function and the simultaneous inscription of multiple and often contradictory versions of the "same" story. Stein's delight in many different accounts of the same event is mentioned in *The Autobiography*: "Gertrude Stein rather liked [Wyndham Lewis]. She particularly liked him one day when he came and told all about his quarrel with Roger Fry. Roger Fry had come in not many days before and had already told all about it. They told exactly the same story only it was different, very different" (166). *The Autobiography* repeatedly presents the "same" story from different points of view in this way. For instance, three different descriptions of the battle of the Marne are included (202–3). There are many other examples of this practice. Concerning Matisse's painting, which "infuriate[s] the public" at the first autumn salon showing "the outlaws of the independent salon," the narrator first tells Stein's version of the story and then goes on: "And so this was the story of the buying of La Femme au Chapeau by the buyers and now for the story from the seller's point of view as told some months after by Monsieur and Madame Matisse" (46).[4]

The way in which *The Autobiography* constantly repeats the same story in different versions parallels the way in which the text itself is only one version of a story, the true story of Alice B. Toklas, which is also repeated elsewhere. If the pattern of telling and repeating stories is related to what is said about multiple stories in *The Autobiography*, three conjectures can be made. First, multiple stories that contradict each other may be enjoyed (and the storytellers liked) rather than considered unreliable and unacceptable in their incongruousness. Second, the existence of very different versions of exactly the same story does not necessarily prove that one version is correct and the others are lies. Third, a wife's story may sometimes take precedence over the story of a genius. The question of the "Good Stein" and the "Bad Stein" may then be reframed to set aside the questions of truth and lies, literary experiment and literary conventionality for a moment and instead think about the way in which a new *double focus* on Stein and Toklas transforms the critical debate. At the same time, the simultaneous inscription of several different stories complicates the task of recovering Toklas in the text. *The Autobiography* inscribes Toklas as indispensable to Stein's life and Stein's work but also blanks out her name, disguises her, denies her significance in relation to her genius husband, thus making it easy for a critic so disposed to invoke and then hastily retreat from the "other woman."

Because of the fundamentally evasive nature of *The Autobiography*—the way in which the text is centered on important omissions, silences, evasions, and distortions—my study must necessarily try to account for a certain elusive category of noncontent or nonidentity, a signifying absence that does not necessarily indicate a failed world/word connection but instead becomes part of discursive and intertextual considerations. The centrality of noncontent has occasionally been recognized by other critics: "Almost wherever one looks hardest for causes in the *Autobiography* 'there is a blank'" (Alkon, 864, quoting from *The Autobiography*). The way in which Toklas *herself* represents a signifying absence in the text is often overlooked, however. Sidonie Smith points out that "using 'Alice' as a piece of camouflage, Stein can make herself the egotistical center of [*The Autobiography*] and the influential center of twentieth-century modernism. . . .

[T]he art of camouflage can also be seen as a strategy for normalizing a culturally abnormal sexual relationship" (Sidonie Smith, quoted in Davis, 42, n. 21). Davis adds to Smith's suggestion that "Stein's use of camouflage is marked by the play of absence and presence in this text. Beneath the camouflage of Toklas, Stein is at once herself and not herself—at once present and absent" (42, n. 21). What is interesting about this interpretation is the way in which *Toklas* as camouflage disappears, steps aside to allow the critic to ascertain that Stein, "beneath" her, is both present and absent. In other words, the radically ambivalent present-absent function of Toklas in the text, the crucial intermediary level, is a critical blind spot. This is where my own investigation provides a much-needed counterdiscourse in relation to the general tendency among critics to invoke Toklas in passing and then to retreat quickly from a full consideration of her work and her indispensable role in relation to Stein.

It is remarkable that Toklas has been overlooked to such a great extent in Stein criticism and in literary history generally, considering the prominent spot in which "her" first autobiography positions her. The follow-up Stein autobiography, symptomatically called *Everybody's Autobiography* as if moving from the particular to the general level, generally avoids mentioning Toklas but still indicates that *The Autobiography* consists of a Stein–Toklas duet, a dialogue, with opinions and memories of both women intertwined and mixed up. On the one hand: "I said in the Autobiography that when one is young a great deal happens in a year" (91). On the other: "Alice Toklas . . . says she was raised in a temperate climate and she never can forget it" (93). Both these opinions are famously represented in *The Autobiography*, and it seems as though the "double" construction of this text can be seen as an opportunity for both women to speak their minds. Norris rightly suggests that the very *form* of *The Autobiography* would seem to resist a reduction of Toklas to Stein's other: "The political gender benefits of such a move [the narrative gimmick of *The Autobiography*] should include the feminization produced by a deauthorized authorial voice that lets itself be intersected by difference—a memoir in a dialogical (rather than monological) voice" (81).

At the same time, "if Toklas seems to write up *The Autobiography*, Stein writes her down in *Everybody's* [*Autobiography*]. . . . Stein casually and quickly dismisses Alice as the author of *The Autobiography*. So doing, she erases Alice as the gaze, the eye, that fixes Stein's identity, Stein's 'I'" (Stimpson, "Gertrude Stein," 159). Stein opens *Everybody's Autobiography* by revealing (or asserting) that in naming her wife, she was, according to the wife, in fact *mis*naming her: "In the first place she did not want it to be Alice B. Toklas, if it has to be at all it should be Alice Toklas and in the French translation it was Alice Toklas in French it just could not be Alice B. Toklas but in America and in England too Alice B. Toklas was more than Alice Toklas. Alice Toklas never thought so and always said so." Stein goes on: "This is the way any autobiography has to be written" (3). In the first few sentences of *Everybody's Autobiography*, then, the issue of naming, unnaming, and misnaming returns. Significantly, Toklas's very name is a source of contention, and her own version (Alice Toklas) is dismissed. Stein seems to be saying that any autobiography must misname its subject. Moreover, in this follow-up autobiography, her partner's name begins to signify *the book Stein wrote*, rather than the historical person Toklas: "I told in Alice B. Toklas how we found the house" (*Everybody's Autobiography*, 22).

One possible reading of these gestures in *Everybody's Autobiography* is that Stein, reportedly envious of anybody else's claim to fame, regretted having put Toklas in the limelight in *The Autobiography* and for the sequel decided to place herself safely back at center stage. As *Stanzas in Meditation* intimates, Stein may have been troubled by the mix-up of her and Toklas in *The Autobiography* and found it necessary to separate her authorial "I" from the "I" of the "other woman": "I am I / And that no one beside / Has my pride / And for an excellent reason / Because I am not only / All alone / But also / The best of all / Now that I have written it twice / It is not as alike as once" (LXX:V, 457–58). In this passage, "I am I" partly because "I am . . . all alone." In other words, Stein's identity *as a writer* depends partly on Toklas *not* being one. In any case, Toklas retreats to a position of obscurity in Stein's autobiographical work, where the emphasis is firmly placed on Stein as a solitary genius. But the writing of *The Autobiography* may also have worried and disturbed Toklas, who, according to her biographers, truly and completely wanted to remain a private person. It is quite possible, likely even, that Toklas asked Stein to play down the significance and influence of the companion-secretary in her later autobiographical writing in order to repair as far as possible the damage to her cherished anonymity after *The Autobiography* had made Toklas a household name. In other words, Stein's stepping back from a focus on her partner can be seen as the result of a marital (dis)agreement in which Toklas in fact demanded to be left out of the public eye. Knowing

Toklas's biography, it is impossible for the literary critic to "blame" Stein for abandoning the technique of lesbian dialogue used for *The Autobiography*. Indeed, I am not primarily interested in Stein's appropriation or disappropriation of Toklas, but above all in the way in which today's critics claim that this text speaks a lesbian dialogue surpassing the logic of either/or and then *still* proceed to drop Toklas out of the picture, thus reinstating the same binary structure. Even those critics of *The Autobiography* who seem to foreground the articulation and performance of a lesbian couple or coupling in the text have generally overlooked the full critical potential of a reading that suspends or troubles the question of authorship, and then takes the vast ramifications of such rethinking seriously. (For an example of this tendency, see for instance Karla Murphy's "'Convincing Lies' of Gertrude Stein: Cubism in *The Autobiography of Alice B. Toklas*.")

The evasive move of momentarily invoking Toklas and then utterly marginalizing her has been repeated again and again in literary critical and historical discourses. Critics who applaud *The Autobiography* for speaking in what may be called a dialogic lesbian voice and acknowledge the radical indeterminacy of its authorial signature typically turn away from the revolutionary potential of such indeterminacy as they call upon and then drop Toklas in order to define this text as the product of a single authorial and authoritative imagination (Stein's), despite the fact that this move would seem to call for a deconstruction of the myth of the solitary author along the lines of Trinh Minh-ha's call for a critical revolution: "Why view these aspects of an individual which we imply in the term 'writer' or 'author' as projections of an isolated self? . . . To confer an Author on a text is to close the writing. Eureka! It makes sense! This is it! I hold the key to the puzzle! Fear and seek. Fear and seek. . . . Seek and lose. Lose, freely. . . . Writing is born when the writer is no longer" (*Woman, Native, Other*, 35). The threatening nature of the Stein–Toklas union, even to complete strangers such as literary historians and critics, can apparently be related not only to its lesbian inflection but also to its departure from a certain normative construction of the great modernist writer as solitary and independent.

The Autobiography has been recognized as a challenging text that pulls a trick on the reader: "The joke is on the reader who believes that genre definitions control a writer and, therefore, that Toklas is really the author," Georgia Johnston says (595). Gilmore puts it this way: "If we ask:

'Whose autobiography is it?' Stein challenges the answer such a question seeks, as well as the assumptions that produce it" ("Signature," 63). I agree that *The Autobiography* amounts to a test for the reader. But most critics, like Johnston and Gilmore in these quotes, recoil at the uncertainty that characterizes *The Autobiography* and refuse to leave it open, even as they admonish the reader for wanting to settle the question. By reinscribing Stein as the solitary author in control of the text and its challenges, they foreclose the possibility of rethinking the category of authorship. Several other critical texts similarly seem to suggest a new double focus on Stein *and* Toklas but then proceed to reiterate the traditional narrative of Stein's authorship. My critique of this tendency constitutes a troubled and troubling counterdiscourse in relation to a certain critical conversation that may at the same time be said to constitute its closest ally. My ambition is to challenge the dominant practice of combining a professed focus on the lesbian couple as the new and radically nonunitary referent for the autobiographical "I" with a thoroughly conventional reinstatement of Stein as the solitary author in control of the text. It is my contention that this move simultaneously cancels out a potential threat to the (hetero)sexism of the genre and a potential feminist rearticulation of Stein *and* Toklas.

In "One As One Not Mistaken but Interrupted," Laurel Bollinger points out that the figure of Stein as popular writer after the publication and success of *The Autobiography* depended on the illusion of Stein's and Toklas's voices merging—that is, on the partial collapse of the wife/genius distinction. Bollinger suggests that Stein's famous writer's block after the publication of *The Autobiography* was the result not only of the well-known tension in her authorship between "real" writing and money-making writing, but in fact the result of a certain breakdown of the category of genius through the open display of a strong and supportive relationship behind the work. Even Bollinger's conceptualization of (inter)subjectivity, however, positions Stein as the operator. Toklas remains the *"other woman,"* entering into Stein's experiment in (inter)subjectivity as *material* rather than partner. Bollinger's discussion leads up to the assumption that "Stein seems to suggest that the answer to the Wife/Genius dichotomy lies within herself: she can be the dual figure who writes the successful novel and also the solitary genius who writes the experiments in language. She need not choose one over the other." Despite having stressed the ambiguity between relational and isolated positions in Stein's work, then, Bollinger drops Toklas altogether at the end of her article and brings Stein squarely back into the position of the solitary author in terms that almost suggest a parody of literary critical discourse, reducing dialogue to monologue: "The self can be dual, finding within its own fragmentation the necessary distance to make conversation possible and sustainable" (254–55). Bollinger's concept of (inter)subjectivity is revealed as distinctively ineffectual as it merges with thoroughly conventional constructions of individual authorship invested with unlimited knowledge and agency and the power to contain and reconcile paradox.

Another example of the same tendency to shy away from a destabilization of solitary authorship in *The Autobiography* is the important 1992 article "A Signature of Lesbian Autobiography," where Gilmore reprimands those who find fault with Stein's strategy of using Toklas's voice: "Readers who object to the troubling appropriation of Alice's voice evidence a confused and confusing homophobia" (67). Gilmore introduces her subject by defining *The Autobiography* as "a long love letter to Alice, a compensatory gift Gertrude wrote to appease her partner" but goes on to say that this move should be seen as a caution, since a focus on biography could "naturalize Stein's discourse as an 'expression' of identity," "miniaturize her as a member of a spatting couple," and "foreclose an inspection of Stein's autobiographical experimentalism, . . . her extended inscription of lesbian identity" (56). Gilmore's concern that Stein must not be "miniaturized" is striking, especially since her article is trying precisely to recover "the other woman as a lesbian" and articulate "a lesbian subject position in autobiography" (72, 63). In relation to these concerns, what is Stein if not "a member of a . . . couple"? If the most important aspect of *The Autobiography* is the inscription of a "double" lesbian subject, as Gilmore suggests, then why would it be amiss to emphasize the relational aspects, not only of the text, but also of its production? Apparently, a relation of proximity to Toklas and her "little" world threatens the (re)construction of Stein as a great modernist writer. It is significant that Gilmore speaks of "Stein," on the one hand, and "Alice," on the other, throughout her discussion. (At times Davis, Dydo, Norris, and several other critics likewise refer to "Stein" and "Alice" in a way that mirrors the patronizing treatment of women married or otherwise related to famous men.) The fact that "invocation and hasty retreat" is Gilmore's own term also speaks to the paradoxical nature of this tendency in Stein criticism. What does it mean that even she ends up dropping Toklas, in the light of her evident awareness of the problem of the "other woman"?

Judy Grahn similarly but less elegantly expresses concern that Stein runs the risk of being miniaturized—in Grahn's words, "exiled" in her "smaller self"—if Toklas is given too much space, allowed too much influence on the genius writer. "It is very important to distinguish between the two women, as otherwise we might try to read the bulk of Stein's work as if it is literary gossip, is arch, or snide, is sarcasm or wit," Grahn cautions and goes on to say that "most of [Stein's] writing came from her largest Self, the large, sweeping mind of a major language philosopher. . . . But by writing a slick, popular book full of famous, arty, cafe society names and observations from her lover's point of view, quite inadvertently she created a mask, named Alice B. Toklas, behind which we have exiled her in her smaller self" (132–33). Grahn goes on to give examples of Stein's and Toklas's styles of writing, which are meant to further distinguish between Stein's "largest Self" and the "smaller" gossipy wit of Toklas. In an extended argument (134–35), Grahn observes, first, that "Toklas' mind" in *What Is Remembered* is "trucking along in the linear anecdotal fashion of most people when they tell stories . . . stories on the order of snapshots, meaningful to those showing them; . . . not meaningful otherwise." She then claims that, in *The Autobiography*, "Stein's interpretation of Toklas' perspective retains her lover's linear story telling style but adds deeper meaning," and finally, a passage from *Everybody's Autobiography*—which is "Stein being more typically Stein"—is used to show how in *her own* work "Stein opens the meaning out still further." In Grahn's reading, Toklas's story is trivial, while Stein's version of it adds depth, although the close association with Toklas's "linearity" puts Stein at risk of being "exiled . . . in her smaller self," whereas Stein's *own* story is open and expansive, the limitless vista of Stein's "largest Self." In Grahn's reading, as in Gilmore's, association with the lesbian lover diminishes or miniaturizes the great author.

Although Dydo's work contains unprecedented acknowledgment of Toklas's role in Stein's life and work, and even though she recognizes that "text and context become enmeshed and are no longer easily separated. Reading Stein involves reading both" (*Gertrude Stein*, 43), even she seems to participate in the project of "liberating" Stein the genius from the influence of Toklas, the "other woman." Dydo may serve as an example of a certain general reluctance in critical discourses to accept Toklas's revisions of, and influences on, Stein's manuscripts as valid parts of the finished literary text. Her extensive archival research shows that the conflict between Stein and Toklas over the manuscript of *Q.E.D.*, an early Stein piece chronicling a youthful lesbian relationship with a woman named May Bookstaver, left concrete traces in Stein's writing, most strikingly since "the word *may* or *May* in all its forms is eliminated" from the manuscript of *Stanzas in Meditation* in "an attempt to purge the text" from the ghost of Stein's ex-lover (Dydo, "*Stanzas*," 13). Dydo's argument in relation to this discovery is that it is possible to *restore* the "original" text of *Stanzas* by disregarding Stein's substitution of "can" for "may" throughout. She proudly underlines the fact that both the sixth volume of the posthumous Yale edition and *The Yale Gertrude Stein* print the "revised, corrupt text," in other words, the text that supposedly reflects Toklas's input, whereas her own *Stein Reader* "restore[s] *Stein's original text*" (*A Stein Reader*, 568–69, my emphasis). The restoration is possible and necessary, Dydo argues, because "The revisions are personal and not literary" ("*Stanzas*," 13–14). This argument presupposes the existence of an "original" text, the master narrative untouched by the "other woman." In terms that indicate the possibility of unearthing Stein's master narrative from beneath the influence of Toklas, Dydo claims that a researcher must turn into a detective to penetrate the Stein–Toklas collection in the Yale archive (especially before it was properly organized, by Dydo herself and others): "And behind it all was the still, small voice of Alice B. Toklas. For all the long late years she answered questions and gave guidance out of her own appropriation of Stein. . . . Even beyond her death, in an archive largely set up on her terms, her voice can still be confused with Stein's own" (*Gertrude Stein*, 8).

It is true that, in her later work, Dydo seems to question the possibility of this very distinction between literary and personal dimensions, writing and biography, and text and context in relation to Stein's work (see *Gertrude Stein*, 43). She also retracts her earlier version of the story of Toklas flying "into a jealous rage" about *Q.E.D.*: "I was wrong. Even though Toklas later read the love affair into the poems, she knew nothing of it in the early summer, for she did not read *Q.E.D.* until much later in the year." Even though she changes her mind about the order of events, however, Dydo holds onto the conception of the revised version of *Stanzas in Meditation* as "adulterated" (491–92): "It is clear that the text of 'Stanzas' in the posthumous Yale volume is corrupt" (510). Moreover, her early interpretation of the way in which Stein's writing reflects her and

Toklas's private life, and how tensions in this private realm sometimes "corrupt" the text, has greatly influenced the entire field of Stein scholarship and may (or can) therefore be made to provisionally represent more general tendencies in literary critical debates. As I see it, the question of originality is vexed to such a great extent by sexual/textual tensions in the Stein–Toklas relationship that it is impossible to revert to a sense of pure original before corruption.

There are many examples of the same tendency to exclude Toklas from a consideration of Stein's work. Lynn Bloom, by way of a momentary focus on Toklas, arrives at the conceptualization of Stein as all-powerful author: "So Stein, both through selecting and revealing the real Alice's real views and through creating the persona of Alice-as-narrator-of-Stein's-autobiography, remains fully in control not only of her material but of her readers' reactions as well" (86). Bloom enumerates the advantages of *The Autobiography* (in her words, an "autobiography-by-*Doppelgänger*") over Stein's later autobiographies and points out that "Alice, even as a created persona, functions effectively as an editor in the *Autobiography*." She is unwilling, however, to consider Toklas beyond her status as a "created persona," a device testifying to "the uniqueness, innovativeness, and memorability of its creator [Stein]." Instead, Bloom repeatedly argues that "Stein, through Toklas, controls the reader as well as her material" (90–91) and plays down (even as she acknowledges) the importance of Toklas's contribution to the actual production of the text: "For the purposes of the first volume of Gertrude Stein's own autobiography, *The Autobiography of Alice B. Toklas*, Alice B. Toklas is no more of an independently functioning person than is Robinson Crusoe." Bloom goes on: "This is true even though, unlike Robinson Crusoe, Alice Toklas not only read but typed the manuscript and provided occasional corrections, interpretations, and cancellations" (81). Bloom's line of reasoning strikes me as remarkable in its refusal to consider the ways in which the "created persona" of Toklas in *The Autobiography* may challenge the conception of its "creator" as unitary, solitary, singular. To my mind, the acknowledgment of Toklas's editorial labor necessitates a critical engagement with her (as person *and* persona) beyond the facile dismissal of her as Stein's construction.

In the first paragraph of "Narratologies of Pleasure," Johnston specifically mentions Stein's "*own* text" twice and Stein's "*own* ending" once, as if to immediately establish singular authorship/ownership of *The Autobiography* (590–91, emphases mine). At the end of her article, Johnston argues for the necessity of "digress[ing] from the generic focus of Toklas writing the autobiography" and in the final sentence centers "Stein, who, *as author of the autobiography*, has moved herself to the margins while she is also ostensibly at the center of this text" (599–600, my emphasis). This insistence may not seem at all remarkable, since (as Bridgman acknowledged twenty-five years earlier) the manuscript *is* in Stein's hand, and the question of authorship may appear to belong exclusively to the text, Stein's "own" text, as a joke, as an experiment in style and genre. Moreover, as Lejeune points out, authorship is not a question of writing or composing but rather a question of being *recognized* as author: "the fact of writing is not sufficient to be declared an author. One is not an author in the absolute. It is a relative and conventional thing: one becomes an author only when one takes, or finds oneself attributed, the responsibility for the emission of a message" (192–93). It is true that Stein has been attributed the responsibility for authoring *The Autobiography* and that she therefore *is* the author. So why is Johnston trying so hard to exclude Toklas from a consideration of the text?

Johnston's article follows Ellen Berry's theory that "Stein's texts engender . . . the reading practices that must take place in order for the texts to be read" (601, n. 1). Referring to Hélène Cixous's "Laugh of the Medusa," Johnston promotes the "alternative" reading of *The Autobiography* presumably offered by the author: "A reader who digresses from the generic focus of Toklas writing the autobiography '[s]hatter[s] the framework' of autobiography's definitions," which enables the creation of "a 'brand new subject' like Ada" (599). In Johnston's reading of *The Autobiography*, Toklas is presented as author only in order to "articulate an alternative type of narrative and reading" (595) for the communication between Stein as author and her readers. Johnston briefly acknowledges that in *The Autobiography*, "Stein and Toklas switch places as 'I's. They merge; they stand not as individuals but create a lesbian couple" (595), but then she immediately moves on to focus on Stein as author on the one hand and, on the other, the reader who is free to choose the alternative reading offered by Stein. Johnston argues that "from the act of displacement itself, an alternative reading practice emerges, at least on the conceptual level. A reader may choose to move from this theory of alternative reading to the practice of alternative reading" (596). Johnston's assessment of *The Autobiography* as a whole, and this interplay between the author's concept and the reader's practice, is that "A traditional practice of reading, which separates subject and object and actively promotes mastery, is subverted in this autobiography from within its text" (595). What Johnston herself does in her analysis is *precisely* to separate "subject and object and actively [promote] mastery," since she so persistently emphasizes the solitary authorship/ownership of Stein and ignores the consequences of a lesbian "merger," which she dutifully mentions and then neglects. In short, Johnston seems to say that when Stein and Toklas "switch places," Stein is doing all the switching, and when Stein and Toklas "create a lesbian couple," Stein is the solitary creator.

Toklas is not merely *ignored* by Johnston, however, but eliminated in another, more elaborate way. Like many other critics, Johnston invokes Toklas and then hastily retreats from consideration of her role in *The Autobiography* and in Stein's literary production as a whole. After initially establishing Stein as the solitary author of "her own" text, Johnston moves on to momentarily open up her critical perspective in interesting ways to include the context of *The Autobiography* and the role of its ostensible subject, but then she takes a step back to once again foreground singular authorship/ownership of the text at the end of her article. Midway into her discussion, Johnston describes Toklas as a "conduit" between *The Autobiography* and its intertexts and even momentarily acknowledges the context of literary production and distribution as she draws a parallel between Toklas as "conduit" within and between texts and Toklas as "conduit" in the sense that she published Stein's work (596). As I see it, this part of Johnston's article represents a widening of her critical perspective to actually begin to consider the ramifications of saying that Stein and Toklas in *The Autobiography* "merge; they stand not as individuals but create a lesbian couple" (595). It is true that Johnston throughout emphasizes her unwillingness to suspend the basic analytical premise of Stein's solitary authorship/ownership of the text: "The joke is on the reader who believes that genre definitions control a writer and, therefore, that Toklas is really the author" (595). Nonetheless, her recognition of Toklas as agent in an intertextual web, and as publisher of Stein's work, indicates an awareness of the complexity of the question of authorship in relation to *The Autobiography*. In the last paragraph of her article, however, Johnston clearly and literally transfers the very role earlier given to Toklas to the reader, on the one hand, and to Stein as solitary author of her own text, on the other: "The reader becomes *a conduit* between the two texts. Rather than masterful subject who will be consumed, the reader becomes *catalyst, parallel to Stein, who, as author of the autobiography*, has moved herself to the margins" (600, my emphases).

In this way, Toklas is erased from Johnston's analysis. This maneuver is carried out under the code name of intimacy. Johnston intriguingly argues that the alternative reading of *The Autobiography* offered by Stein through "its intertextual web" creates "a widened angle," and Johnston includes an excerpt from Mildred Aldrich's book *A Hilltop on the Marne*, which is mentioned but not described or quoted in the text. According to Johnston, moving outside the text to get acquainted with its intertexts enables the reader to "enter into the reading position of Alice B. Toklas, a position of intimacy" (598). The reader and the author can, in Johnston's reading, freely choose reading/writing practices and create for themselves positions and roles at will. What are they if not "masterful subject[s]"? Over the last two pages of the article, by way of a powerful reader choosing freely to enter into Stein's alternative reading position ("a position of intimacy"), Toklas as *agent* in all senses of the word is eliminated, and the conduit is bypassed in a gesture of critical short-circuiting.

At the end of her article, Johnston mentions Toklas only to dismiss "the generic focus of Toklas writing the autobiography" (599), which, intriguingly enough, is a nonissue or a tactic of evasion, since the twist effected in the ending of *The Autobiography* has, generally speaking, prevented readers and critics from *ever* reading this text as a straightforward instance of the autobiographical genre (where the author's name on the cover, the narrator in the text, and the real-life writer "correspond"). Instead of this threatening imaginary reading of Toklas as author, Johnston presents us with, on the one hand, an "intimate reader" who, through "enter[ing] into the reading position of Alice B. Toklas" (598), in fact usurps or replaces her, and, on the other, a solitary author in control of the text who is singularly responsible for the switching of places and the doubling of the "I" in it. In my reading, contrary to Johnston's, the greatest challenge of reading *The Autobiography* is not to suspend the generic presupposition of Toklas having authored her own autobiography, which is a nonissue anyway because Stein did, but to take seriously the (im)possibility that *she might have*, in a certain strategic fashion that destabilizes the construction of authorship as singular and uncomplicated, and above all leaves the question open.

There are ways of reading *The Autobiography* as a record of the centrality and indispensability of the "other woman," without making her the author in a reversal of roles. In the present study, it is my argument that Toklas *enabled* Stein's work, not that she wrote or cowrote *The Autobiography*. This has been a controversial question in the history of Stein scholarship. In his landmark Stein study, *Gertrude Stein in Pieces* (1970), Bridgman remarks that the manuscript of *The Autobiography* is entirely in Stein's hand, indeed with fewer corrections and changes by Toklas than customary for a Stein manuscript: "The physical evidence indicates that *The Autobiography of Alice B. Toklas* was written by Gertrude Stein alone, with few hesitations or changes." Bridgman also seems to suggest, however, that Stein was persuaded, most likely by Toklas, to write in a style different from the one she chose originally: "There is at Yale . . . a preliminary notebook in which [Stein] made several false starts at the book. They are false, that is, if compared to the Alice Toklas who appears in the book. Otherwise, they are altogether characteristic of Gertrude Stein, the writer who found it difficult to maintain a single tone or topic for very long" (212).

Bridgman seems reluctant to define Stein as the solitary author despite his manuscript check. As Neuman points out, Bridgman's "conclusions stop just short of Alice's picking up the pen" (*Gertrude Stein*, 31). This critical inclination can be related to the fact, discovered by Bridgman, that the *cahier* manuscript of "Ada" in the Yale collection of unpublished documents is, in large part, in Toklas's hand (Yale Collection of American Literature, Beinecke Rare Book and Manuscript Library, MSS 76 and 77. From now on, I will refer to this collection as YCAL and indicate number of MSS and folder). This would mean, Bridgman argues, that "Alice Toklas composed the major part of her first, brief autobiography." His argument is that "given the manuscript in two hands; and given the conclusion that the two people are one, the evidence is persuasive that this was a collaboration of symbolic significance, sealing the relationship between the two women" (210–11). Bridgman's intimations made other critics, for instance Gilbert and Gubar, ask, "Is it possible that Alice B. Toklas actually wrote *The Autobiography of Alice B. Toklas*?" They go on to argue that "Toklas's authorship of other texts raises . . . doubts about the creator of *The Autobiography of Alice B. Toklas*, a work which is completely idiosyncratic in Stein's oeuvre, but which very much resembles Toklas's cookbook and her late memoir, *What Is Remembered*" (252–54).

Dydo's subsequent research at Yale has shown, however, that there is an original "*carnet*" of "Ada" in Stein's hand preceding the "*cahier*" copy upon which Bridgman based his hypothesis. (*Carnets* and *cahiers* are Dydo's terms for the small pocket notebooks and slightly larger manuscript notebooks, respectively, used by Stein.) On this basis, Dydo conceptualizes the "Ada" collaboration differently: "In the manuscript of *Ada* Stein and Toklas joined hands by sharing the labor of copying the text from the pocket notebook. Transcribed in both hands, the manuscript of *Ada* links Toklas' inspiring storytelling with Stein's story writing in a testament to a symbiotic relationship in which living and writing become one" (*A Stein Reader*, 100). Like Toklas herself, Dydo dismisses the very idea of actual cowriting: "Surely union in love is central for Stein and Toklas, but union in writing. . . . The very thought is preposterous. Where [Toklas's] hand is visible in the manuscripts, even with no first drafts preserved, it is because she copied, not because she composed" (*Gertrude Stein*, 35). Instead, Dydo describes the way in which Toklas as both "the beloved and the muse" makes Stein create "masterpieces of sexual fulfillment on the instrument of her body" and "literary masterpieces with the instrument of language" (28). Even as Dydo has helped establish the persistent image of Toklas as Stein's muse, which I find unfortunate and unsatisfactory in its lack of specificity and its resistance to considerations of history and labor, she also demonstrates her insight, gained during many years of research in the archive, into *the concrete practices of writing* that took place in the Stein–Toklas household: "What look like dog-eared corners at the outside top and bottom of many *carnets* appear to contain elaborate private signals from Stein to Toklas, showing her where to begin, what to do, how far to read or copy. Toklas apparently folded corners with return signals when she left the *carnets* for Stein to pick up again" (32). This type of (con)textual "evidence" is crucial not only for an enhanced understanding of Stein's work, but also for the expansion of critical attention to include Toklas and her indispensable role in relation to it.

In relation to Bridgman's ambivalence about the authorship of *The Autobiography*, Johnston suggests that Stein's "play with genre expectations" was so "overwhelming" that "even Richard Bridgman, one of Stein's first strong critics," was momentarily fooled by the hoax (603, n. 16). My argument, contrary to Johnston's, is that Bridgman in his early discussion concerning the question of authorship in *The Autobiography* comes closer to a rigorous recognition of Toklas's role than many other critics who have since prided themselves on looking through Stein's little joke, especially the red herring of ambiguous authorship. Although I challenge certain tendencies in the construction of literary history, the purpose of my study is not to commit heresy in Bridgman's sense of the term, in other words, to establish Toklas as the "real" author of *The Autobiography*, to elevate her to the rank of Stein and other great writers, or to bring Stein "down" to Toklas's level (for comments on the futility of such gestures, see Gilmore, "Signature," 56, and Grahn, 132–33). As many Stein critics have pointed out, it is impossible to find out the extent of Toklas's contribution to the writing of *The Autobiography* beyond the customary editing and typing she did for all Stein works. Precisely for that reason it might be possible and it might be desirable to suspend the regime of dominant knowledge for a moment, to dwell in the uncertainty or crisis that Bridgman identifies, to risk heresy perhaps, *but still not to settle the question*. Such a gesture must necessarily displace the reductive logic of either/or.

Bella Brodzki and Celeste Schenck define *The Autobiography* as "the ultimate female autobiography—with a difference. . . . Being *between two covers* with somebody else ultimately replaces singularity with alterity in a way that is dramatically female, provides a mode of resisting reification and essentialism, and most important, allows for more radical experimentation in autobiographical form than recent critics . . . have been willing to attribute to women writers" (11, emphasis in original). Brodzki and Schenck also posit the existence of "a textual third place" where Stein and Toklas are inseparable: "readers expecting a traditional autobiography feel compelled to choose between the biography of Toklas and the autobiography of Stein. Reading, in fact, requires no such choice: the blurred boundaries between Stein and Toklas as the autobiography constitutes them creates a textual third place from which 'she' speaks" (11). Unfortunately, however, Brodzki and Schenck do not go on to explore the specifically *lesbian* inflection of "being between two covers with somebody else" and do not problematize the construction of Stein as author/ity. In order to advocate their argument that Stein should not be "deprived her rightful place in a 'tradition' of ruptures in autobiographical practice" (11) on the grounds of her gender, Brodzki and Schenck seem to "choose" a conventional conceptualization of her as a modernist writer, utterly independent and in charge of her own text and her own experiments. As I see it, however, there is a need for further attention to the way in which solitary authorship is destabilized from inside the text itself, as well as an extended consideration of the level of production as another "third place," where boundaries between the one and the other cannot be easily upheld. This study is an attempt to push forward, between (book) covers, where others have turned around.

In the present study, I venture beyond momentarily invoking Toklas and then retreating from an extended consideration of her role to instead envision her as *indispensable*—in relation to Stein's work as well as to today's critical conversations. Like Johnston, I am interested in creating a widened critical perspective on *The Autobiography* by taking intertextuality into account. My primary emphasis, however, is not on intertexts referred to in *The Autobiography* but instead on various inscriptions of the ongoing text of "Alice B. Toklas," especially the three Toklas autobiographies that I have selected for study. The expanded critical angle that I apply to *The Autobiography* also includes a persistent focus on the *production* of the text in the specific context of the domestic, sexual, and literary coupling of Stein and Toklas. This is not merely to say that Toklas influenced Stein's work like many other wives, husbands, brothers, sisters, and friends of geniuses have influenced the work of a genius, but to instead insist on a concept of radical reciprocity, an irreducible dimension of *being between two covers with somebody else*, which undermines the hierarchical model implied in the genius/wife dichotomy, much like *The Autobiography* itself unsettles this binary.

As I see it, Stein is a great author precisely *on account of* Toklas's authorizing presence/absence, manifested for instance in her function as a gatekeeper. At the Saturday evening salon at 27 rue de Fleurus, "Alice acted both as a sieve and buckler; she defended Gertrude from the bores and most of the people were strained through her before Gertrude had any prolonged contact with them" (Imbs, 121). This is a position of considerable power and authority. In relation to the "mixing" or, rather, interface between two worlds, Toklas maintains order. As a "hovering presence," she patrols the boundaries between outside and inside and keeps separate spheres reasonably separate (Scobie, 124). Many of those who turned up to look at paintings and meet Stein testify to Toklas's role as "the gatekeeper and guide to [the] emotional states" of Stein as a Roman emperor (Stimpson, "Gertrice," 130). Imbs, who manages to pass the test of Toklas and take his place among Stein's favored "young men," is clearly impressed with Toklas's technique as gatekeeper: "She talked a blue streak. Without fluttering, or losing the trend of thought, or say anything superfluous, Alice Toklas could keep up a most intense, elaborate and rapid flow of conversation. If you really listened you very quickly fell under the mild hypnotic state which her mental pyrotechnics induced" (120–21). Toklas is generally considered the authority on conversation, whereas Stein did not excel in this particular art and knew it: "The continuous pleasant hesitating flow of conversation, the never ceasing sound of the human voice speaking in english, bothered her" (*The Autobiography*, 172). While Stein is the eccentric genius, the recluse, the infant prodigy who is easily bored and often cannot find anything to say, Toklas is the expert conversationalist.

Toklas in her role as gatekeeper to Stein's domain is not only famous for her excellent conversation skills and delicious baked goods. Among her contemporaries, she was also notorious and disliked for her unrelenting refusal to let certain people through the gate. Beach, for instance, recalls bringing Sherwood Anderson over to see Stein and indicates, less bitterly of course than some other people who were themselves victims of Toklas's "straining" techniques, that Toklas operated as an insurmountable obstacle for some people, notably wives, trying to get through to Stein: "Sherwood's wife, Tennessee . . . didn't fare so well. She tried in vain to take part in the interesting conversation between the two writers, but Alice held her off. I knew the rules and regulations about wives at Gertrude's. They couldn't be kept from coming, but Alice had strict orders to keep them out of the way while Gertrude conversed with the husbands" (55). This description of Sherwood and Tennessee Anderson's first visit with Stein is remarkable not only in terms of its reiteration of the familiar story of Stein's and especially Toklas's "cruelty to wives," but also in relation to a very different account of the "same" event in *The Autobiography*. Here, the narrator testifies that Beach was not even present at the time: "She later ceased coming to the house but she sent word that Sherwood Anderson had come to Paris and wanted to see Gertrude Stein and might he come. . . . he came with his wife" (266–67). What is even more interesting, *The Autobiography* claims that Toklas *herself* was absent on the day when she, according to Beach, wife-proofed Tennessee Anderson: "For some reason or other I was not present on this occasion, some domestic complication in all probability, at any rate when I did come home Gertrude Stein was moved and pleased" (267). Who is to be trusted?

Tennessee Anderson was not the only visitor subjected to Toklas's "wife-proofing cruelty." Despite the fact that she, as Picasso's wife, is actually allowed access to Stein immediately, Françoise Gilot records the experience as torture in *Life with Picasso*. With Picasso passively listening, she is thoroughly questioned by Stein and finds the questioning "worse than the oral examination for the *baccalauréat*," but Toklas is her main problem: "She looked as though she had dressed for a funeral. . . . She looked hostile, as though she were predisposed against me. . . . Her voice was very low, like a man's, and rasping, and one could hear the air passing loudly through her teeth. It made a most disagreeable sound, like the sharpening of a scythe. . . . whenever I said anything displeasing to Alice Toklas, she would dart another plate of cakes at me and I would be forced to take one and bite into it. They were all rich and gooey and with nothing to drink, talking was not easy" (172–74). Like Imbs and Beach, Gilot emphasizes the way in which Toklas uses the full range of her domestic expertise to regulate access to Stein, utilizing different means according to who wants it. Imbs, not a wife but a promising young man, is impressed by her conversation, enjoys her refreshments thoroughly, and is finally let through to Stein after taking his time with the gatekeeper: "I realized instinctively that Alice was important and required attention. My one idea, having arrived, was to be invited again" (122). The tormented Gilot, on the other hand, describes how Toklas's "heavenly" baked goods, much relished by other visitors, in fact in very concrete terms disturb the communication between her and Stein, silencing her. In her experience, Toklas's offerings are not nourishing or life-giving, but rather associated with silence and death (the sharpening of a scythe, the funeral attire). Stein invites Gilot back, but she has had enough of Toklas: "I might have gone back if I hadn't been so terrorized by Miss Stein's little acolyte, but I was and so I promised myself never to set foot in that apartment again" (174). Gilot seems to echo the sentiments of several potential friends of Stein who proclaim themselves scared off by Toklas when she points out that it is "easier to get along without [Stein] than to take her in tandem with Alice B. Toklas" (175).

It can be argued that readers and critics, too, must either "get along without Stein" or "take her in tandem with" Toklas. Not only in Stein's life but also in *The Autobiography*, Toklas functions as a medium or conduit between Stein and the world, specifically Stein and her readers. Ever since *The Autobiography* was published, critics have recognized Toklas's function as a go-between, creating a link between Stein and her readers. In *The Autobiography*, Toklas's blue-streak conversation, ostensibly "imitated" by Stein, hypnotizes the reader and submits her or him to the procedure of being "strained through" Toklas. Imbs's sieve and buckler image is attractive and helpful as we move into the text but at the same time invites simplification. It could be interpreted as another way of saying that the ideal reader (who is neither boring nor annoying) will be able to get past Toklas, enter Stein's domain, and thereby leave Toklas behind, which is precisely what many critics do or claim to have done. Obviously, the impulse to wish the gatekeeper out of the way is part of the dominant construction of interior and exterior, where the gatekeeper turns into a dispensable obstacle on someone's path to reach the supposedly independent and preexisting interior. This is a model that does not acknowledge the way in which the "frame" *constitutes* that which it frames. If Toklas the sieve and buckler is ignored, there is no core or interior to be found, since she, by patrolling its borders, enables the very existence of the interior. The introduction to Dydo's latest book seems to suggest that it is possible to bypass Toklas as the gatekeeper of Stein's literary production and to avoid confusing her voice with Stein's by concentrating on Stein's work as it can be traced in manuscripts. In my mind, however, Toklas in her gatekeeper function cannot be evaded, not even by the literary critic in search of an essence uncorrupted by the presence of the "other woman." In other words, Toklas is not dispensable.

Toklas's reason for not writing her own autobiography is explained immediately before the exposure of the authorial ruse of *The Autobiography*: "I am a pretty good housekeeper and a pretty good gardener and a pretty good needlewoman and a pretty good secretary and a pretty good editor and a pretty good vet for dogs and I have to do them all at once and I find it difficult to add being a pretty good author" (342). This is Toklas's rationale for letting Stein "write it for her," turning her into an unlikely descendant of Robinson Crusoe. In an abundance of biographical materials, and in their own autobiographical writings, Stein and Toklas seem to inhabit a fixed and unchanging economy of power, pleasure, and labor where writing, cooking, gardening, driving, and a number of other occupations are organized in intricate ways in relation to certain rigid dichotomies. Toklas's work, available to us in various texts, is part of an economy that regulates the relations and responsibilities of an unconventional lesbian marriage along the lines of traditional patriarchal marriage structures. Generally speaking, Toklas spent most of her life with Stein thoroughly occupied with domestic and editorial labor, all the while conscious of the fact that her husband did not like to see her work—"Six white pigeons to be smothered, to be plucked, to be cleaned and all this to be accomplished before Gertrude Stein returned for she didn't like to see work being done" (*Cook Book*, 40) and moreover refused to do any work herself: "It is quite true what is known as work is something that I cannot do it makes me nervous, I can read and write and I can wander around and I can drive an automobile and I can talk and that is almost all, doing anything else makes me nervous" (*Everybody's Autobiography*, 316). In this way, and even as their copy subverted not only the original but also the very concept of originality, the two women took their gender-bending performance of patriarchal marriage structures very seriously.

It seems as if, in the highly structured Stein–Toklas marriage, Stein *only* wrote and therefore was a real writer, whereas Toklas was the secretary-companion and therefore was not expected to produce writing of her own. At night, after Toklas went to bed, Stein the genius was trying to bring the English language into the twentieth century. The next day, Toklas the secretary juggled typing, editing, cooking, and housekeeping chores. The division of labor and alternate arrangement of day and night, work and sleep, are well known in the legend of Stein and Toklas. When both women are awake, Stein's immediate needs govern Toklas's every move. It is true that Stein, as the husband, also did all the driving and helped some with the gardening, which was primarily Toklas's domain. There are many hilarious stories, however, about the way in which Stein and Toklas upheld a strict division of labor, according to which Toklas took care of everything practical and Stein was unable, unwilling, and probably not allowed by Toklas to do much of anything (except writing). In *Everybody's Autobiography*, Stein describes an encounter with a photographer on their 1934 U.S. tour. He wants her to "do" something in the photos, and she asks for suggestions: "Why he said there is your bag supposing you unpack it, oh I said Miss Toklas always does that oh no I could not do that, well he said there is the telephone suppose you telephone well I said yes but I never do Miss Toklas always does that, well he said what can you do, well I said I can put my hat on and I can take it off and I can put my coat on and I can take it off and I like water I can drink a glass of water all right he said do that so I did that" (218–19). This is the well-known legend of the Stein–Toklas marriage as it has been organized for popular history. Based upon abundant biographical and autobiographical "evidence" of this kind, the story of Stein and Toklas can be simplified into a stark binary model, in which Stein exploits her wife's labor, in general sleeping, resting, reading, and wandering around all day except for short writing sessions, while her wife toils endlessly in the kitchen and the garden.

These roles were probably partly invented for, or at the very least exaggerated in, the Toklas autobiographies and other textual representations of the couple. At the same time, I recognize the validity of Stimpson's biographical analysis: "We, who value freedom and options and flexibility, must accept the possibility that the very firmness of [Stein's and Toklas's] roles helped them to surmount the difficulties of their [sexual] deviancies" ("Gertrice," 129). But the power balance of the relationship and the daily routines organizing it are more complex than it may seem, and there are accounts that depart from the dominant narrative of the Stein–Toklas relationship. Luhan, for instance, speaks of Toklas in a way that seems to exclude the dimension of manual labor: "She was forever manicuring her nails. Her hands were small and fine and with the almond-shaped, painted, glistening nails they looked like the hands of a courtesan. Every morning, for an hour, Alice polished her nails—they had become a fetish with her. She loved her hands" (324). Luhan makes Toklas's nails stand for her entire existence: "I couldn't understand Alice. Her life seemed to me so featureless. Gertrude had her writing and I had my struggle with my body and its continual 'Sturm und Drang'; it was my tension. But Alice seemed to me to have only her polished, painted nails" (*European Experiences*, 332). Considering the elaborate preparations for Stein's breakfast and the manicure habit reported here, it seems as though Toklas had very long mornings. The combination of high-maintenance nails, household drudgery, and incessant gardening is only one among many incompatible combinations suggesting that there may not be only *one* true story of Alice B. Toklas.

There are other ways in which the rigorous division of labor and fixed roles in the Stein–Toklas relationship at times seem to shift and crumble. Despite Toklas's background position in the official version of the Stein–Toklas legend, many friends have testified that Stein was almost completely dominated by her strong-willed companion in their private life. Diana Souhami's version of the events that led up to the writing of *The Autobiography* is that Toklas *demanded* that Stein produce something profitable. She was, according to Souhami's conjecture, fed up with the pile of unpublished manuscripts and the lack of money: "Alice, quite simply, wanted [Stein] to write something that made money. She did not like selling their paintings to pay for private publishing. Shove is proof of love, said Gertrude, and reluctantly agreed to go commercial" (187). This is a remarkable reversal in relation to the dominant narrative of the Stein–Toklas division of labor and would seem to displace the common conception of Toklas as a submissive and self-sacrificing wife: The wife demands that the genius get to work, even to the extent of lowering her aesthetic standards, in order to support them. It is important to note, however, that exceptions from and destabilizations of the description of the Stein–Toklas union as a patriarchal marriage are not necessarily truer than the dominant version of the story of the relationship. The many true stories of Stein and Toklas compete for dominance on the level of discourse without secure anchoring in reality. Even as I try to take into account Toklas's labor in a material and historical sense, as it bears upon the writing of literary history and the distribution of literary value, I am necessarily still dealing with the *legend* of Stein and Toklas and their division of labor.

My own research at Yale, and my exploration of Dydo's work, have resulted in an enhanced awareness of the intricate ways in which texts passed back and forth between Stein and Toklas—not only how Toklas (an early riser) in the morning typed Stein's handwritten pages from the previous night, while Stein slept until noon, but also how Stein and Toklas frequently took turns copying by hand into *cahiers*, how Stein sometimes seems to imitate Toklas's neat handwriting (which means that her writing suddenly becomes legible), and how Toklas's domestic to-do lists are frequently folded in with Stein's literary exercises: "[Stein's] notebook has a draft of an essay in her own hand on one page, with a shopping list in French in Alice's hand on the next. Alice's list also includes, in English, some crucial household tasks, such as taking their poodle Basket to the 'farmacy.' The daily tasks outlined in Alice's unselfconscious writing, and undertaken solely by her, made possible Gertrude's self-conscious writing on the next page, which, appropriately enough, Gertrude titled 'how to write'" (Weiss, 66). Weiss pinpoints the way in which Toklas's enabling labor pertains not only to the realm of living (the practical aspects of having a dog) but also to the realm of writing, and she thus indicates that the separation of the two, and the exclusion of Toklas from a consideration of Stein's work, must be considered an impossible critical undertaking.

A few critics have analyzed the division of labor in the Stein–Toklas household in such a way as to take Toklas's indispensable role into account. For instance, my own work follows Blair's "Home Truths," which in a very intriguing way suggests "a dense entanglement between modernist culture making, avant-garde practices, and bourgeois commodity logic" (427). Blair points out that many historians and critics have identified "antidomestic fervor" as "a leading feature of modernist . . . postures of cultural response." What is rejected is the "social logic of separate spheres" (429). Blair argues, however, that the imagined community of reception remains firmly located in the "bourgeois domestic," with culture being "a consumer good to be delivered into the privacy of [one's] own home" (429). In relation to my own focus on the division of labor and the butch-femme role-play in the Stein–Toklas marriage, Blair's insights are highly pertinent: "In 27 rue de Fleurus, doing the marketing refers simultaneously (if not equally) to the work of domestic management and the strenuous labor of culture" (429). The point of Blair's survey of overlapping domestic and avant-garde spaces is to ask "how prevailing notions of avant-garde literary production shift when we understand the latter as embedded in the changing form of domesticity. The very notion of the avant-garde itself . . . looks very different when we consider not only the isomorphism of the bourgeois home and the modernist salon, but the fluid, bidirectional circulation of texts, tastes, and fantasies between those sites" (419). In fact, Blair points out, "the circulation of avant-garde texts and bourgeois objects, the architecture of distinct zones of reading, are mutually determining processes" (433).

If, in a very simplified scheme, Stein can be said to stand for "avant-garde literary production," and Toklas for "domesticity," Blair's argument that prevailing notions of the former sphere may change as the two are reconsidered as "embedded" (in bed together) and overlapping is extremely relevant to my own attempt to insert Toklas into the ongoing debate on Stein in general and *The Autobiography* in particular. According to Blair, Man Ray's famous photographs from inside 27 rue de Fleurus, which show a space distinctly divided between "bourgeois bric-a-brac and avant-garde masterworks," represent Stein and Toklas as "joint producers of a space or realm of experience, in which 'pleasure in a home' . . . is ultimately coextensive with the auratic zone of an authentic avant-garde" (424–25). Blair mentions Toklas only in passing, since she is talking specifically about Stein's "If You Had Three Husbands" and its publication in *Broom* as indication that both writer and journal recognize "the coextensiveness of avant-garde and domestic spaces" and "render visible the material circuits through which the literary travels" (431). In my opinion, however, Blair's ideas can be applied to the texts under consideration in the present study. The same overlapping of spaces and open display of the concrete materiality of literary production characterize not only *The Autobiography* but indeed all three Toklas autobiographies.

My own reading of the Toklas autobiographies has been particularly influenced by Blair's argument that "we need to consider the effects of spatial proximity, contiguity, and simultaneity: the bracing unevenness of cultural fields that are at the same time built environments, forms of metropolitan sociality, sites of labor, pleasure, and reception, and dwelling places" (433). With Blair's argument in mind, it is interesting to consider a number of passages from the Toklas autobiographies where the "separate spheres" of Toklas's domestic and editorial labor and Stein's avant-garde literary production are brought into critical proximity and made to overlap and sometimes merge. For instance, Toklas reading "Ada" for the first time while complaining that dinner is getting cold, Toklas embroidering Picasso motifs, and Toklas "domesticating" some of Stein's most famous experiments in language and literature: "Speaking of the device of rose is a rose is a rose is a rose, it was I who found it in one of Gertrude Stein's manuscripts and insisted upon putting it as a device on the letter paper, on the table linen and anywhere that she would permit that I would put it. I am very pleased with myself for having done so" (*The Autobiography*, 187). Blair argues that a reconceptualization of "the place of the literary" as a question of material and social spatiality entails an understanding of literary objects as "embedded in the life-worlds they register, reimagine, address, and reject" (433). I would like to add that "life-worlds" are not only registered but also partly *created* by literary acts and by the domestic labor that organizes and enables both worlds and words. It is impossible to determine which comes first, life or text. Toklas is indispensable in both realms.

In my exploration of the issue of labor, and my emphasis on the existence of an alternative true story of Alice B. Toklas in *The Autobiography*, I am also very much indebted to Norris's brilliant but little-known article "The 'Wife' and the 'Genius.'" Norris rightly argues that, in *The Autobiography*, "Stein overwrites the work of male genius with what underwrites it: the wife's double labor." I agree with her that *The Autobiography* (like the *Cook Book*) can be seen as "a form of portraiture in which the variety of creative labors performed by wives—including modeling, millinery, domestic art, cooking, needlework, typing, proofreading, and publishing—can be restored to visibility and equalized in value with the fine art of genius" (89–90). Norris quite rightly points out that the great men of *The Autobiography* are often eclipsed "with the shadow of interesting or heroic women" like Fernande Olivier (Picasso's lover), Hélène (Stein's cook), and Madame Matisse (85) and that Stein seems to use these great men as a corrective: "As she portrays geniuses painting the portraits of their wives, her own implication in the same gesture is as vulnerable to demythification as that of a Matisse, who serves as her cautionary mirror" (89).

Norris's alternative reading of *The Autobiography* does not lead up to the exclusion of Toklas from the picture. Instead: "The alternative reading would require readers to assume the sight and interest of Alice's implied reader of *The Autobiography*: that of a wife" (86). Norris specifies the "ideal reader" of *The Autobiography* as "an essentially *new gender*: the intellectual wife" (91). This ideal reader position would then constitute a position of solidarity, perhaps, with the wives behind the scenes of modern art, including Toklas (who is not eliminated but instead made part of a group). Norris argues that Stein's aim is "to transform the *effacement* of wives into a *refacement* that is different from their portraiture in the works of genius. . . . [T]his becomes a project of *repopulation*—a recasting of the history of modern art replete with all the obscure contributions of wives, mistresses, servants, and sisters" (86). In Norris's opinion, then, Stein in *The Autobiography* presents "a revisionary gendered economics of modern art that encompasses overdetermined contributions by women of capital, patronage, domestic labor, technical labor, domestic art, publishing, and so on" (93). The reward for women who support modern art and modernist writing, it seems, is when genius recognizes and acknowledges the value of their aid: "Against this exploitation of the wife . . . for unpaid technical labor, Stein prominently foregrounds Toklas' contributions as typist, proofreader, and publisher. . . . The question of whether or not Alice actually contributes to the writing of Stein's texts . . . implicitly sustains the prestige gulf between various kinds of creative labors that *The Autobiography* may, in fact, be radically revaluating" (95).

I find Norris's reading eminently useful, above all her insight that "Stein overwrites the work of male genius with what underwrites it: the wife's double labor," and the way in which she then goes on to complicate the picture in order to distinguish between wives of various circumstances: "The hats of some wives of geniuses are underwritten by the wives of others. Fernande and Alice's celestial hats might, hypothetically, have been made by a poverty-stricken Madame Matisse" (89). In this way, Norris opens up *The Autobiography* beyond a narrow reading of ventriloquism and genius/wife asymmetry into an extensive consideration of gender, class, and labor issues in the text. My own reading of the "other" narrative in *The Autobiography*, the story of Toklas as indispensable in Stein's life and Stein's work, is greatly indebted to Norris's article. Despite the potential for a very interesting connection to Toklas autobiographies in the plural, however, Norris ignores the question of Toklas's own writing and dismisses the question of influence on Stein's writing: "The question of whether or not Alice actually contributes to the writing of Stein's texts . . . implicitly sustains the prestige gulf between various kinds of creative labors that *The Autobiography* may, in fact, be radically revaluating" (95). Contrary to Norris, I still think the question is worth asking, although the most sophisticated reading will defer the answer. Norris also neutralizes the ambiguously but inescapably exploitative nature of the genius–wife relationship by arguing that the "troublesome political implications" of *The Autobiography* can be reinterpreted as a "politically benign" gesture on Stein's part: "What must be repressed by critics both hostile and friendly to Stein, it seems, is the reading of *The Autobiography* at a kind of face value, as the memoir that disrupts the master–slave dialectic of its gender conventions utterly by having genius, for once, offer recognition and prestige to a wife—indeed, not just to an individual wife but to the collective wives of modern art" (84). The problem is that the master–slave dialectic *remains*, in part, despite these destabilizations of the genius/wife binary, and is brought to a much higher level of visibility in the second chapter of *Everybody's Autobiography*, entitled "What Was the Effect upon Me of the Autobiography" and dealing primarily with money and the significance of money. Here, Stein not only emphasizes the crude economical benefits of publishing her partner's autobiography but also unashamedly excludes Toklas from enjoyment of the profit from *The Autobiography*, "all honestly earned": "first I bought myself a new eight cylinder Ford car and the most expensive coat made to order by Hermes and fitted by the man who makes horse covers for race horses for Basket the white poodle and two collars studded for Basket. I had never made any money before in my life and I was most excited" (40–41).

A new car for herself, expensive gifts for the dog—but Toklas is hardly mentioned at all, except as admitting that she was wrong about the bestseller potential of "her own" autobiography: "While I was writing it I used to ask Alice B. Toklas if she thought it was going to be a best seller and she said no she did not think so because it was not sentimental enough and then later on when it was a best seller she said well after all it was sentimental enough" (46). Dydo's question seems highly pertinent in this context: "Fame . . . belonged to Gertrude Stein as a well-known writer; did Alice, who shared Stein's life but not her name, share in the fame?" ("*Stanzas*," 9). It is true that Toklas sometimes seems to surface in *Everybody's Autobiography* as the other party in an ongoing dialogue that is impossible to suppress entirely in a narrative concerning Stein's life: "Well Alice B. Toklas would say that depends on who you are" (87). Stein also admits from time to time that Toklas's labor is her privilege: "Alice B. Toklas is always forethoughtful which is what is pleasant for me so she said she would make copies of all my writing not yet published and send it to Carl Van Vechten for safe keeping" (11). On the whole, however, Toklas is marginalized in, or even excluded from, *Everybody's Autobiography*. Stimpson compares *The Autobiography* and *Everybody's Autobiography* and concludes that the latter text, unlike the former, "asserts the authority of the self, especially that of the genius/author" ("Gertrude Stein," 160). As I have indicated above, I think Norris is right about the "dehierarchized gender configurations that emulsify wives and geniuses" in *The Autobiography*. But I also think this is a fractional reading. A "prestige gulf" still remains to some extent between the worlds of fine art and "wifely" arts, and I think Norris is stretching it when she locates the impetus for a destabilization of these categories in a "political gesture" on Stein's part.

A quick look at the text itself indicates the way in which the issue of labor in *The Autobiography* is fundamentally ambiguous and must not be settled prematurely. The narrator famously argues that her own primary way of relating to art and literature, that is, dusting, typing, and proofreading, is superior (in terms of knowledge, recognition, and aesthetic sensation) to Stein's habit of just looking and reading: "I always say that you cannot tell what a picture really is or what an object really is until you dust it every day and you cannot tell what a book is until you type it or proof-read it. It then does something to you that only reading never can do" (153). The passage on the value of dusting must, however, be read with caution. This is one of many examples of textual themes that can be read both in terms of the alternative version of *The Autobiography* as a record of Toklas's indispensable and qualified role *and* in terms of Stein's exploitation and devaluation of Toklas's drudgery, a subtext impossible to divest oneself of completely in a rigorous reading of the relationship. Significantly, the narrator's words of wisdom return with a malicious slant (almost the same but not quite) in relation to Hemingway, who copied and proofread for Stein at one point: "Correcting proofs is, as I said before, like dusting, you learn the values of the thing as no reading suffices to teach it to you. In correcting these proofs Hemingway learned a great deal and he admired all that he learned" (294). In relation to this latter passage, and to the portrait in this text of Hemingway as "a rotten pupil," the effect of dusting and proofreading is transformed from a superior ability to "tell" what something "really is" into a realization and acceptance of inferiority. This type of ambiguity must be acknowledged in any reassessment of the Stein–Toklas division of labor.

Many critics have claimed that *The Autobiography* is in fact Stein's autobiography and have pointed out that it is almost entirely *about* Stein, so that Toklas is completely marginalized in the very text that first names her. It is true that Stein, or more particularly her genius and her importance as the "first twentieth-century writer" (72), dominates *The Autobiography* in terms of space and general prominence. In terms of the structure of the text, however, and certain points of particular emphasis, another version of the gist of *The Autobiography*, one that instead centers Toklas and her enabling function, can be constructed. The first part of *The Autobiography* revolves around what Toklas saw as she first arrived in Stein's world, that is, her first impressions. In connection with this there is an insistent focus on origins, on initiation, on beginnings. A related theme has to do with knowledge and Toklas's (and the reader's) gradual acquirement of insider knowledge pertaining to this inaugural moment and setting, when "two americans," in other words, Gertrude and Leo Stein, "happened to be in the heart of an art movement of which the outside world at that time knew nothing" (37). This is where the narrator most forcefully operates to create connections between her own sphere and the sphere of geniuses and great artists. The movement performed by the text is that of an outsider entering the insider realm of specific knowledge and of imparting that knowledge to other outsiders (the readers): "of course I did not know what [the vernissage of the independent] was all about," Toklas says. "But gradually I knew and later on I will tell the story of the pictures, their painters and their followers and what this conversation meant" (19–20). Statements such as these, recurrent throughout the first part of *The Autobiography*, not only create tension and expectation but also *enact* the trajectory of Toklas moving toward the very center of this insider realm of specific knowledge: Stein. In instances such as these, it becomes quite obvious that Toklas in the text functions as a conduit or go-between, who by staging her own gradual initiation to Stein's world enables the reader to follow at a certain pace and to a certain point.

The story, in other words, is not only about the beginning of modern art and literature, but also and above all about the way in which Toklas arrives from outside and, through a gradual acquisition of insider knowledge, begins to *recognize* this moment in history. Back then, the outside world knew nothing, but now, at the moment of writing *The Autobiography*, through the recreation of origins as Toklas saw them, and the rehearsal of knowledge as Toklas gradually gathered it, the reader can be initiated and enlightened, too—much like people who knew Toklas personally and relied on her for information. About one visitor to the salon, the narrator says: "He never dared to criticise anything to [Stein] but to me he would say, and you, Mademoiselle, do you, pointing to the despised object, do you find that beautiful" (134). Similarly, Aldrich is troubled by the art of Matisse and Picasso and asks Toklas for the truth, her conception of insider knowledge: "One day she said to me, Alice, tell me is it alright, are they really alright, I know Gertrude thinks so and Gertrude knows, but really is it not all fumisterie, is it not all false" (164). As a liminal figure, Toklas not only possesses insider knowledge but also a position that allows her to impart such knowledge to the outside. This is the position that makes possible *The Autobiography*. It is also a position of authority and power in relation to the story. As I see it, therefore, the question is not so much "Could *The Autobiography* have been written without Stein?"—the answer being no without a doubt—but what is more interesting, "Would this text have been possible without Toklas?" My argument is that Toklas is indispensable for *The Autobiography* in the same way that she was indispensable in Stein's life and work from 1907 onward.

It is somewhat surprising, considering the emphasis on *the* beginning in *The Autobiography*, that there is an abundance of beginnings in the text itself. Chapter 5, entitled "1907–1914," starts: "And so life in Paris began and as all roads lead to Paris, all of us are now there, and I can begin to tell what happened when I was of it" (116). Notwithstanding the intriguing mix of past and present in this sentence, of course this story was begun already at the end of chapter 1. The proliferation of references to the beginning in this text, the way in which the *firstness* of Toklas's arrival in Paris is emphasized again and again, in fact subverts the meaning of originality as *the first time* is described in different variations. Also, the emphasis on chronology, a time line starting in those "first days," is contradicted by an impulse to freeze the original moment and make it timeless: "But to return to the beginning of my life in Paris. It was based upon the rue de Fleurus and the Saturday evenings and it was like a kaleidoscope slowly turning" (120). In the beginning 27 rue de Fleurus is a strangely unchanging place: "And everybody came and no one made any difference. Gertrude Stein sat peacefully in a chair and those who could did the same, the rest stood. . . . My memory of it is very vivid" (167).

The chronology of the narrative is sometimes obviously skewed, for instance, at the juncture of chapters 3 and 4. The last sentence of chapter 3, having told the story of "Gertrude Stein in Paris—1903–1907," moves ahead to the next phase of Stein's life—her life with Toklas: "But this last was after I came to Paris" (92). Indeed, Toklas arrived in Paris in 1907, and the way in which this chapter takes the reader up to a point when she is present is not surprising. It all becomes more confusing, however, since the beginning of chapter 4, which concerns "Gertrude Stein before She Came to Paris," connects back to the last sentence of chapter 3: "*Once more* I have come to Paris and *now* I am one of the habitués of the rue de Fleurus. Gertrude Stein was writing The Making of Americans and she had just commenced correcting the proofs of Three Lives. I helped her correct them" (93, my emphases). After this touchdown of the narrative, not at the moment of writing *The Autobiography*, but at that inaugural moment in 1907, and in words that would seem to entail a doubling of that moment, the much earlier story that the title of the chapter indicates is started: "Gertrude Stein was born in Allegheny, Pennsylvania" (93). The way in which the end of chapter 3 and the beginning of chapter 4 are connected by way of Toklas's presence, then, creates confusion and a breakdown of chronology rather than a smooth transition, since the order of the two chapters is reversed in relation to linear time. The indispensable role of Toklas as mouthpiece not only for her own story but also for Stein's part of the story in *The Autobiography* is foregrounded.

The first short chapter, "Before I Came to Paris," leads up not only to the first meeting between Stein and Toklas, but also and most significantly to Toklas's intuitive ability to recognize genius: "I may say that only three times in my life have I met a genius and each time a bell within me rang and I was not mistaken, and I may say in each case it was before there was any general recognition of the quality of genius in them. The three geniuses of whom I wish to speak are Gertrude Stein, Pablo Picasso and Alfred Whitehead. . . . In no one of the three cases have I been mistaken. In this way my new full life began" (6).[5] As Gygax points out, "Although Stein makes Toklas present her as a genius, Toklas herself is also given a very special status as she is capable of knowing whether a person is a genius or not" (68). Instead of focusing only on the way in which Toklas thankfully acknowledges that meeting Stein launched her "new full life," in other words, the conventional reading of an overconfident ventriloquist Stein making her partner/dummy praise her, it is possible to reconsider the ending of the first chapter as an indication that *Stein's* life, too, changed immeasurably as a result of this first meeting, from *wanting* to be a genius to *becoming* one, through the recognition and enabling labor of her new love.

Toklas's enabling function in relation to Stein pertains not only to the smooth operation of the household, but also to Stein's writing and her subsequent identity as a famous writer. As *The Autobiography* makes clear, when Stein wins Toklas over, she not only acquires a lover and a dependable typist but also begins writing her word portraits, the first of which is Toklas's first autobiography, "Ada," and other famous works such as *Tender Buttons*, which clearly takes its subject matter—the domestic preoccupations of "Objects," "Food," and "Rooms"—from the domain of her wife. Thomson indicates that Toklas provided Stein with the influence and inspiration she so desperately needed to become a successful writer, since she was "alone in having almost no visible poetic parents or progeny. Her writing seemed to come from nowhere. . . . There was nevertheless, in Alice Toklas, literary influence from a nonprofessional source. As early as 1910, in *Ada*, . . . Gertrude imitated Alice's way of telling a story" (Thomson, 176). Neil Schmitz similarly points out that Toklas's arrival on the scene radically changed Stein's writing "from the philosophic to the poetic, from painful self-examination to humor" (paraphrased in Benstock, *Women of the Left Bank*, 162). The "transitional work" between Stein's textual production before and after meeting Toklas is, according to Benstock, *Tender Buttons*, in its composition of "a grammar of lesbian domesticity." "In accepting Alice's love," Benstock says, "Stein learned a new language. . . . Her writing suddenly ceased imitating the patriarchy" (*Women of the Left Bank*, 163). Gilbert and Gubar define the Stein–Toklas marriage as the remedy for a lack in Stein's desire to be a genius: "To certify the authority identified with both maleness and genius, [geniuses such as Shakespeare, Tolstoy, William James, Whitehead, Einstein, Picasso, and Matisse] had what Stein needed: a wife. Exploiting a strategy of male impersonation . . . to appropriate male authority and to reclaim the muse for herself, Stein evolved some of her most innovative aesthetic strategies after she 'married' Alice B. Toklas" (239).

In her article on *The Autobiography*, Gilmore admonishes readers who go looking for "referentiality" and asking "whose autobiography it 'really' is." In her terms, this is a nonquestion, because "this is exactly the kind of interpretation that cannot be sustained when we read the autobiography as a gift" ("Signature," 68). As I see it, Gilmore's construction of *The Autobiography* as a gift from Stein to Toklas is not completely convincing. For one thing, *The Autobiography* is not very likely as a conciliatory gift, because it seems to have been an offering that the recipient did not really want. Not only did Toklas, according to her biographers, wish to remain in the background, but, as Rogers points out, she also resented the way in which *The Autobiography* cast doubt upon the independence and autonomy of Stein's genius (33). She kept repeating in interviews throughout her life that Stein was fully in charge of the text. In a 1952 interview, Roland Duncan asks Toklas if she contributed to the writing of *The Autobiography*. "What could I contribute?" Toklas says, adding that she had to remind Stein of two important things that she had forgotten: "That's all. That was my contribution, and the typewriting. No, it was a great joke" (Duncan interview, 85–86). More specifically, a gift, after it is presented to the recipient, belongs *at least in part* to the person who received it, not only or primarily to the one who gave it away. In Gilmore's article, however, Toklas never really receives her gift—it remains Stein's to give throughout. Stein remains in control of the text as the solitary author of its challenges, and Toklas remains the "other woman," although recognized by Gilmore as lesbian. As a counterdiscursive critical move, an alternative to Gilmore's concept of *The Autobiography* as a gift, I would like to turn the exchange around, so that it becomes possible to say that *Toklas* offers her name and her story to *Stein* as a gift or a privilege. It is true that, as the beginning of *Everybody's Autobiography* indicates, Toklas was willing to "give" Stein "Alice Toklas"—"if it has to be at all"—but not the "B." (For a comment on the "B."—to be or not to be—see Dydo, *Gertrude Stein*, 459, n. 70.) In relation to Toklas's predilection for secrecy and modesty, however, even conceding to offer "Alice Toklas" to Stein as a gift to be used in writing is extraordinary. (Moreover, after Stein's death Toklas named her *own* work *The Alice B. Toklas Cook Book*—not *The Alice Toklas Cook Book*—as if referring back to herself as legend rather than to herself as opinionated individual.) By means of the gift of her own auto- biography, as well as a certain confusion of the categories of presence and absence (sometimes downplaying her own presence in Stein's life and work to the point of an authorizing absence), Toklas authorizes (enables) Stein not only to write but above all to be an author.

My argument regarding *The Autobiography* is that the famous passage on Toklas's talent for recognizing genius and the massive demonstration of her enabling Stein's genius throughout, culminating in the last chapter where she turns publisher as well beyond her role as first reader, editor, typist, manager, and agent, all invite a reading of Stein's bestseller as a text that may seem to center Stein but in fact by doing so *enacts* another crucial but less obtrusive narrative: the story of Toklas's indispensable part in the Stein–Toklas literary enterprise, which to a large extent operates by such tactical moves of centering (Stein) and decentering (herself). Toklas enables Stein's genius not only in the sense of an ahistorical or ethereal muse, but above all in the sense that her labor in very concrete ways makes Stein's writing and publishing possible. Toklas launched the Plain Edition in 1930 and speedily issued *Lucy Church Amiably* (1930), *Before the Flowers of Friendship Faded Friendship Faded* (1931), *How to Write* (1931), *Operas and Plays* (1932), and *Matisse, Picasso, and Gertrude Stein* (1933). Appar- ently this was not enough to create a substantial readership for Stein's work, so in 1932, Toklas presumably presented her name and her story to Stein as a gift by means of which fame and fortune could be acquired. Dydo says that Toklas's "great efforts for the Plain Edition could not satisfy Stein's enormous need for recognition" (*Gertrude Stein*, 499) and notes that "sales were limited, expenses were high, and efforts, especially on the part of Toklas, were enormous. . . . Now, however, the *Autobiography*, join- ing as one the words of Stein and the voice of Toklas, created the key to publication, audience, fame, and money" (*Gertrude Stein*, 544–45). It is impossible to say whether the writing of *The Autobiography* was Toklas's idea or Stein's, but the very fact that *we do not know* is crucially important in relation to my argument, which privileges ambiguity.

Apart from the fact that she provides ever greater amounts of "material" (stories, gossip, domestic concerns, her own distinctive talent for conversation) for Stein's writing and finally publishes it, there are from the very beginning two principal domains for Toklas's enabling labor: on the one hand, typing and editorial work, and, on the other, domestic toil. As regards the former part of her new job, Toklas steps in to fill a vacuum, since Stein never types. "Gertrude Stein had at that time a wretched little portable typewriter which she never used. She always then and for many years later wrote on scraps of paper in pencil, copied it into french school note-books in ink and then often copied it over again in ink," the narrator of *The Autobiography* says. "Gertrude Stein tried to copy Three Lives on the type-writer but it was no use, it made her nervous, so Etta Cone came to the rescue" (69–70). Of course, very soon Toklas would be the one to relieve Stein of the task that made her nervous. From 1907 onward, she "effected important alterations in the rhythm of daily life at 27, rue de Fleurus" (Benstock, *Women of the Left Bank*, 163–64), and Stein's writing practices were among the habits that changed. The way in which Toklas becomes a "habitué" in Stein's home is described not only in terms of her visits to the Saturday evening salon and the vernissage of the independent, but primarily in terms of her labor, and in terms of the purchase of a certain commodity, a new typewriter to replace the old one: "I helped Gertrude Stein with the proofs of Three Lives and then I began to type-write The Making of Americans. The little badly made french portable was not strong enough to type this big book and so we bought a large and imposing Smith Premier which at first looked very much out of place in the atelier but soon we were all used to it and it remained until I had an american portable, in short until after the war" (*Autobiography*, 116).

Toklas, too, may have seemed "out of place" in Stein's atelier at first, but then as she gradually made herself indispensable, everybody got used to her (or, as I have indicated above, fell out with Stein). The indispensability of Toklas is related not only to her ability to type without getting nervous but also to her unique status as the only reliable interpreter of Stein's handwriting: "As a matter of fact her handwriting has always been illegible and I am very often able to read it when she is not," (*Autobiography*, 102). This remark follows upon an anecdote from Stein's childhood. One of Stein's writing exercises in school was to be "copied out on beautiful parchment paper. After she had tried to copy it twice and the writing became worse and worse she was reduced to letting some one else copy it for her. This, the teacher considered a disgrace. She does not remember that she herself did" (*Autobiography*, 102). As a great avant-garde writer, Stein is certainly not "reduced" by letting Toklas copy/type for her and decipher her handwriting. This arrangement instead only seems to enlarge her and boost her ego. Of course this is the way that many male artists and writers have always exploited their wives' invisible labor for the purposes of supporting and making possible their public work. At the same time, the way in which each Stein text on its way to publication passes between the two women (is "strained" through Toklas in her function as sieve, as it were, and might never emerge in the outside world without her interpretive abilities) again points to Toklas's role as medium or conduit. Toklas's function as interpreter of Stein's writing parallels her role as gatekeeper and go-between in Stein's salon. She is the interface between the inside and the outside of Stein's world, just like she is the indispensable conduit through which Stein's text passes to become legible and publishable. Indeed, as Weiss has shown, the very literary *practices* carried out by Stein and Toklas defy the concept of a solitary author: "Alice's creative deciphering of Gertrude's illegible scrawl, and her correction of Gertrude's mistakes or introduction of new textual errors [raise] interesting questions about authorship" (63). The fact that Toklas alone is able to decipher Stein's handwritten work in its entirety also brings to mind Derrida's claim about the definition of writing: "A writing that was not structurally legible—iterable—beyond the death of the addressee would not be writing" ("Signature Event Context," 315). It can be argued, then, that Toklas is indispensable for the status of Stein's work as "writing."

Throughout their life together, Toklas enabled Stein not only to be a genius, write, and publish, but also to travel comfortably, eat well, and enjoy a carefully preserved domestic interiority, a well-guarded inner space. Toklas's role in Stein's household can be interpreted in terms of household drudgery, a wife's submission to a husband's demands in a lesbian marriage mirroring patriarchal patterns in heterosexual relationships. By way of a rereading that centers Toklas, however, and takes into serious consideration her contribution to the Stein–Toklas writing relationship, it is possible, without losing sight of these very same hierarchical structures undoubtedly present in Toklas's life with Stein, to articulate the significance of Toklas's labor in other, more open-ended, terms. The narrator of *The Autobiography* points out that Stein is "passionately addicted to what the french call métier and she contends that one can only have one métier as one can only have one language. Her métier is writing and her language is english" (103). In the second to last paragraph of *The Autobiography*, the narrator then names her own functions in the Stein–Toklas household (housekeeper, gardener, needlewoman, secretary, editor, veterinarian) as well as her proficiency in them. Toklas's *métier*, then, can be seen as not only recognizing genius, and enabling it through domestic and cultural labor, but also creating it.

The search for a new young painter to aspire to the status of genius (following Picasso), and the tentative nomination of Francis Rose, has been seen as the principal theme of the last chapter of *The Autobiography*. To my mind, however, the focal point of the last part of *The Autobiography* is Toklas becoming a publisher, learning her trade. As Norris puts it, "Stein displaces discussion of her own creative problems in writing *Lucy Church Amiably* and *How to Write* with an elaborate narration of Alice's industry, resourcefulness, and management of the problems of printing, bookbinding, and distributing the books" (95). At one point in the text, Harry Gibb persuades Stein and Toklas that Stein's work must be published even though the previous publisher is no longer active: "turning to me he said, Alice you do it. I knew he was right and that it had to be done. But how" (281). After this passage follows a lengthy section of the chapter dealing with modernist art, Stein's writing, getting settled in Bilignin, the trip to England for lectures at Oxford and Cambridge, and above all some twelve pages on Hemingway. Elliot Paul's new job as the editor of a Paris magazine is mentioned: "Gertrude Stein was naturally all for it. After all, as she said, we do want to be printed. One writes for oneself and strangers but with no adventurous publishers how can one come in contact with those same strangers" (325). Adventure is mentioned again in relation to publishing: "There are many Paris picture dealers who like adventure in their business, there are no publishers in America who like adventure in theirs" (328). And then Toklas proceeds to describe her own efforts to be an adventurous publisher: "At first I thought I would associate some one with me but that soon did not please me and I decided to do it all by myself" (329).

Toklas's gradual initiation into publishing is carefully described. She learns from others, from her own achievements, and from her mistakes: "I turned over the Paris work to a french agent. This worked very well at first but finally did not work well. However one must learn one's trade" (330). The narrator's growing confidence in herself as publisher is obvious in the text: "I decided upon my next book How To Write and not being entirely satisfied with the get up of Lucy Church Amiably, although it did look like a school book [like Stein wanted it to], I decided to have the next book printed at Dijon and in the form of an Elzevir" (330). Significantly, in this passage *How to Write* is referred to as *"my* book." Is this Stein the author's lapse into her own level, bypassing the level of the narrator? Maybe, but an alternative reading is more interesting. It can be argued that the narrator, speaking of *How to Write* as *"my* book," is claiming (co)ownership through the function of her trade, her labor. With the publisher's rightful claim on the text comes the authority to make independent decisions, and also the desire to expand her publishing enterprise: "I was getting more ambitious. I wished now to begin a series of three, beginning with Operas and Plays, going on with Matisse, Picasso and Gertrude Stein and Two Shorter Stories, and then going on with Two Long Poems and Many Shorter Ones." At the moment of writing *The Autobiography*, this project is underway and Toklas points ahead: "Now I have an up to date list of book-sellers and I am once more on my way" (333).

The Autobiography, both structurally and thematically, emphasizes Toklas's arrival as the crucial event that, through her immediate and instinctual recognition of Stein's genius, in fact inaugurates or creates it, and then goes on to enable it for the rest of Stein's life and beyond. I am not alone in thinking so. Scobie similarly points out that the list of functions at the very end of *The Autobiography*, which outlines things that Toklas is "pretty good" at doing, "defines her role in the household as that of an *enabler*: she creates the domestic space within which it is possible for Gertrude Stein to function as a genius—in Stein's own terms, as a writer, and as a man. It is this domestic role of Toklas which is literalised in her position as the narrator of Stein's autobiography. Quite literally, *she enables Stein to speak*" (128–29, my emphases). Coupled with a loyal partner who recognized genius in her, and at the very same moment set out to enable it, not only supporting it in a general way like most wives of writers and artists would, but actually providing a great deal of the material and helping shape the finished product, Stein can start *becoming* a genius.

The real trick of *The Autobiography* may be that while it thwarts the reader's expectations for an autobiographical or even straightforwardly *bio*graphical account of Toklas's life, it offers instead a subdued but sustained story of her *labor*, her indispensability and her sexual/textual relationship with Stein, partly hidden by the tall tale of Stein's genius. The relationship between these two layers of text may be compared to the asymmetrical effect in photos of Stein and Toklas, where photographers find it difficult not to have Toklas hidden from view by her partner, larger in body and personality. "They were quite a startling-looking couple," photographer Cecil Beaton says in *Photobiography* (1951). "In whatever juxtaposition I took them the effect was incongruous and strange" (138–39). Another way of relating to the coexistence of two very different versions of the same story, one that is submerged and the other manifestly visible, is to take the lead from the narrator herself who, in the first page of *The Autobiography*, professes: "I like a view but I like to sit with my back turned to it" (3). In the text, Stein the genius and other (male) geniuses are constantly in plain view, but, just as there are ways of straying (deliberately) from the path at the Père Lachaise Cemetery to find Toklas's name on the back of Stein's tombstone, there are other ways of looking strategically at the text, other places to look, other potential critical pathways, which allow for an alternative "wife-centered" take on the first Toklas autobiography. As I have pointed out already, I do not wish to argue that Toklas composed her own autobiography in 1932, but I consider her contribution to *The Autobiography*, and to Stein's writing in general, more substantial and more extensive than the general support and influence of many other silent wives (and husbands, friends, brothers, sisters, mentors) of literary geniuses. By highlighting Toklas's role in the production of *The Autobiography*, the common analysis of this text as a gift from Stein to Toklas can be problematized, and an alternative version, one that shifts the balance of power and authority to reformulate the authorship/ownership of Toklas's first autobiography as a (reluctant) gift from Toklas to Stein, can be put forward.

Chapter 3

Mimicry and Sexual/Textual Difference in What Is Remembered

In a sense, all signification takes place within the orbit of
the compulsion to repeat; "agency," then, is to be located
within the possibility of a variation on that repetition.
JUDITH BUTLER, *Gender Trouble*, 145

Can you recollect any example of easy repetition.
I can and I can mention it. I can explain how by twice repeating
you change the meaning you actually change the meaning. This
makes it more interesting. If we attach it to a person we make
for realization.
GERTRUDE STEIN, *Geography and Plays*, 260

Let us return once again to the paradoxical leitmotif for my discussion: Bridgman's (probably misguided) comment that, however unorthodox it may seem, maybe "Toklas composed her own autobiography" (209). Each element of his statement is in question in the present investigation: the name "Toklas" and the person(a) it (de)signifies; the authorial/authoritative act of writing/composing a text; the assumptions behind labeling a text someone's "own"; and the generic framework of autobiography, including the expectations and fantasies that adhere to it. At the same time, the fact that *she did*, at least twice, and each time with a significant difference, remains the basis and justification for an intertextual study of the Toklas autobiographies. In this chapter, I will discuss the third Toklas autobiography, *What Is Remembered*. The reason the first text-based chapter on *The Autobiography* is followed by a reading of *What Is Remembered* rather than the *Cook Book*, despite the order of publication (as if modeling my study on the disrupted chronology of *The Autobiography*), is my emphasis on the way in which *What Is Remembered* mimics or echoes *The Autobiography*, and my conceptualization of the *Cook Book* in terms of a certain departure, not *from* but *within* this particular intertextual conversation.

It is fairly apparent that *The Autobiography* and the *Cook Book* relate to each other, and to the genre of autobiography, in complex and not-quite-straight ways. What about *What Is Remembered*, the apparently least remarkable of the Toklas autobiographies? Is this finally the "straight" memoir where the autobiographical contract is observed, the representation of autobiographical material creating a semblance of straightforward referentiality and unmediated access to the autobiographer? I do not think so, and the passive construction of the title may serve as an emblem of the way in which Toklas is missing from the third Toklas autobiography as well. The phrase "what is remembered" effectively excludes from view the person remembering something, and this evasive maneuver characterizes the text as a whole. It is my argument that *What Is Remembered* (re)creates a persona that is at least as far removed from the "real" Toklas as the persona ostensibly created by Stein for *The Autobiography*. Indeed, as I have already mentioned, *What Is Remembered* seems to refer back to the narrator of Stein's *Autobiography* to a far greater extent than the "actual" past experiences of the "real" author. What *is* "remembered," then, is perhaps not so much what happened as what stories were told and written and infinitely rewritten, privately and publicly, in a lesbian marriage that lasted four decades. It can be argued, of course, that every autobiography masks its subject to a greater or lesser extent. In this case, however, it seems as though the autobiographer's refusal to pretend transparency, assume a revealing pose, or even pretend that the autobiographical persona is always the same and self-identical, is carried out with fewer excuses and more audacity in such a way as to confuse and even, as we will see, enrage people.

Considered in isolation, *What Is Remembered* reads like an emotionally restrained and stylistically straightforward memoir and does not go out of its way to invite further critical inquiry. In other words, the final Toklas autobiography does not thematize its own textuality in the same way as the two previous autobiographies. If the context is taken into account, however, *What Is Remembered* relates to the earlier texts and to the fantasy of a preexisting autobiographical truth in such a way that intriguing questions of repetition, mimicry and difference arise. In the present study, the significance of the third Toklas autobiography resides in strategies of repetition and mimicry and in small but important differences from generic expectations, "original" texts, and heterosexual conventions. These traits can ultimately, by means of a certain practice of intertextual reading, be seen to transform the stylistically "straight" memoir into a skewed writing of the self that could, like the two earlier Toklas autobiographies, be provisionally defined as "almost the same but not quite/not straight" in relation to a variety of sexual/textual discourses. Two of these discourses are of primary interest in the present study: first, the protocol of normative heterosexuality, and second, the generic contract of autobiography, including the fantasy of a preexisting autobiographical truth that can be accurately communicated in writing. *What Is Remembered* may seem less transgressive than the two previous Toklas autobiographies in relation to laws of gender/sexuality and genre/textuality. Despite the impeccable decorum of the Stein–Toklas relationship as depicted in this text, however, the husband in this particular marriage is still another woman. Despite the apparent conventionality of *What Is Remembered* as autobiography, moreover, the textual persona still does not seem to match the historical person.

Despite the fact that he was wrong about the authorship of "Ada," Bridgman's analysis of *The Autobiography* indicates that the origin of Stein's text is impossible to establish with certainty: "The tart economy of the *Autobiography* can be found in only one other book—Alice Toklas' own memoirs, *What Is Remembered*. The question inevitably arises of who influenced whom" (213). Bridgman's findings have since been displaced by Dydo and others, but the challenge that he identifies lingers *in the texts themselves*. As Stein mimics Toklas, and Toklas mimics Stein (or herself, in which case the concept of mimicry as it has typically been defined is thrown into question), Bridgman's question remains important and even necessary, especially in relation to a recognition of the "other woman" as a lesbian, but a simple answer is unlikely and perhaps irrelevant.

As I turn to the least well known of the Toklas autobiographies, my ambition is to show that it deserves critical attention as a text that, through strategies of mimicry and silence, repetition and difference, relates in not quite/not straight ways to *The Autobiography* as original text, to heterosexuality as the norm, and to autobiography as a genre. The apparent sexual/textual conventionality of *What Is Remembered* can then be displaced as a category of interpretation and replaced by an emphasis on (inter)textual practices and strategies such as mimicry, a particular form of repetition with a difference. "Repeating a word over and over gradually breaks the bond of word and reference. A form of punning, repetition gives body to the word and assaults meaning," Dydo says (*Gertrude Stein*, 16). Derrida similarly argues that "pure repetition, were it to change neither thing nor sign, carries with it an unlimited power of perversion and subversion" (quoted in Hilti, 37). The issue of repetition speaks to the troubled status of autobiography in Stein's aesthetic philosophy, one of the main themes of *Everybody's Autobiography* and also discussed at length in "What Are Master-pieces and Why Are There So Few of Them." In this lecture, Stein famously distinguishes between "identity" and "entity." "Identity is recognition," she says, "you know who you are because you and others remember anything about yourself. . . . I am I because my little dog knows me but . . . that is what destroys creation" (355). Stein goes on to say that "the master-piece has nothing to do with human nature or with identity, it has to do with the human mind and the entity that is with a thing in itself and not in relation" (358). According to Stein, then, identity is based on remembering, repetition, and relation, and these qualities rule out creative eminence. In his reading of her lecture, Breslin points out that Stein's "desire to live and write in a continuous present thus turns her against the necessarily retrospective act of autobiography. . . . [T]o live in a continuous present, to *be* rather than to *repeat*, one must constantly break down identity" (150).

The negative connotations of repetition in Stein's aesthetic philosophy are somewhat surprising, given the fact that Stein's literary style is famous above all for being precisely *repetitive*. Stein redefined the constant reiteration of the same words and phrases in her own work, however, as "insistence." As Weiss points out, Stein "created new relations between words, even between the same words. She did not call this repetition, but rather insistence, since through the repeating, meanings change" (68). The Toklas autobiographies, taken together, can be construed as similarly performing a discursive act of insistence, where the category of the same is radically transformed not only through its repetition but also through the inclusion of change and difference (almost the same but not quite/not straight). These texts, written decades apart by two separate writers, were certainly not meant to be read together in this way, but it is possible to draw upon the implications of Stein's term *insistence* to make sense of the Toklas autobiographies as intertexts that repeat the "same" autobiographical material in slightly different ways and thereby change meaning (even to the point of redefining meaning as change and difference). At the same time, it must be noted that I, as critic and audience, hereby submit these texts to the very dubious treatment described by Stein at the end of her lecture on the scarcity of masterpieces: "After the audience begins, naturally they create something that is they create you, and so not everything is so important, something is more important than another thing, which was not true when you were you that is when you were not you as your little dog knows you" (363).

In this chapter, I will turn first to critical expectations for authenticity in autobiography, and specifically to the way in which *What Is Remembered* has typically been categorized as a failed autobiography ever since it was published more than four decades ago. The tendency to see Toklas's "own" autobiographies as records of the autobiographer's true voice, instances of autobiographical failure, or both, entails certain critical consequences: textual strategies and intertextual connections are ignored, and Toklas is largely neglected in critical conversations on autobiography. I engage with the critical tendency to lament Toklas's absence from her own autobiography by way of a counterargument that locates her agency precisely in the right to remain silent/absent, and by way of an alternative intertextual approach. As an illustration of the way in which *What Is Remembered* thwarts expectations for straight autobiography, I will also repeat the legend of Toklas and her prospective ghostwriter. In a section of intertextual close readings, I will then focus on the issue of repetition with a difference, and give examples of a number of passages in *The Autobiography* and *What Is Remembered* that describe the "same" events. I will also discuss the repressed lesbian subplot and the theme of heterosexual (im)possibility in *What Is Remembered* as a reformulation of sexual/textual corruption. The final part of this chapter redefines *What Is Remembered* as *writing* in its own right, on the one hand, and, on the other, as a *supplement* to Stein's work. These two functions are not opposites, but rather, as Derrida has shown in *Of Grammatology*, two sides of the same coin.

Bridgman locates the difference between *The Autobiography* and *What Is Remembered*, which he finds stylistically very similar, in the representation of Toklas: "Even if her autobiography [*The Autobiography*] was written by a surrogate, in it Alice Toklas developed a distinctive character. That character differs somewhat from the one who appears in her own memoirs, *What Is Remembered*. There, her impudent, raffish, gypsy wildness is given much greater latitude" (219). Bridgman seems to imply that various aspects of the "real" Toklas are present in the two texts to different degrees, rather than the more radical possibility that Toklas is always already a textual phenomenon, rather than the reflection of a human being in the real world. Several critics have noted that the relationship between the Toklas autobiographies and the various Toklas personas in them is one of ambiguity and uncertainty, but they generally tend to return to a conventional conception of autobiographical truth and of the authentic voice of the "real" Toklas. For instance, Michael Hoffman says that "a few critics have noticed resemblances between the style of *What Is Remembered* and that of *The Autobiography of Alice B. Toklas*, an observation that leads to one of two conclusions: either Stein was a wonderful mimic, or Toklas played a greater hand in writing *The Autobiography* than is commonly believed" (15).

Why is *What Is Remembered* typically seen as representing the voice of the "real" Toklas (which, because of the resemblance between this memoir and Stein's earlier text, would *prove* that Toklas contributed to *The Autobiography*) rather than problematized, for instance, as Toklas mimicking *Stein's* previous text (making her, too, a "wonderful mimic," but not necessarily a reliable autobiographer)? The same assumption, that Toklas's "own" autobiographies represent her "own" authentic voice, recurs everywhere: "Not until publication of *The Alice B. Toklas Cook Book* twenty years later, and Toklas' own memoir *What Is Remembered* a decade after that, was it apparent how uncannily accurate Stein had been in capturing the waspish, acidulous voice of her friend" (Kellner, 21). What if Stein did not exactly "capture" Toklas but rather *produced* her back then, or if Toklas deliberately produced *herself* for Stein's text, as if giving "dictation," and then imitated—or *continued*—Stein's version of "Alice B. Toklas" in her "own" subsequent autobiographies?

In order to understand certain critical tendencies in relation to Toklas and her work, it is instructive to consider the contemporary reception of *What Is Remembered*. Ray Lewis White's *Gertrude Stein and Alice B. Toklas* provides a survey of critical reactions following its publication, and all the following examples of reviewers' opinions are taken from the 1963 section of White's reference guide, pages 168–82. Many reviews compare the third Toklas autobiography to Stein's "original" and find *What Is Remembered* vastly inferior, lacking not only in relation to norms for literary or autobiographical greatness, but specifically in relation to *The Autobiography* as the official (indeed, *authorized*) version of Toklas's life. For instance, the *New Statesman* writes that these two texts "recount the same incidents, tell the same stories. Oddly enough, however, the version of Miss Toklas, to whom the events happened, seems neutral, numb, even denatured compared with Gertrude Stein's vitality and gaiety" (178). The *Woburn Times* agrees that *What Is Remembered* does not "compete" with *The Autobiography* but rather constitutes a "terse condensation" of it: "Is this deliberate or did Stein so completely reveal the real Alice that she cannot emerge as a different person in her own book?" (177). Again, assumptions concerning the "real" Toklas dominate the response to the text. The *Chicago Daily News* is dismissive of the latter "version" of Toklas's autobiography: "Do not expect any confessions of the heart nor vivid, probing experiences of the famous personalities parading through these pages—least of all, a portrait of Gertrude Stein. None of the style and wit of Gertrude Stein's autobiography, *The Autobiography of Alice B. Toklas*, is even hinted at" (172). Similarly, the *Fort Worth Star* complains that whereas *The Autobiography* reads like "a witty and charming novel," *What Is Remembered* is "similar to a catalog, replete with listings of people and places but with only the most fragmentary comments about either" (172). What is per definition (but perhaps not "factually") *remembered* by the autobiographer is in this case deemed inferior, in autobiographical terms, to what is written for/about her by someone else.

As these examples indicate, most reviewers dismiss *What Is Remembered* as a text distinguished by lack, incompleteness, and autobiographical failure. The sparse style of *What Is Remembered* is often seen as particularly unacceptable: "Miss Toklas has . . . an extraordinarily staccato and urbane writing style, often to a point where she gives the impression that she is jotting down a series of notes for a larger, more detailed life story, rather than the finished product itself" (the *Phoenix Republic*, quoted in White, 169). This characterization of *What Is Remembered* as a fragment of what it *should have been* recurs again and again: "Alice Toklas' *What Is Remembered* would make a good preface for *a real book*. . . . Not what is remembered here, but what has been forgotten, might be truly worth a book" (the *Washington Post*, quoted in White, 173, my emphasis). Reviewers tend to wish for something *more*, in accordance with a certain model of completeness or fullness in autobiography: "The reader will frequently wish for longer descriptions which simply aren't there" (the *Nashville Tennessean*, quoted in White, 178). *What Is Remembered* is seen by the *Buffalo Courier-Express* as "an annotated supplementary text. Miss

Toklas drops famous names with wild abandon. . . . The sparse prose, ret-
icent accounts and terse phrases leave much to be desired. Miss Toklas
left much unsaid that the reader would like to have had amplified and
analyzed" (173). The *Oakland Tribune* reviewer similarly complains that
What Is Remembered "is not the book for which I had hoped and waited.
As a memoirist, Miss Toklas has the privilege of selection, of course. But
with it goes a responsibility, and here she fails me. The book . . . simply
excludes too much" (179–80). And finally, the reviewer at the *Des Moines
Register* laments "an arid lack of critical comment on most of [the
famous], a prevalence of trivia and a seemingly intentional reduction of
literary style to the copybook manner adequate for enumeration of unim-
portant incident. And one will read on in vain expecting to find somewhere in her memories a reference of real warmth about the companion,
an expression of even 'cordial' affection" (181).

Measured not only against a notion of "reality," then, but primarily
against the "original" Toklas autobiography and against a certain standard of autobiographical confession, in contemporary reviews *What Is
Remembered* is described as a failure. Some of the contemporary reviews
are mildly laudatory, but with a tendency to express sympathy and admi-
ration for Toklas herself rather than for her work. *The Saturday Review*
relies upon the fantasy of authorship as ownership and agency to describe
Toklas as a tragic figure: "Did she never wish for a life of her own, for anything of her own?" *Time*'s reviewer famously calls *What Is Remembered*
"the sad, slight book of a woman who all her life has looked in a mirror
and seen someone else." Toklas was seen "to have disappeared without a
trace into Gertrude Stein's life." This is apparently because "Predictably
but a little pathetically, [*What Is Remembered*] reads like Gertrude Stein"
(both *Saturday Review* and *Time* quoted in Simon, *Biography*, 247).

Ever since the first wave of either mildly sympathetic or strongly
dismissive reviews, *What Is Remembered* has been almost completely
ignored, both by Stein scholars and by critics of autobiography. Apart
from the anecdote about Toklas's conflict with her would-be ghostwriter,
which recurs in several Stein and Toklas biographies, and which will be
repeated yet again in this study, there has been practically *nothing* written
on *What Is Remembered* beyond the compulsory brief reference in
overviews of Stein's and Toklas's work. Those few recent comments on
What Is Remembered that do exist seem to envision more agency on Toklas's part than did reviews from the time of publication, even as they still

emphasize the weaknesses of the text. For instance, Bruce Kellner characterizes the third Toklas autobiography as "often inaccurate, elliptical, and woefully lacking in substantive detail, but its terse and pithy wit sustains it, and at least it tells the reader all that Toklas cared to share" (324). Similarly, "If *What Is Remembered* was not autobiography it was, nevertheless, what Alice set out to write" (Simon, *Biography*, 247). Bloom even indicates that *What Is Remembered* is more "truly" autobiographical than Stein's *Autobiography*: "In her own autobiography [*What Is Remembered*] Toklas discloses, among other selves, a private, vulnerable self of the sort which Stein-as-autobiographer rarely reveals" (88).

Despite a slight shift in emphasis, however, it is interesting to see how attitudes about autobiography as potentially or ideally *accurate* (as opposed to inaccurate), *direct* (as opposed to elliptical), and *complete* (as opposed to lacking in substantive detail) are at work in commentary on *What Is Remembered* from the early 1960s onward. In other words, over the four decades since *What Is Remembered* was published, reviewers and critics seem to generally agree that Toklas is "missing" from her "own" autobiography, provided that her text can even be categorized as such. I cannot refute this, because *of course* the "real" Toklas is not to be found in the text, and furthermore that is precisely my point, but I would like to modify and problematize the verdict upon *What Is Remembered* as a failed autobiography somewhat by asking why any reading of the text would assume to find presence and completeness in it in the first place. As this chapter will show, the text itself signals a very different inclination.

First, the verdict upon *What Is Remembered* as the "sad, slight book of a woman who all her life has looked in a mirror and seen someone else" and moreover "disappeared without a trace into [that other woman's] life" is not convincing. In fact, the first part of *What Is Remembered* very clearly shows Toklas claiming her independence. En route to Paris, Toklas must abandon a thoroughly traditional feminine position as her father's and grandfather's housekeeper and her brother's substitute mother, which she had occupied since age ten when her mother died. It is interesting that she also calls herself unyielding and difficult in relation to Mike and Sarah Stein, who invite her to go with them to Europe after the San Francisco earthquake in 1906: "I was cool about accepting this invitation, so they compromised with *a more accommodating and charming young girl*" (22, my emphasis). Once arrived in Paris, there are recurring hints that Toklas is not a sensitive, vulnerable lady like Harriet Levy, her travel companion:

"Gertrude told me that Fernande considered Alice Derain's conversation too frank and not suitable for Harriet. For me it was all right" (39). Before turning to Toklas's life with Stein, then, the text establishes her as part of a historical context, and moreover as a strong and independent woman who leaves a life of stability and convention, complete with male suitors and male members of the household who rely on her for domestic duties, for a more adventurous life "living history" (60) and living literature (51) in an unconventional lesbian marriage in Paris, a life that she moreover takes on without hesitation, fear, or exaggerated delicacy.

It is true that *What Is Remembered* as a whole foregrounds Stein at the expense of Toklas in a way that closely resembles the layered structure of *The Autobiography*. As Derrida and other critics have shown, autobiographies typically thematize and prefigure the death of the autobiographer. *What Is Remembered* instead centers the death of the autobiographer's partner. The narrative ends many years before the writing moment, with the death of Stein, as if *she* were the center of this autobiography as well, and the narrative necessarily stops when she dies.[1] *What Is Remembered* as an epitaph is interesting in relation to the general preoccupation with death in autobiography, typically identified and theorized as a problematization of the *autobiographer's* subjectivity (see Marcus's discussion of "the thanatographical interests of deconstruction," 208–10). The "I" of the third Toklas autobiography is attached so closely to Stein's life (falling silent as she dies) that *What Is Remembered* looks like *The Autobiography* in reverse. Is this Toklas ventriloquizing *Stein* like Stein ventriloquized *her* for *The Autobiography*? Maybe, but since *What Is Remembered* also echoes *The Autobiography* to such a great extent, this would mean that the "I" ostensibly created by Stein for *The Autobiography*, not the aging Alice B. Toklas writing in the early 1960s, returns after Stein's death to speak in her place. In other words, it may *still* be Stein who (from beyond the grave) "speaks for" Toklas, if Toklas in 1963 speaks (through) the "I" that Stein created for the first autobiography. These patterns can be seen as a more literal form of ghost writing.

In its content and temporal scope, furthermore, *What Is Remembered* almost entirely stays within the frame established by *The Autobiography*. Instead of placing the emphasis on her childhood, which was neglected in the first autobiography, or her life after its publication, which would seem to provide a natural complement to Stein's bestseller, Toklas chooses to primarily cover the same time period as the earlier work and to repeat (more or less in the same vein) many of the stories and anecdotes from *The Autobiography*. What we get in *What Is Remembered* beyond what we get in *The Autobiography* is the story of the 1934 U.S. tour, a brief section on World War II, and the final short chapter on Stein's illness and death. The bulk of the book, however (148 pages out of 186), deals with the same events, the same time period, and the same people as *The Autobiography*. Some passages seem almost *copied* from *The Autobiography* (see, for instance, the story of Avery Hopwood, in *The Autobiography* 187–89, in *What Is Remembered* 134–35, and the story of the banquet for Rousseau, in *The Autobiography* 138–45, in *What Is Remembered* 61–64). I will give several examples of such correspondences in the section on repetition below.

One highly interesting aspect of *What Is Remembered* is that, even as it echoes and in a sense duplicates *The Autobiography*, it almost completely ignores Stein's text in that it does not mention it directly. In *What Is Remembered*, the 1934 U.S. lecture tour, which was a *direct* result of Stein's success with *The Autobiography*, is described without any allusion whatsoever to the reason for it, namely a bestseller with Toklas's name on the cover. In fact, *What Is Remembered* quite conspicuously tries to bypass *The Autobiography* and its bestseller status by emphasizing occasions during the U.S. tour when Stein mentions her "real" writing, the obscure material, as the reason for her popularity. Even when Stein and Toklas meet the publisher for the bestselling *Autobiography*, the emphasis is shifted to the (imaginary) appeal of Stein's inaccessible writing: "Mr. Harcourt said, I had no idea you were going to be as popular as this. Gertrude said, No, but you should have thought so because it is the things they do not understand that attract them the most. Mr. Harcourt thereupon sent for Mr. Brace and said, Listen to what she says, she says the public is attracted to what it does not understand" (155). A little later, the same displacement of attention from the bestselling success of *The Autobiography* to the obscurity of Stein's "real" writing recurs: "The film directors gathered around Miss Stein and said, We like to know how you came to have your enormous popularity, and she said, By having a small audience, whereupon they shoved their chairs away from her, discouraged with what she had to advise" (164). Of course, Stein was popular in the United States at this time precisely because she had attracted a *large* audience with *The Autobiography*. Nevertheless, throughout the whole of *What Is Remembered*, *The Autobiography* is mentioned only once, in passing, and seemingly only to "blame" someone else for the idea: "It was Bertie, Sir Robert Abdy, who had said to Gertrude, You should write the history of your friends and time. Which she did, *The Auto-biography of Alice B. Toklas*" (172).

The way in which *The Autobiography* is mentioned only once and in an offhand, indifferent way in *What Is Remembered* is interesting and adds to the impression (and her own repeated statement) that Toklas would like to deflect attention away from her role in Stein's life. At the same time, and keeping in mind Toklas's talent for disguise and camouflage, this tendency need not indicate that she is *sadly* missing from her autobiography, or that her autobiography is failed, but rather that her agency in the text resides precisely in the right to remain silent, and that the literary value of *What Is Remembered* should be sought in aspects of text and intertext rather than in a notion of autobiographical truth. As I see it, a consideration of Toklas's penchant for tricks of evasion may usefully inform a recovery of her as a cultural laborer and a writer, who not only coproduced Stein's modernist masterpieces and Stein herself as a modernist genius but also crafted challenging texts of her own that thwart the reader's expectations for confession and revelation. As we have seen, Toklas is notorious among critics, biographers, and commentators for the lack of these dimensions in her autobiographical writing. Paradoxically, the most famous aspect of *What Is Remembered* is the version of it that never got written, the ghostly pretext that exists only as a forever deferred (im)possibility in the story of Toklas and her would-be ghostwriter.

When Toklas returned to rue Christine in June 1961 from her yearly stay at a convent in southern France, she found that her beloved collection of paintings had been removed to a bank vault by Stein's relatives, who worried about their inheritance. James Lord, who visited Toklas shortly afterward, describes Toklas's home after the confiscation in dramatic terms: "The apartment had not been repainted for more than fifteen years with the result that where each picture had hung a discolored area of its exact size now remained. Like drab and disconsolate ghosts, these shapes were far more insistent and inexorable presences than the paintings themselves had been, because they never for a moment allowed one to forget that what had been was now no more." Lord's description of the appearance of Toklas's rue Christine apartment after the removal of the paintings is strangely reversed. It must be assumed that the *original* color had been preserved in spots where there had been pictures, and that the rest of the walls had been discolored over time. This confusion relates to the present subject, since the original or true color (of Toklas) seems ghostly in comparison to the corrupted surface, which appears natural by force of habit and familiarity.

When Lord lamented that "it's sad to see all those blank spots where the pictures were," however, Toklas, who was at this time slowly going blind, reportedly replied: "Oh, not to me dear. I can't see them. But I can see the pictures in my memory" (quoted in Simon, *Biography*, 250). In a 1961 letter, she expresses the same sentiment of quiet acceptance: "The pictures are gone permanently. My dim sight could not see them now. Happily a vivid memory does" (*Staying On Alone*, 403). The confiscation of the pictures happened around the time that Toklas started writing *What Is Remembered* and provides a useful parallel to the production of the third Toklas autobiography. When Toklas recalls her past for her memoirs, she is almost blind to the world but "sees" with her memory and makes the exact sizes and inexorable presences of certain absences and silences signify in the story of her life, like ghosts, alongside the substance of what is actually told. Samuel Steward suggests that Toklas's apartment was ghostly even before the pictures were taken away, because Toklas had turned it into a memorial of Stein and the old days: "It was a haunted room, and ghosts were talking" (87). Indeed, Toklas could well be called her own ghostwriter, just like Stein once played the part of her ghost-writer in *The Autobiography*. As Lejeune points out, "*Anyone* who decides to write his life story acts as if he were his own ghostwriter" (188, empha-sis in original). There was originally, however, another, "external" ghost-writer for *What Is Remembered*, and the story of his futile attempt to make Toklas's ghosts materialize is illuminating in relation to the text and its reputation as a failed autobiography. The struggle between the old lady and her ghostwriter is well known, and the legend appears in lengthy ver-sions both in Simon's Toklas biography and in Souhami's *Gertrude and Alice*. All quotes in the following discussion, unless otherwise stated, are from Simon's text, pages 244–46.

When Toklas in her old age was encouraged by American publisher John Schaffner to start writing her memoirs, she herself suggested "collabora-tion" with writer Max White, and he immediately launched a misguided attempt to procure from Toklas autobiographical truth. To his dismay, how-ever, he soon realized that "Alice's version of her life . . . was nothing but a store of well-wrought anecdotes" and that Toklas's notion of remembering did not correspond to his own: "As the note-taking got underway, I began to notice that Alice kept staring into the corner of the room beyond Picasso's tawny nude on pink. She was watching a silent film of her own years before she met Gertrude. It was too good in spots: the truth would never have needed all that plausibility. This could only harm the book." It is significant that White emphasizes the way in which Toklas's memories are "too good," they are neat and plausible in excess of what is appropriate for direct, truthful representation of past events and emotions. Part of what he is trying to get at, of course, is the unspoken lesbian content of Toklas's story—what is left out of the silent film, the nudity that Toklas disregards and "stares beyond" for the official record. White tries to unsettle Toklas by means of a "reflector that would show her to herself" and offers Barney's version of Remy de Gourmant's *Lettres à une Amazone*. Toklas reacts to this prod for the submerged lesbian content of her story with disbelief and dismay but refuses to respond to it with greater candor, and White describes how "she glanced into the corner from which so much fiction of her own had come. . . . Then she resumed smoothly. I had got a probative answer and she would go on pretending there had never been a question. Unable or unwilling to recognize the danger or to be the good friend to Gertrude's work she meant to be she returned to her manipulation of what was already tainted material turning comic." When White complains about Toklas manipulating, fictionalizing, even *tainting* her own autobiography by refusing to provide "enough information" or "real material," he is apparently measuring Toklas's "fiction" against a conception of autobiographical truth as preexisting, factual, pure, complete, and verifiable *and* its representation at the same time as emotional and "direct," and finding it unsatisfactory on these grounds. In relation to this model of autobiography, the autobiographer's "own" version of the story can be rejected as flawed and even corrupt.

The conflict between White's and Toklas's versions of autobiographical truth peaks as Toklas reaches the end of the story. White hopes and expects that the memory of Stein's death will unsettle Toklas into giving him what he wants and is deeply disappointed when even her account of this event turns out, in his opinion, "washed of all emotion and . . . turned into legend." Toklas supposedly reverses the order of Stein's famous last words, and "The tone of that afternoon, as of her story over the weeks, was hollow." It is interesting in this context to consider White's reliance on earlier installments of the legend of Stein and Toklas. Toklas was alone with Stein on the day she died (at least that is what she claims). It would seem she alone was in a position to know what "actually" happened, and she was most certainly the one who later reported the details of Stein's last moments to the public, in effect *establishing* the famous last words, as well as their order, as "fact." In *What Is Remembered*, Stein's death is described as follows: "I sat next to her and she said to me early in the afternoon, What is the answer? I was silent. In that case, she said, what is the question? Then the whole afternoon was troubled, confused, and very uncertain, and later in the afternoon they took her away on a wheeled stretcher to the operating room and I never saw her again" (186). Again, it is impossible to arrive at a sense of unambiguous correspondence between what *happened* and what is *told*. Who knows whether Toklas reversed the order of the two questions *then* and actually set the order *straight* when rehearsing her memories in conversation with White? Who knows whether these were Stein's last words at all? Obviously the story, as it is written down, is also the result of a process of selection.[2]

White presupposes preexisting autobiographical truth, but naturally he knows it only through previous texts and hence expects Toklas not only to go through the motions of providing him with unmediated autobiographical material and cater to readerly expectations for entertaining disclosure, but also to be loyal to the earlier versions of her own life, including other people's interpretations of her relationship with Stein. Despite the fact that Toklas sticks very closely to the official version of her life story as it was established in *The Autobiography*, White is not satisfied, because he fails to procure from her the exposure of a few gratifying secrets. Thwarted, he fumes, "All [Toklas] can do is lie and deny it and contradict herself. If this were amusing stuff, I'd have been able to make something of it." After weeks of hard work trying to get Toklas to open up, White realizes that she is going to remain unyielding in her refusal to deliver autobiographical truth as he defines it, and abruptly he breaks off the collaboration. So dissatisfied is White with Toklas's memories that he rids himself of his notes and typewritten pages in what seems like a ritual of purification: "I went the three short blocks from the rue Christine to my hotel in Git-le-Coeur where I tore my notes into tangled strips and stuffed them into a linen mail sack and took them the few steps that brought me to a public trash receptacle on the boulevard des Grands Augustins. I made sure no last piece of paper clung to the inside of my mail sack. The dustmen would empty the S.V.P. before dawn."

White later tells his lawyer that "Miss Toklas couldn't remember her memories. . . . I'm the only one capable of judging just how incapable

Alice is of any sort of collaboration. She's completely incapable." *Miss Toklas couldn't remember her memories*. What happens to the definition of memory and remembering in White's attack on Toklas? Clearly he was hoping for the revelation of secrets and the "amusing" disclosure of intimate details, but Toklas wrote in a letter: "We are agreed that the reminiscences should be centered on Baby [Stein] and her work. That mine be discarded. . . . I am nothing but the memory of her" (quoted in Souhami, 266). Toklas's definition of memory is based on selection (her own reminiscences are "discarded") and the potential for displacement (she is "nothing but the memory of [Stein]"). This is "legend" to White, who expects and demands emotion and a semblance of autobiographical truth, a seemingly *straight* line from historical person to autobiographical persona. Simon claims that, while White "took the book [project] seriously as biography," Toklas regarded it as a "novel," in other words, "as her final opportunity to gild the legend which she had created" (*Biography*, 246). I am not entirely convinced by Simon's argument. Instead, if I were to momentarily speculate on the intentions of the author, I would suspect that Toklas to a very high degree "took the book seriously" as autobiography, but her conception of autobiography and autobiographical truth differed critically from that of her would-be collaborator. This biographical conjecture is supported by the way in which, in Toklas's version of the story of her life, absence, silence, and difference signify along with what is present, spoken, and mimetic.

Weiss claims that *What Is Remembered* "might as well have been titled What Is Forgotten" because of Toklas's "loss" of memory (99). White, on the other hand, seems to argue that Toklas intentionally distorts and "taints" her memories, so as to hide the "*real* material" from him on purpose. My argument, contrary to both these explanations, is that it is impossible to establish the level of authorial intention and agency in the "failure" of *What Is Remembered* as straight autobiography. I would even go so far as to say that it does not even matter whether Toklas was actually *unable* to remember by the time she wrote *What Is Remembered* or whether she in fact *chose* to manipulate her memories in such a way as to redefine the meaning of autobiographical truth. As I see it, it is more productive to engage with the text precisely as a *text*, as a practice of *writing*, and as part of an intertextual relationship, specifically as one of the Toklas autobiographies, than to try to grasp for a sense of authorial agenda and intention, which in itself bespeaks a yearning for autobiographical truth. In relation to this alternative approach, it is interesting to return to Stein's thinking on the topic of remembering and identity.

In *Everybody's Autobiography*, Stein remarks that "identity is funny being yourself is funny as you are never yourself to yourself except as you remember yourself and then of course you do not believe yourself. That is really the trouble with an autobiography you do not of course you do not really believe yourself, why should you, you know so well so very well that it is not yourself, it could not be yourself because you cannot remember right and if you do remember right it does not sound right and of course it does not sound right because it is not right. You are of course never yourself" (68). With this problematization of autobiographical discourse and remembering in mind, it is possible to reconsider *What Is Remembered* as a potential masterpiece, in the sense that it does not pretend to remember a true self. In fact, it actively forgets or suspends the truth about the autobiographer's self and seems to *enact* Stein's statement that "you are of course never yourself" to the point of excluding the autobiographer not only from the passive construction of the title, but also from this particular "true story of Alice B. Toklas."

Toklas considered finding another collaborator when White deserted the project but then went ahead and (re)wrote her memoir herself. As if to defy White, she then published her book, the impossible memoirs of a lady who cannot or will not remember her "own" memories, under the title *What Is Remembered*.[3] White's version of Toklas's story never happened, and there is no way of knowing whether or how the notes that White destroyed differed from the published version, but in relation to White's ghost story, the published version (Toklas's "own") presumably resembles the blank spaces on the walls of Toklas's apartment after her collection of paintings were removed. The autobiographical truth of *What Is Remembered* (de)signifies precisely by silence and absence—and yet it is all there.

The Toklas autobiographies, taken together, enact a series of "easy repetition." They repeat anecdotes, names, autobiographical "facts," an autobiographical "I" with the "same" referent, and a certain summoning forth of the generic assumptions of autobiography. The repetition of autobiographical material creates a sense of extratextual autobiographical truth that can be referred to with authority and accuracy and also creates a sense of oral history feeding into text, the recurrent momentary manifestation in writing of an ongoing life narrative. Each time that repetition occurs, however, a dimension of difference is also opened up, unsettling both the fantasy of preexisting autobiographical truth and the hierarchical difference between speech as originary and writing as supplementary. In Stein's words, "I can explain how by twice repeating you change the meaning you actually change the meaning. This makes it more interesting. If we attach it to a person we make for realization" (*Geography and Plays*, 260). In other words, only by repeating the story of Toklas in such a way that meaning (identity) turns into change (difference) will this particular narrative signify. It could be argued, then, along the lines of Butler's concept of "a variation on . . . [the] repetition," that the only way to "realize" Toklas (both in the sense of *understanding* her and in the sense of *making her real*), to arrive at a sense of her "identity" in the text, is to include difference, the opposite of identity, in the category of identity.

One of the anecdotes included in *The Autobiography* and repeated in *What Is Remembered* may illustrate the type of identity that rests fitfully on difference. In *The Autobiography*, the narrator describes the arrival of Constance Fletcher to the Villa Curonia as follows: "Constance Fletcher came a day or so after we arrived and I went to the station to meet her. Mabel Dodge had described her to me as a very large woman who would wear a purple robe and who was deaf. As a matter of fact she was dressed in green and was not deaf but very short sighted, and she was delightful" (*The Autobiography*, 175). *What Is Remembered* describes the "same" arrival like this: "One day Mabel asked me to go to the railroad station to meet Constance Fletcher, who was coming from her home in Venice. You will know her, said Mabel, because she is deaf and will be wearing a purple robe. When I got to the railroad station Miss Fletcher came up to me. She was wearing not a purple robe but a bright green one, she was not deaf but nearly blind and peered through her lorgnons" (*What Is Remembered*, 72). The Toklas autobiographies, seemingly true to autobiographical generic conventions, similarly suggest that you will know and recognize Toklas because she is, does, and says certain things. Through a maze of repetition, mimicry, and difference, however, Toklas turns out to be almost the same but not quite in relation to every definition offered— and still you "know" her, as you would know Constance Fletcher at the railroad station, despite everything. The recurrence of this particular anecdote in two almost-the-same-but-not-quite textual representations, written and published thirty years apart, gives the impression that Fletcher's arrival at the railway station is a historical fact; it is an event in reality that can be referred to with authority. At the same time, the very occurrence of repetition introduces a small but significant difference (the "same" story told twice is *almost* the same but not quite) and the possibility of a mismatch between world and word. "Knowing" what really happened has shifted from a category of world/word correspondence to a proliferation of minute shifts and aberrations, taking place primarily on the level of discourse.

There are many examples of autobiographical anecdotes that recur, with more or less significant variations, in one or another of the three autobiographies. For instance, at a dinner party described in the *Cook Book*, Toklas is "paralysed to find [herself] placed next to Mr. James Branch Cabell, but his cheery, Tell me, Miss Stein's writing is a joke, isn't it, put [her] completely at ease so that [they] got on very well after that" (130). This episode is included in *What Is Remembered* as well but described a little differently: "At dinner I sat next to James Branch Cabell who asked me, Is Gertrude Stein serious? Desperately, I replied. That puts a different light on it, he said. For you, I said, not for me" (161). In the present study, the recurrence of the same anecdotes is significant not only in relation to an analysis of specific variations, but above all in relation to the rhetorical figure of "almost the same but not quite," referring to a slippage of signification that is problematic in the context of the expected "sameness" of a person's identity and the presumed factuality of events in a person's life. Such slippage is everywhere in the Toklas autobiographies. Compare the following autobiographical openings (stories of origin):

> I was born in San Francisco, California. I have in consequence always preferred living in a temperate climate but it is difficult, on the continent of Europe or even in America, to find a temperate climate and live in it. My mother's father was a pioneer, he came to California in '49, he married my grandmother who was very fond of music. She was a pupil of Clara Schumann's father. My mother was a quiet charming woman named Emilie. (*The Autobiography*, 3)

> I was born and raised in California, where my maternal grandfather had been a pioneer before the state was admitted to the Union. He had bought a gold mine and settled in Jackson, Amador County. A few years later he crossed the Isthmus of Panama again and went to Brooklyn, where he married my grandmother. There my mother was born. When she was three years old, they went to Jackson. (*What Is Remembered*, 5)

These two openings, similar as they may be, are not *the same*—they are *almost* the same but not quite. I am not talking primarily about the way in which music figures in the first paragraph of *The Autobiography* and the grandfather's gold mine in the first paragraph of *What Is Remembered*, although differences of that order are significant, too. Had the first sentences of *What Is Remembered* been copied directly from *The Autobiography*, the two stories of origin would *still* not have been the same. Repetition entails a certain crease in representation, a fold that destabilizes the notion of sameness in relation to two representations of a person or a life and ultimately the notion of sameness between the signifier and the signified. Also, compare the way in which *The Autobiography* features *two* autobiographical beginnings or stories of origin, splitting or splicing the text and underlining its double-voicing tactics: "I was born in San Francisco, California" (3) and "Gertrude Stein was born in Allegheny, Pennsylvania" (93). In this way, *The Autobiography* both merges and separates Toklas and Stein, "she" and "I," west and east, in the vertiginous movement of a double take. Another example of a double take is the legendary first meeting between Stein and Toklas, which holds a prominent place in both *What Is Remembered* and *The Autobiography*.[4] Like the two texts in general, the following two accounts of the "same" event are linked by both resemblance and difference:

> Within a year I also had gone and I had come to Paris. There I went to see Mrs [Sarah] Stein who had in the meantime returned to Paris, and there at her house I met Gertrude Stein. I was impressed by the coral brooch she wore and by her voice. I may say that only three times in my life have I met a genius and each time a bell within me rang and I was not mistaken, and I may say in each case it was before there was any general recognition of the quality of genius in them. The three geniuses of whom I wish to speak are Gertrude Stein, Pablo Picasso and Alfred Whitehead. I have met many important people, I have met several great people but I have only known three first class geniuses and in each case on sight within me something rang. In no one of the three cases have I been mistaken. In this way my new full life began. (*The Autobiography*, 5–6)

> In the room were Mr. and Mrs. [Mike and Sarah] Stein and Gertrude Stein. It was Gertrude Stein who held my complete attention, as she did for all the many years I knew her until her death, and all these empty ones since then. She was a golden brown presence, burned by the Tuscan sun and

with a golden glint in her warm brown hair. She was dressed in a warm brown corduroy suit. She wore a large round coral brooch and when she talked, very little, or laughed, a good deal, I thought her voice came from this brooch. It was unlike anyone else's voice—deep, full, velvety like a great contralto's, like two voices. She was large and heavy with delicate small hands and a beautifully modelled and unique head. It was often compared to a Roman emperor's, but later Donald Sutherland said that her eyes made her a primitive Greek. (*What Is Remembered*, 26)

Even as the similarities between these two narratives call upon the autobiographical convention of world/word correspondence and the iterability of autobiographical "facts," the differences indicate the problem of retaining a notion of unmediated access to "real life" in autobiography and ultimately the difficulty of trying to pin down autobiographical truth. The description of the first meeting in *The Autobiography* to a great extent highlights Stein's genius, whereas the description of the "same" occasion in *What Is Remembered* focuses instead on her physical attributes. In the latter text, moreover, the famous proclamation of three geniuses is saved for later, and its emphases shifted: "I did not know who [Dr. Alfred North Whitehead] was at the time, and only when I saw his face under a lamp did I recognize him. He had a most benign sweet smile and a simplicity that comes only in geniuses. He was my third genius for whom the bell rang. The first two had been Gertrude Stein and Picasso" (90). The way in which Toklas in her "own" autobiography mentions her talent for hearing bells ringing in the presence of genius in passing and without drama, and even with a certain deferral added (some extra time and a lamp are needed to recognize this genius), very much unlike the bombastic declaration of the same capability in *The Autobiography*, can certainly be interpreted as yet another sign that Toklas is merely following Stein's lead in singing praise to Stein's genius, while nobody does it better than Stein herself. The quiet manner in which this skill is mentioned in *What Is Remembered*, however, can also be seen as an aspect of intertextuality. Writing *What Is Remembered*, Toklas may assume that her readers have read *The Autobiography*, or at least that they are familiar with the legend, that they *know* about the bells ringing.

Another example of an anecdote that is included in *The Autobiography* and then repeated, with a difference, in *What Is Remembered* relates a dinner party at rue de Fleurus:

We had just finished the first course when there was a quick patter of foot-steps in the court and Hélène opened the door before the bell rang. Pablo and Fernande as everybody called them at that time walked in. He, small, quick moving but not restless, his eyes having a strange faculty of opening wide and drinking in what he wished to see. He had the isolation and move-ment of the head of a bull fighter at the head of their procession. Fernande was a tall beautiful woman with a wonderful big hat and a very evidently new dress, they were both very fussed. I am very upset, said Pablo, but you know very well Gertrude I am never late but Fernande ordered a dress for the vernissage to-morrow and it didn't come. (*The Autobiography*, 15)

As we were sitting down at table there was a loud knocking at the pavillon door. Helene came to announce, Monsieur Picasso and Madame Fernande, who in an instant came in, much flustered, both of them talking at the same time. Picasso, very dark with black hair, a lock hanging over one of his mar-vellous all-seeing brilliant black eyes, was explaining in his raucous Spanish voice, You know how as a Spaniard I would want to be on time, how I always am. Fernande, with her characteristic gesture of one arm extended above her head with a Napoleonic forefinger pointing in the air, asked Gertrude Stein to excuse them. The new suit she was wearing, made for the next day's vernissage of the Salon d'Automne, had not been delivered on time and there was of course nothing to do but wait. (*What Is Remembered*, 30–31)

A comparison of these two textual representations of the "same" dramatic arrival supports the common critical claim that *The Autobiography* and *What Is Remembered* are written in the same "style," presumably mirroring Toklas's conversation. There are also, however, small but important differ-ences. There is a bell that does not have time to ring in *The Autobiography*, a "loud knocking" in *What Is Remembered*. Picasso is defined as a Spaniard in both texts, explicitly in *What Is Remembered* and through his resem-blance to a bull fighter in *The Autobiography*. His "all-seeing" eyes are simi-larly emphasized in both texts, but differently. In *The Autobiography*, Picasso apologizes to Stein, but in *What Is Remembered*, it is Fernande, with her Napoleonic forefinger in the air. (This is one of the many little ways in which *What Is Remembered* in fact appears to tell the "same" story as *The Autobiography* but effects a slight shift of emphasis to center wives, and women in general, at the expense of male genius.) The scene, unsettled by a double take, begins to shift away from a notion of autobiography as mimesis, the representation of what *happened*, to an emphasis on the way a story is *told* and told and told again, on autobiography as process. In comparative close readings like these, it becomes increasingly clear that the reader of the Toklas autobiographies is let in on a lifetime of personal anecdotes shared and constantly renegotiated by two women, and repeated with a difference in many intertexts in an ongoing (de)construction of autobiographical "truth." A double aspect of obvious similarity (the way in which people, events, and autobiographical "facts" appear to be the "same") and simultaneous noncorrespondence (the way in which the texts constantly exceed, fall short of, contradict, and redefine each other) necessarily characterizes an intertextual reading of the Toklas autobiographies.

Part of my argument with regard to the Toklas autobiographies as a series of "easy repetitions" is that, through an intertextual reading of the Toklas autobiographies, it is possible to show that Toklas in her "own" autobiographies, even as she by all accounts stays eminently loyal to Stein's "original," still repeats and mimics Stein's text in such a way as to unsettle the fantasy of originality. *What Is Remembered* enacts a multitude of small but significant slippages and displacements not only in relation to its primary intertext, *The Autobiography*, but also to the historical-biographical context, the presumed pre-existing story of the "real" Toklas. The third Toklas autobiography imitates or approaches both registers of text and context but differs from them in a way that unsettles the conception of autobiography as mimesis, as an unmediated record of factual events. The fact that there are several versions of the "same" life story throws into doubt the simple equation of world and word in autobiography. Toklas's autobiographical "I" is *almost the same but not quite* in relation to Stein's "I" in *The Autobiography*. Moreover, the "I" in the *Cook Book* and the "I" in *What Is Remembered* are almost the same but not quite in relation to each other as well. These differences indicate that Toklas in the text(s) may also be *almost the same but not quite* in relation to the "real" Toklas, so that the fantasy of autobiographical transparency is displaced in favor of a more complex conception of the relation between world and word. Moreover, this foundational ambiguity displaces the idea of a truer or fuller picture of Toklas in *any one text*. Therefore, the fantasy of singularity functions as an enabling paradox or irony at the center of my investigation, the ever-receding referent for the impossible "true story of Alice B. Toklas."

I have been talking about autobiographical material repeated in and among the three Toklas autobiographies. These texts also "repeat" or mimic the discourses and protocols of heterosexuality, and again we are talking about repetition with a difference, almost the same but not quite. The unspoken crux of all three Toklas autobiographies is the issue of camouflaged homosexuality in a context of normative heterosexuality. In "An Exercise in Analysis" in *Last Operas and Plays*, Stein is unusually outspoken about the outlawed status of her and Toklas's marriage. "We have suffered," she complains. "Please be mannish. . . . Please be womanish. . . . Please me. / Do please me. / Please me pleasantly." Toklas replies "Yes I will." "What is the name of the bedding. . . . It is different." Stein meditates. "Then don't explain," Toklas says (quoted and interpreted as dialogue in Simon, *Biography*, 263). Although unspoken in the more accessible works, the "difference" of the "bedding" is the *sine qua non* as the Toklas autobiographies perform a movement of almost the same but not quite/not straight in relation to the heterosexual norm. With Butler's theory of gender trouble in mind I argue that, in Stein's and Toklas's very *performance* of gender and sexuality, in their constant untiring repetition of this particular narrative, a crucial dimension of difference is opened up in the seam between categories of theory and practice, invisibility and visibility, worlds and words. The submerged lesbian content in *What Is Remembered*, specifically when it is manifested through the subplot of heterosexual (im)possibility, can be interpreted as a reformulation of textual/sexual corruption.

There was considerable resistance to acknowledging the lesbian relationship of Stein and Toklas as such when the question of Stein's sexuality and its role in her writings first appeared, most famously in the works of Thomson and Bridgman, after Toklas's death in 1967. In a 1971 letter to the editors of the *New York Review of Books*, Patricia Meyerowitz complains about a recent "flow of strange writings about Gertrude Stein" which "seeks to explain Gertrude Stein's work in terms of her alleged perverse sexuality." Meyerowitz finds these critical tendencies "destructive" and argues hilariously that the title *Tender Buttons* refers precisely to the chaste tenderness that Stein felt for her collection of buttons, before she goes on to grapple with the crux of the matter, "the vexed problem of Gertrude Stein's alleged lesbianism." According to Meyerowitz, Stein's attachment to her brother and dislike of her father made it difficult for her to relate sexually to any other man, but her celibacy should not be interpreted as homosexuality. It is interesting to note that Meyerowitz's argument against the critical turn to Stein's "perverse sexuality" is based to a great extent on her scorn for Toklas as Stein's presumed sexual partner: "With whom did she indulge? Alice Toklas. Ridiculous. Totally ridiculous even to contemplate it but I shall nevertheless do so. Alice Toklas emerges as a prudish spinster. Gertrude Stein summed her up soon after they began living together. . . . She told her she was 'an old maid mermaid.'" Meyerowitz seems to have misunderstood the import of the passage in *What Is Remembered* that concludes by stating that "by the time the buttercups were in bloom, the old maid mermaid had gone into oblivion and I had been gathering wild violets" (48). In a surprising interpretation, Meyerowitz points to this passage to prove Toklas's asexuality. Stein, on the other hand, is in Meyerowitz's opinion merely celibate, not "unaware" of her sexuality. Meyerowitz ends her letter with her own preferred conception of the Stein–Toklas marriage: "Simply stated, Alice and Gertrude made a home for themselves with an emotional attachment as the bond that kept them together. But lesbianism—never" (*New York Review of Books*, 7 October 1971).

In a paradoxical not-quite-straight version (reversal) of the sentiments expressed by Meyerowitz, Toklas in her own writing sometimes pretends to be so shocked by heterosexual "perversion" or corruption that she refuses to believe that it exists. In a letter to the Van Vechtens, for instance, Toklas describes a situation that can only mean an out-of-bounds (hetero)sexual liaison between the servant Thérèse and the painter Genia and then goes on to refute its possibility, while clearly campaigning for her own conception of honesty and decency: "Baby went down the hall and knocked on Thérèse's door—no answer. Baby opened the door. No Thérèse—the bed had not been slept in. Baby heard voices from the room Genia occupied. There was no clue—neither Baby nor I believed Thérèse was in bed with Genia—definitely not. She came from a family of honest women" (*Staying On Alone*, 389). *What Is Remembered* includes a great number of similar incidents, where the corruption of heterosexual couples is decorously hinted at and mildly but firmly reproved: "When we got back to Palma we found that Jeanne and our Breton cook had got to know each other and gone on a walk carrying a hot gigot, which our cook had baked. This intimacy made the situation a bit difficult" (97). During the war, Stein and Toklas throw a party for English soldiers and governesses, and when Toklas describes this event in *What Is Remembered*—the same "unfortunate incident" is recounted in the *Cook Book* (65–66)—she again depicts herself as a guardian of (heterosexual) respectability and decency: "Miss Larkins, the prettiest of the English girls, said to me when the party was over, The officer in the bedroom next to the one I am occupying, when I went into mine he knocked at the wall and said, 'Shall I light my fire?' To which I said, I hope you did not answer. Oh no, she said, of course I did not" (107). Toklas also laments, in subtle and ironic tones, the complicated love life of Juan Gris (145) and Ford Madox Ford, who "was amusing but he made trouble for Violet Hunt." Once again, Toklas refuses to sanction heterosexual license: "The next to the last time I saw Ford was one evening when he came to the rue de Fleurus with a very pretty redheaded girl and said to me, Alice tell her she should marry me. I, knowing the circumstances of his real marriage, said, Oh Ford I cannot" (123). The same type of situation recurs as Imbs writes to Stein and Toklas that he intends to bring a Polish girl with him back to Paris: "Gertrude wrote him a sharp letter saying, You can't do that, Bravig, you can't bring a girl to whom you are not married back to Paris. And Bravig said, What do you propose I should do? Marry her, said she, which Bravig proceeded to do" (140).

The theme of heterosexual license, and Stein's and Toklas's reproach of it, can be found in all three Toklas autobiographies. In *The Autobiography*, Stein performs the same sly commentary on the transgressions of straight couples as can be found in *What Is Remembered*. As Stimpson points out, Stein is "reminding her readers that heterosexuals can sin, too," and that in her version, "the lesbian couple upholds the principles of monogamy" ("Gertrude Stein," 155, 158). Elsewhere, Stimpson describes how, in their insistence on monogamy, Stein and Toklas differ not only from the licentious straight men and women mildly admonished in their autobiographical writings, but also from other Parisian lesbians: "They visited in lesbian circles in which monogamy was a trifle. They were apparently hugely faithful" ("Gertrice," 134). As Turner similarly describes the situation, Stein and Toklas "outdid their lesbian contemporaries. . . . While Radclyffe Hall fretted neurotically over her 'inversion,' and Vita Sackville-West tried to have it both ways, . . . Gertrude and Alice simply married, set up house, had sex, and stayed together" (22–23).

In the *Cook Book*, Friedrich the perfect Austrian cook is torn between his "angel" fiancée and a "devil" woman who threatens to kill him if he will not marry her and then tries to poison him. In the end, he disappears with "the devil," but Stein and Toklas soon receive a wedding announcement from his abandoned fiancée: "She had entered a well-established bourgeois family with nothing more to fear" (46). In this way, the Toklas autobiographies both reaffirm and problematize the picture of heterosexual relationships as the norm, portray Stein and Toklas as unlikely guardians of (heterosexual) respectability and decorum, and implicitly offer their relationship as a model for a specifically *lesbian* decency. This can be seen as a way to deflect attention from an unconventional and outlawed marriage, but it can also be seen as a way to emphasize the flawed nature of other (mainly heterosexual) relationships as a contrast to the solid mutual commitment of these two women. At the same time, the sexual aspect of the Stein–Toklas relationship is almost entirely unspoken in all three Toklas autobiographies. In *What Is Remembered*, it exists only as a repressed subplot that sends a ripple through the text just once, in the episode where Toklas comes to visit Stein for their first "date" and fails to arrive on time:

> When I got to the rue de Fleurus and knocked on the very large studio door in the court, it was Gertrude Stein who opened it. She was very different from the day before. She had my petit bleu in her hand. She had not her smiling countenance of the day before. She was now a vengeful goddess and I was afraid. I did not know what had happened or what was going to happen.
>
> Nor is it possible for me to tell about it now. After she had paced for some time about the long Florentine table made longer by being flanked on either side by two smaller ones, she stood in front of me and said, Now you understand. It is over. It is not too late to go for a walk. You can look at the pictures while I change my clothes. (27)

In a significant statement, at this point in the text the unspeakable makes itself known: "Nor is it possible for me to tell about it now." The quotation seems innocent enough when considered out of context, but this passage, with its breathless style and mysterious reference to some sort of crisis— the somewhat ominous exposure of attraction and desire and the beginning of a lesbian love story, presumably—constitutes a sharp contrast with the bulk of the text, where the relationship between the two women is represented in chatty, everyday language freed from mystery or suggestion: "When our work at Perpignan was over, we returned to Paris. On the way up I gave Gertrude a half cold chicken to eat in one hand while she was driving, so as not to waste any time" (104). In her old age, many years after Stein's death and more than half a century after their first meeting, Toklas still cannot allow the lesbian inflection of their relationship to come to the surface—it is impossible to tell.

Even as Toklas is unwilling to speak openly about her lesbian relationship with Stein, she does indicate her own sexuality by including in *What Is Remembered* a slight but significant subplot of heterosexual (im)possibility. The narrative of heterosexual possibility and its gradual turn to impossibility revolves largely around Toklas's (final) romantic relationship with a man, aboard the boat to Europe: "On board was a distinguished old-ish man, a commodore, who got into conversation with me when I was reading on the deck after lunch. We spent the greater part of the voyage together. Harriet did not speak to me of the episode but I could see that she considered that I lacked discretion" (23). On the day that Toklas arrives in Paris, she meets Stein, and their relationship takes off almost immediately. The brief fling on board the transatlantic ship is then radically reevaluated as Toklas describes how she received "a most compromising letter from the commodore. There was no question of my answering it. I carried it in my handbag into the Tuileries Gardens where I sat down near the artificial lake and tore the letter into shreds, hoping when I dropped them into the lake that no one was seeing me do so. I then walked up the Champs Elysees to the hotel. Well, that episode was closed" (29).

"Distinguished" has been changed to "compromising," and the heterosexual love life of Toklas is "closed." It is true that Toklas may already have experienced lesbian relationships by the time she arrives in Paris, perhaps with Harriet Levy. I am talking here, however, about the way in which a shift from heterosexual possibility to impossibility is effected *textually*. It is interesting that the description of Toklas's elaborate destruction of the written indication of a potentially tainted *sexual* liaison, the invitation to a love relationship that never happened, reads very much like White's description of his getting rid of the evidence of a ruined *textual* relationship, notes for the version of *What Is Remembered* that never happened. Toklas refuses both these invitations, the commodore's and White's, to *straight* sexual/textual intercourse and goes on instead in her "own" writing to position herself as almost the same but not quite/not straight in relation to the generic contract of autobiography *and* to heterosexuality as the norm. In this manner, Toklas performs a reformulation of textual/sexual "corruption," which brings us back to Dydo's concept of textual corruption as the trace of the "other woman" in the "original" text. This time around, even though she may not be "accommodating and charming" in relation to proponents of such norms and contracts, Toklas makes sure that she is not "lack[ing in] discretion" (*What Is Remembered*, 22–23).

In the present study, I engage with the *Cook Book* and *What Is Remembered* as writing and as supplements to Stein's *Autobiography*. Writing and/as supplementarity must be recognized as one of the most central and well-known aspects of Derridean theory. The Toklas autobiographies, taken together, and the issues actualized by the three texts as intertexts, bring to mind Derrida's famous reading in *Of Grammatology* of Jean-Jacques Rousseau's *Essay on the Origin of Language*. His discussion of Rousseau's "dangerous supplement" is highly useful for the present study, not only because it provides a way of thinking about Toklas's "own" autobiographies as supplements to Stein's original *Autobiography* that at the same time challenge the very *idea* of originality, but above all because it offers a radical possibility for the strategic coupling of textuality and sexuality, genre and gender. According to Rousseau, masturbation is "dangerous" as a supplement to sexual intercourse, and writing is "dangerous" because it poses as "presence and the sign of the thing itself," even as it is supposedly only a substitute for speech. With atypical simplicity, Derrida says that Rousseau "considers writing as a dangerous means, a menacing aid, the critical response to a situation of distress. When Nature, as self-proximity, comes to be forbidden or interrupted, when speech fails to protect presence, writing becomes necessary. It must *be added* to the word urgently" (144, emphasis in original). Moreover, "Within the chain of supplements [in Rousseau], it [is] difficult to separate writing from onanism. Those two supplements have in common at least the fact that they are dangerous" (165). Derrida's analysis ultimately shows that Rousseau ends up inadvertently establishing the very opposite of what he intends to prove, namely the foundational and primary supplementarity of language, society, and human relationships. Derrida's reconception of supplementarity is summed up by Seán Burke as follows: "the thought of an originary presence is destined to discover a supplement at the origin, the supplement of an origin itself supplementary, a presencing absence, an absenting presence" (125).

The Derridean supplement is characterized by a fundamental paradox since it "harbors within itself two significations whose cohabitation is as strange as it is necessary." On the one hand, the supplement "adds itself, it is a surplus, a plenitude enriching another plenitude, the *fullest measure* of presence." On the other, the supplement precisely *supplements*: "It adds only to replace. . . . If it represents and makes an image, it is by the anterior default of a presence" (*Of Grammatology*, 144–45). Derrida's concept of supplementarity as a dimension of abysmal textuality, the insertion of repetition in the fantasy of presence, and the introduction of a split in the category of the "self" has greatly influenced my reading of the Toklas autobiographies. At the same time, it must be acknowledged that Derrida's theory of the supplement may frame a discussion of lesbian autobiography only provisionally, and with constant awareness of complications, such as possible complicity with prevalent (hetero)sexist constructions of lesbian sex as two women touching each other *as if touching themselves*, in a simplistic doubling of Irigaray's construction of woman as two lips constantly touching each other (*This Sex Which Is Not One*). It should be noted that many Stein critics talk about Stein's work in ways that strongly suggest affinities with Irigaray's notion of *écriture féminine*: "In joining the substance of Stein to the voice of Toklas, she is both distinguishing the two and making them one—one of two, two of two" (Dydo, *Gertrude Stein*, 540). In the present study, I am not trying to identify a form of *écriture féminine* in the Toklas autobiographies. Instead, my ambition is to rethink these texts as (practices of) writing, and this is why Derrida's reading of Rousseau may provide a useful theoretical framework for a discussion of supplementarity in the Toklas autobiographies.

As I have argued throughout, the Toklas autobiographies inhabit a complex relation of originality and supplementarity in relation to each other. Both the *Cook Book* and *What Is Remembered* supplement Stein's *Autobiography*, but not in exactly the same way. Unlike the *Cook Book*, *What Is Remembered* openly and without excuses performs the act that Toklas defined as impossible a decade earlier. In short, it repeats Stein's move in writing "a book about her life with Gertrude Stein and about the many people and adventures they had shared" (*Cook Book*, vii). Another difference between the two autobiographies authored by Toklas is that *What Is Remembered* centers Stein to an even greater extent than the *Cook Book*. Of course, this can be seen as a function of the way in which *What Is Remembered* repeats or mimics *The Autobiography*, which has been described as *Stein's* self-writing. The *Cook Book*, however, deals extensively with the domestic domain, where Stein stayed out and Toklas ruled supreme. Therefore, the *Cook Book* reads less like a tribute to Stein and more like the deeply personal and surprisingly amusing account of a lifetime in housekeeping. But both the *Cook Book* and *What Is Remembered* very clearly "follow upon" *The Autobiography*, not only in terms of simple chronology but, in the case of the *Cook Book*, extratextually (according to the publisher's note, which is of course also a text, this work takes the form of a "cook book . . . with memories" precisely because the *Autobiography* is already "done") and, in the case of *What Is Remembered*, textually (it rehearses the same material as the *Autobiography* and generally seems to refer back to the previous text rather than "real life"). It can be argued that the two Toklas autobiographies authored by Toklas follow upon Stein's *Autobiography* in a more critical sense than Stein's own *Everybody's Autobiography*, which is explicitly situated in relation to the earlier text as a "sequel," dealing with what happened after *The Autobiography*.

What is interesting, of course, is the fact that the "originality" of the first autobiography is a fantasy, not only in the sense that originality in textual representations is *always* a fantasy, but also in the sense that the ruse, the scam of originality and transparency, in this case is the very point of the work and is thoroughly exposed in the text itself. Furthermore, the supplementarity of the two autobiographies authored by Toklas proves impossible to reduce to "additionality." These supplements not only add to but also modify the "original" in such a way that the supplementary discourse takes precedence and endangers the construction of the first Toklas autobiography as the "original." This perspective departs from the dominant version of the relation between these texts, which has been unproblematically reproduced by many critics: "Mapping the set of contradictions that defined this relationship [between Stein and Toklas] is difficult, since the only record that survives is Stein's, a record in which Alice is central to observations that rest in Gertrude's perceptions. After Gertrude's death, Alice loyally attested to the accuracy of this record; if there were discrepancies, they were never admitted" (Benstock, *Women of the Left Bank*, 165).

The assumptions behind Benstock's version of the story are not to be taken for granted. The origin of the "I" speaking in *The Autobiography* is forever deferred. It is a classical chicken/egg situation, which inserts a certain ambiguity in each consideration of the relationship between the Toklas autobiographies. For instance, in *What Is Remembered*, often described as an "echo" of *The Autobiography*, is Toklas mimicking Stein or herself? Or is she perhaps not mimicking at all, but speaking "straight"? As we have seen already, the relationship between Stein and Toklas was complicated and has been conceptualized in many different ways. Flanner says, "While Gertrude orated and made the pattern of the conversation, Miss Alice B. Toklas was sitting behind a tea tray. It was as if Gertrude was giving the address and Alice was supplying all the corrective footnotes" (quoted in Weiss, 78). In this version of the story, Toklas's contribution, albeit apparently secondary and less prolific, is not only a supplement in the sense of an addition, but also a *correction*, a supplement that forever exceeds and alters the "original" address. Toklas's "correction" of Stein should perhaps not be seen as the presentation of a "truer version," or even the one and only "true story," but rather as a necessary condition for the existence of the "original," in the sense that it makes possible the concept of originality but at the same time shows that the only possible "truth" of the story resides in its multiplicity and elasticity, and in its resistance to the fantasy of a "truly" and ultimately truth-telling autobiography.

In this context, it is interesting to recall once again the supplementary issue of *transition* magazine, which was intended to "correct" what Stein said about friends, acquaintances, and an entire era in *The Autobiography* (see Weiss, 96, and my own discussion of the *transition* document). Toklas's "correction" of Stein is different, however, because it is combined with the foundational assumption that "Gertrude [is] always right" (Thomson, 171). This is presumably why the *Cook Book* and *What Is Remembered* leave the official story from *The Autobiography* intact to such a high degree. Moreover, this postulation is a mutual one in the Stein–Toklas marriage. In *Everybody's Autobiography*, Stein says that Toklas "is always right so much so that I often ask her does it not tire her" (123). Moreover, Bridgman points out that Stein defines herself as "stupid" in relation to Toklas, using the very same construction ("always right"): "Gertrude Stein realized that she was not equipped to exercise the selectivity that a history required. . . . She relied therefore upon the judgment of Alice. 'I can be as stupid as I like because my wife is always right'" (213).

In his chapter "Portrait of Gertrude Stein," Thomson (like many other Stein commentators) ends up portraying Toklas as well, and he, too, seems to agree that she is "always right." His analysis of storytelling practices in the Stein–Toklas marriage both follows and radically extends Flanner's characterization of the discursive interplay between the two women, as he, too, positions Toklas behind a domestic prop (this time not a tea tray, but a tapestry frame): "How often have I heard [Stein] begin some tale, a recent one or a far-away one, and then as she went on with it get first repetitive and then uncertain till Alice would look up over the tapestry frame and say, 'I'm sorry, Lovey; it wasn't like that at all.' 'All right, Pussy,' Gertrude would say. 'You tell it.' Every story that ever came into the house eventually got told in Alice's way, and this was its definitive version" (177). This anecdote can be taken to suggest a possible reading of Toklas's "own" autobiographies, the *Cook Book* and *What Is Remembered*, as continuations, completions, and even *corrections* of Stein's *Autobiography*, rather than weak follow-ups. This reading would destabilize the hierarchical model that in reviews and other commentaries typically posits *The Autobiography* as the "original," the masterpiece in relation to which *What Is Remembered* is found lacking, and it would reinterpret Toklas's acts of repetition as assertive and even dominant (like Stein's repetition/imitation of Toklas's story and conversation in *The Autobiography*) rather than uncertain, submissive, and secondary. I will now give one important example, on the centrality of art, to indicate the way in which Toklas repeats Stein's account with small but significant differences.

While the famous paintings of Picasso, Matisse, Derain, Braque, and others play a central part in *What Is Remembered*, as they did in *The Autobiography*, Toklas also, through irony and a certain quiet counterdiscourse running parallel to the "official" story, indicates her (in)difference in the latter memoir: "After lunch, [Mike Stein] said, I shall take Alice to the Louvre. It is scandalous that she has not yet found time to go there. I thought she was interested in pictures. Perhaps I was but perhaps it was not my major interest" (*What Is Remembered*, 33–34). The subsequent description of Toklas's first visit to the Louvre indicates to the reader that the experience did not exactly change her priorities: "Down the long gallery I was rushed. So that you may know where to find things, explained Mike as we hurried past miles of pictures. I was exhausted" (34). Like so often in the *Cook Book*, good taste is then redefined in terms of the palate rather than the visual arts, as the narrative shifts abruptly to another domain: "Mike then took me across to the rue de Rivoli, where we had an ice at an incomparable Hungarian pastry shop" (34). The implication seems to be that the ice cream made up for the visit to the Louvre.

It Is significant, moreover, that the vernissage of the independent, where Toklas is initiated to the world of modern art, is described much less exhaustively in *What Is Remembered* (32–33) than in *The Autobiography* (21–26). In *What Is Remembered*, Toklas focuses on a small number of people attending—Picasso, Fernande, and their crowd—and her conversation with Fernande about French lessons. She mentions the show itself only to point out that "The discussions were lively but not entirely friendly" and to present a brief anecdote about modern art: "A very small Russian girl was holding forth explaining her picture, a nude holding aloft a severed leg. It was the beginning of the Russian horrors. She was a student of the Matisse school. The first day Matisse came to criticize the pictures he had asked her, as was his habit, For what are you striving, mademoiselle? She had answered, without a moment's hesitation, The modern, the new. The class applauded" (33). Toklas leaves it at that, creating a profound ambiguity in the text about the author's own opinion. Does she too applaud this ambitious art student? Or does she present this story as a joke, perhaps even as a critique of a certain weakness for the spectacular in art? In any case, *What Is Remembered* does not deal with the vernissage of the independent further. In *The Autobiography*, on the contrary, the same event holds a prominent place in the narrative.

I have quoted Thomson saying that "Gertrude imitated [Toklas's style] three times with striking success. She could not use it often, because its way was not hers" (177). I find it significant that Thomson emphasizes *Stein's* imitation of Toklas in "Ada," *Miss Furr and Miss Skeene*, and *The Autobiography*, treating Toklas's discourse as primary and Stein's as secondary. He also describes Toklas's style, "her unique narrative powers," as exactly that—a *way with words* that differs from Stein's. Like most other critics and commentators, Thomson deals with Toklas in passing and in relation to Stein, but his remarks on her work are significant. As far as I know, he is alone in speaking seriously of *What Is Remembered* as belonging to a certain style and a certain literary tradition: "There is nothing comparable to this compactness [of style in *What Is Remembered*] elsewhere in English, nor to my knowledge in any other literature, save possibly in Julius Caesar's *De Bello Gallico*." Here, Thomson displaces the image of Stein as the Roman emperor, supported not only by a certain famous haircut ("designed" by Toklas) but also by the frequent mention of "Caesars" in Stein's own work, placing the third Toklas autobiography alongside *De Bello Gallico* in a literary tradition of compactness and great "brevity" (176). The text provides many examples of these characteristics. For instance, *What Is Remembered* quietly remarks upon the variety of people congregating in the American West at the end of the nineteenth century and the way in which their interactions suggest enormous differences in status and power but without spelling out the implications to the reader: "One autumn we stayed at a hop ranch in the Snoqualmie Valley for several weeks. A young squaw came and asked us for a pair of shoes in which to bury her child who had always gone barefoot. A beautiful Southern girl who was staying at the ranch gave her a pair of very high-heeled white satin slippers" (12–13). And the narrative moves swiftly on to something else. In passages like these, Toklas seems to draw upon a literary tradition of compactness and emotional restraint (what Bridgman calls "tart economy"), a practice that reminds the reader not only of *De Bello Gallico*, to return to Thomson's suggestion, but also, in a specifically American context, of Hemingway.

Of course, as we have seen in some of the reviews quoted above, not everyone was won over by the compactness of Toklas's style. Many reviewers were quite disappointed to find the brevity and emotional restraint of a Caesar or a Hemingway in the memoirs of Gertrude Stein's eccentric companion. As I have already pointed out, critical and readerly expectations are typically centered on revelation, fullness, and the public display of emotion in autobiography. In *What Is Remembered*, such expectations are thwarted and, more often than not, the text is then defined as a failed autobiography, its author gone missing. As I see it, however, Toklas's refusal to provide disclosure and transparency can be interpreted otherwise in an intertextual reading that takes into account textual strategies and tricks of evasion—in other words, a reading that reconsiders autobiography as *writing* and the autobiographical "I" as an ever-shifting site of resistance. This is an approach that necessarily privileges the dangerous supplementarity of writing at the expense of the fantasy of autobiography as truth, essence, and "the fullest measure of presence."

Chapter 4

The Alice B. Toklas Cook Book **and the Incompatible Combination**

By signing the text—whether a book, a cookbook, an autobiography, or a recipe card—the author promises that this is the "truth." This might be especially important in the context of cookbooks and recipes, for if the "truth" is not given, a dish will fail. . . . Thus, when an autobiography is enhanced by recipes from author to reader, the trust implied by the recipe-sharing tradition affects the autobiographical offering.
TRACI MARIE KELLY, "If I were a Voodoo Priestess," 265

The Alice B. Toklas Cook Book by Toklas can be seen as the neglected counterpart or intertext of Stein's *Autobiography of Alice B. Toklas*. The two texts are inextricably connected. First, both revolve around the details of a life, presumably the "same" life, but neither qualifies as the "straight" autobiography of the person whose name appears in the title. The result of this paradox can be described in a Derridean way as a "deferred" auto-biography (which differs from the norm yet stays close enough to trouble it), since Stein and Toklas both deflect an initial request for a straight autobiography.[1] Already in the choice of a genre for her writing after Stein's death, and true to her predilection for disguise, Toklas avoids a commitment to naming or defining herself in a conventional form of self-writing and instead asserts an alternative generic frame for (un)naming or (re)inventing herself in the text. In an anecdote included in the publisher's note, Toklas posits and then circumvents the impossibility or impasse upon which, paradoxically and intriguingly, follows her idea to write a cookbook with memories:

"Oh," said Alice, "I couldn't do that."
"Why not?" asked the young publisher from New York [Simon Michael Bessie] who had been trying to persuade her to write a book about her life

with Gertrude Stein and about the many people and adventures they had shared.

"Because," said Alice in that cigarette-rough and sensuous voice, "Gertrude did my autobiography and it's done. . . . What I could do," she said as tentatively as she was able, which was not very, "is a cook book." And then, "It would, of course, be full of memories." She kept her promise. (vii)

The peculiar genesis of the *Cook Book*, as reported here, supports my reading of the middle Toklas autobiography as a text that unsettles the very concept of autobiography. Beyond the commonsensical probability that Toklas came up with the idea of an autobiographical cookbook to satisfy Bessie, because her refusal to write a "straight" autobiography disappointed him, the *Cook Book* follows upon *The Autobiography* in an extremely interesting "negative" sense. It can be argued that Toklas's text occupies a position of *absolute difference* in relation to Stein's, in fact, constituting its negative "other." Not an autobiography but "a cook book . . . full of memories," the *Cook Book* enacts the ultimate trick of evasion and seems the very opposite also of *What Is Remembered*, which openly and without excuses does what Toklas defined as impossible a decade earlier, in that it repeats Stein's move in writing "a book about her life with Gertrude Stein and about the many people and adventures they had shared." Toklas's conversation with her publisher can be juxtaposed with a characterization of her found elsewhere. Stewart remarks that "Miss Toklas was somewhat deaf. . . . [S]he misunderstood an inquiry . . . and gave a somewhat different account" (118). Toklas certainly does not "misunderstand" Bessie's inquiry, but she deliberately *rewrites* the demand according to her own conception of possible and impossible and decides to give a "somewhat different account." This rewriting of the task at hand arguably endows Toklas with some freedom insofar as it finds a liminal space for her writing, and I have chosen to conceptualize the *Cook Book* as a renegade autobiography, almost the same but not quite/not straight, following upon Toklas's decision to provide the publisher with a "different account" instead of the straight autobiography that he asks for. At the same time, does writing remain *writing* when it is based upon a (deliberate) departure from generic expectation?

Like the ending of *The Autobiography*, the ending of the *Cook Book* avoids closure and opens onto radical uncertainty. The setting is the garden at Bilignin, Stein and Toklas's country home: "And so we left Bilignin, never to return. And now it amuses me to remember that the only confidence I ever gave was given twice, in the upper garden, to two friends. The first one gaily responded, How very amusing. The other asked with no little alarm, But, Alice, have you ever tried to write. As if a cook-book had anything to do with writing" (280). Without the final paragraph, the ending of the *Cook Book* would have paralleled the ending of *What Is Remembered*, which coincides with Stein's death: "and I never saw her again" (186). The *Cook Book*, however, goes on to comment on its own genesis, its own production, in a way that instead resembles *The Autobiography*. At the same time, the ending of the *Cook Book* also creates a distance between what is remembered in it and the act of writing in a way that differs from the previous text. The two reactions to Toklas's confidence, amusement and alarm, seem diametrically opposed, yet they also appear to have the same *effect*, namely, to dismiss or belittle the writing of the *Cook Book*, the *Cook Book* as writing. Such reactions may seem similar to Hemingway's misnaming and unnaming of Toklas, but what is interesting is the fact that these attempts at dismissal are contained within the text and *themselves* dismissed through a refusal of the very premise for misnaming and unnaming: the status of this text *as writing*. If Toklas herself casts doubt upon the status of her book as "writing," and thus undermines the grounds for judging it in accordance with the norms and standards of that category, she is in a sense immune to, or at least in defiance of, acts of violent unnaming. This discursive effect (again, not a question of authorial intent) parallels the way in which Toklas, in life and in texts, refuses to maintain a stable identity for herself that can then be appropriated by others, myself included, for "the true story of Alice B. Toklas."

I would like to juxtapose this finale, where Toklas unsettles the concept of "writing," and the reported beginning, where Toklas rewrites the request to write an autobiography, and force the two textual moments together in a provisional circle. Between these two textual moments, and quite independently of any consideration of the referential truth of either one, there is a certain space or spacing, the opening up of a liminal discursivity at the borders of several genres or categories: cookbook, autobiography, and literary experiment. In this way, Toklas inhabits the borderlands of dominant discourse, a fundamentally ambivalent and challenging inside/outside position. What happens to "writing" in Toklas's disclaimer? To be sure, not only the concept of cookbook but also the concept of writing is affected by the ambiguity of the last sentence.

Through this radically indefinite "as if," writing, as the norm or model to which the alarmed friend refers, is being called into question and undermined along with the (non)writing that constitutes the *Cook Book*. This vague threat to real writing is probably also the impetus for alarm, rather than concern about the reputation, success, or failure of the friend who confides that she has unexpectedly put pen to paper.

There is another text dealing with the transaction that is described at the very end of the *Cook Book* that further problematizes Toklas's attitude toward the sanctity of writing. In a 1949 letter to Steward, Toklas writes: "My household work seems never ending—always increasing for some mysterious [reason]—but the long projected cookbook has to materialize. . . . Years ago when I spoke of it to Thornton Wilder he only said—but Alice have you ever tried to write. Not since I was ten or eleven years old was the answer—so perhaps one has to have some experience of writing for even a cookbook. But cant one count and build upon conviction—prejudice and passion—my inadequate equipment" (*Dear Sammy*, 169). In this version of the "same" story, Toklas both reiterates her characteristic self-depreciating stance and questions it. Her "equipment" (conviction, prejudice, and passion) is "inadequate," yet she seems to suggest that it can still replace experience (of writing) and enable (some sort of) writing. This ambivalence continues in the *Cook Book* itself. In the text, Toklas downplays her role as a writer in relation to the autobiographical material and highlights the compilation of recipes and the transmission of culinary knowledge as her task.[2] It seems as though Toklas is self-confident as a cook and recipe collector, but not as a "writer," and particularly not as the writer of an autobiography, since "Gertrude did my autobiography and it's done." Toklas seems to worry about encroaching upon her husband's territory (the autobiography).[3]

What is particularly interesting about the ending of the *Cook Book* in the context of the present study is the way in which it can be seen as a *key for reading*, a message to the reader. "The *only* confidence I *ever* gave," Toklas cautions us, referring back to a conversation in the past that is included only as a trace or a fragment, and implying that *this*, the present discourse, relaying the autobiographical material included in the *Cook Book*, is *not* a reliable autobiographer talking straight. A significant point is that exactly *what* the only confidence she ever gave *was* is not spelled out but may be surmised only through the reactions provoked by it. It seems reasonable to think that Toklas's friends would not have reacted very strongly to the idea for her to publish a regular cookbook. After all, she was well known among friends and acquaintances for her expertise in the kitchen, and the cookbook genre would probably not have been considered inappropriate for the wife of a genius. The most plausible cause for amusement and alarm, instead, is the divulgence of an intention to mix genres in a culinary autobiography or autobiographical cookbook, hence the emphasis on *writing* and experience in writing (the compilation of a conventional cookbook would seem to require other, less exclusive skills). The possibility, playfully referred to by Bridgman, that Toklas may have composed her own autobiography is suppressed even here.

In her foreword to the *Cook Book*, M. F. K. Fisher takes the last sentence of this text at face value: "Miss Toklas made comments about the people and the recipes in her book exactly as she talked, so that she felt that her notes were not worthy of being called writing, which was to her a life apart, mostly occupied by Gertrude, with a few lesser geniuses lurking behind her mammoth shadow" (xiv). In Fisher's opinion, then, the ending of the *Cook Book* is to be taken seriously, perhaps as an earnest disclaimer by a modest cook and recipe collector who would not want her petty text production, prompted by financial difficulties, to be placed in the same category as the masterpieces written by her genius companion. This appears to be "true" in the most basic biographical sense. Despite the fact that Fisher may be right in her conjectures about the opinions of the "real" Toklas, however, I am unwilling to accept a reading of the *Cook Book* that ignores or trivializes the striking reversal of the last paragraph. This is why I emphasize the way in which Stein's decision to write Toklas's first autobiography (autobiographies) on her behalf throws the *Cook Book* into a different light—arguably, a much more intriguing one.

The ending of the *Cook Book* can be juxtaposed with the ending of *The Autobiography* to show that both texts might be seen as deferred autobiographies. Like the *Cook Book*, *The Autobiography* ends in a self-reflexive way and with a celebrated twist, and the famous ending is preceded by a reference to the impossibility of Stein writing her autobiography, which resembles the anecdote concerning Toklas's refusal to produce a memoir, even as it also differs from it in significant ways: "For some time now many people, and publishers, have been asking Gertrude Stein to write her autobiography and she had always replied, not possibly. She began to tease me and say that I should write my autobiography. Just think, she would say, what a lot of money you would make. She then began to invent titles for my autobiography. My Life With The Great, Wives of Geniuses I Have Sat With, My Twenty-five Years With Gertrude Stein" (341). Why would it be impossible for Stein to write her autobiography, and why, on the other hand, does she find it appropriate for Toklas to write hers? What is the difference, if any, between Stein's and Toklas's refusals to write their autobiographies? A provisional answer would be that, while Stein seems to think that she is *above* writing her autobiography (she is the Great, the Genius, about whom Toklas should be writing *her* autobiography), Toklas seems to suggest that she is not *worthy* of writing one (Stein already did hers, it is done, and she is not capable of real "writing" anyway). Quite obviously, even as they are part of the affectionate jesting game of two lovers, and Stein is making fun not only of Toklas but also of herself, the titles suggested by Stein for Toklas's autobiography spell out the paramount hierarchical division that runs along the binary lines of great/not great, genius/wife, Stein/Toklas.

To understand Stein's attitude toward the idea of writing her own autobiography and of her wife writing her own autobiography, we need to think about the way in which the reference to money ("think . . . what a lot of money you would make") in relation to a piece of writing possibly alters its aesthetic value and makes it "low" in opposition to "high" modernism or "high" art. The manuscript of *The Autobiography* shows that, at this reference to money, "Toklas adds in heavy, red-penciled capitals, 'NO.' Stein kept the sentence" (Dydo, *Gertrude Stein*, 539). Despite the fact that all three Toklas autobiographies can be seen as commercial to some degree, the widely disparate status of the three texts in relation to commercial success, critical reception, and literary "value" must be taken into account. According to Stein, *The Autobiography* was written in her "money-making style" and hence it is less valuable as a piece of writing than her "real" writing and less worthy of attention. Toklas, who did not have to maintain the aura of genius, exhibited no such qualms about her own work, which was produced in order to relieve the strained financial situation she found herself in after Stein's death. The "incompatible combination" mentioned in Toklas's letter to Steward occurs at the intersection of necessity and writing. In other words, it represents the clash between essential material needs and creativity. The production of Toklas's writing, then, is marked by commercial necessity to an even higher extent than *The Autobiography*, which was written during a period when Stein and Toklas enjoyed a stable, if not lavish, financial situation.

Even though *The Autobiography* can be seen as more "commercial" than other Stein writings—Stein quite simply needed a bestseller—its function as a commodity is not advertised in the text itself: "Not surprisingly, the tact that renders sexuality invisible [in an instance of the subgenre lesbian lie] also renders money invisible. *The Autobiography* is genteel about Stein's income. The circulation of her desire and that of her dollars/francs are each veiled" (Stimpson, "Gertrude Stein," 153). Toklas, on the other hand, is *always* more or less outspoken, and cynical, about the fact that she writes primarily to make money. Steward recalls a conversation with her: "She had just sold an article on cooking and had been 'hideously overpaid' for it. On the proceeds she was going to take a month in Spain and another in Cannes, and had already out of the money taken a trip to Switzerland to see Bernard Faÿ . . . and had bought herself a dress of pure rayon, of which she was much enamored" (*Dear Sammy*, 91).

A recognition of the Toklas autobiographies as commodities and an awareness of the significance of money in relation to writing are crucial aspects of my argument. Toklas's low opinion of her own work and Stein's well-known ambivalence about the welcoming audience-friendly style that she used for *The Autobiography* (and, to a lesser degree, for other autobiographical works) may seem related. Toklas, however, does not have a "high art style" in relation to which her "money-making style" can be defined as inferior. The production of her work is *entirely* based on financial need. In effect, she wrote in order to be able to survive without selling too many paintings from her and Stein's collection. The material necessity of publishing her work contributes to its "low" status, and, according to many letters and other sources, Toklas herself did not consider her writing to have *any* significant aesthetic value beyond its pecuniary worth. For instance, this is the way in which she advises Steward on the treatment of jaundice, the illness that plagued her while she wrote the *Cook Book*: "But go on to it gradually because jaundice likes to return! That's why the cook book was so drab. But I've finally gotten some advance pennies—due in June!—and am blowing them into heating" (*Dear Sammy*, 206). Similarly, in a January 1954 letter to Thornton Wilder, Toklas says, "The pennies that finally were sent as royalties (!) are now royally paying for as near adequate heat as the radiator can produce" (*Staying On Alone*, 292). The value of the *Cook Book* is measured not in literary merit but in the level of comfort in the author's home.

In relation to the *Cook Book*, Toklas speaks of her "inadequate equipment" for writing as a function of the fact that her experience in writing ended when she was "ten or eleven years old" (which was when her mother died and she took over the operation of the household). We may assume, then, that she is not adequately equipped to be a writer simply because, ever since she was a child, she has been a domestic laborer of sorts, responsible for two fairly conventional homes (at least concerning domestic arrangements): first, her grandfather's San Francisco household (see, for instance, Stimpson, "Gertrice," 125); and then, Stein's household. As *The Autobiography* indicates, the "inadequacy" in relation to "composing her own autobiography" in 1932 is relative to the fact that she takes care of the house, the garden, the sewing, the dogs, and the practicalities of *Stein's* writing. Toklas's inability to produce "real" writing, then, is a question of *labor*, not a question of genius, talent, or skill. This would seem to challenge, but also in a sense reinscribe, the genius/wife distinction at the heart of the text as genius begins to look less like an essence, more like a privilege.

What happens as *The Autobiography* closes is that Stein *affirms* the work as writing through comparing it to Defoe's text and through redefining it as a literary experiment rather than as a simple memoir. This is a move that appears directly opposite to Toklas's rejection of the *Cook Book* as writing in the final sentence of that text. At the same time, Stein's decision to dismiss ("not possibly") a request for an autobiography and instead produce a "different account" is more or less identical to Toklas's decision to write "a cook book . . . full of memories." It could be argued, then, that both *The Autobiography* and the *Cook Book* are *deferred* Toklas autobiographies, echoes of two "straight" autobiographies that never got written. Let me be even more specific. Both *The Autobiography* and the *Cook Book* are deferred autobiographies in the sense that (1) they arise from a negativity, the erased origin of an autobiography that never got written, (2) *The Autobiography* erases itself as *autobiography* and the *Cook Book* erases itself as *writing* in a final reversal, (3) both texts operate through mixing genres, and (4) both *The Autobiography* and the *Cook Book* are written from a liminal position, speaking not the strongly present autobiographical "I" postulated in the generic contract, but another, radically uncertain, (inter)subjective positionality. The *Cook Book* effects this uncertainty by mixing the cookbook genre with the register of autobiography and by emphasizing the contributions of various "coauthors."

In *The Autobiography*, autobiographical, biographical, and novelistic traits coexist fitfully, and "I" and "she" are (con)fused in such a way as to perform a splitting or doubling of the authorial function.

In her conversation with the publisher of the *Cook Book*, quoted early in this chapter, Toklas finds a different way to write autobiographically, because her autobiography is already "done." In relation to *The Autobiography*, Toklas as writing subject can be said to be *undone*, fictionalized, and removed from the only immediately available position to the wife of a genius where writing is possible. Toklas's way out of this predicament is to construct a liminal genre of her own, an account that differs from the book that Stein wrote for/about her, and moreover a liminal role for herself in writing it, since the role of "writer" in the Stein–Toklas marriage is occupied by Stein. Biographical evidence suggests that encroaching upon Stein's domain, the domain of genius, was anathema to Toklas, both before and after Stein's death. Toklas lived on for another two decades after her partner died with one paramount ambition determining her every move: to act as the guardian and promoter of Stein's reputation as genius while keeping herself in the background and the specifically lesbian inflection of their relationship a secret. When it comes to cooking, housekeeping, and recipes, however, *Toklas* is the indisputable "genius," clearly in charge of the epistemologies and discourses particular to that domain. In the kitchen, Toklas ruled supreme and Stein stayed away.

Everybody's Autobiography provides an anecdote about the way in which the domestic domain and the recipe genre, unlike the autobiography, were off limits to Stein. Returning to France after the 1934 U.S. tour, a fellow American passenger on the *Champlain* "told Alice Toklas that she was going to have a career that would soon be beginning, and that I [Stein] would go on succeeding, we wondered what the career of Alice Toklas was going to be and when it was to begin and then it almost began she decided to write a cook book and if she did the career would begin and she will but she has not yet had time, naturally enough who can and of course this she would not let me do for her and with reason" (296). Stimpson points out that Toklas's career is discussed here "rather as if she were a housewife thinking about reentry" ("Gertrice," 134).[4] After having written Toklas out of almost an entire book, Stein at the very end seems to gracefully concede that her wife, too, may have a career (while making sure to mention that she herself will go on "succeeding" as well). Again, the fact that Toklas is not (yet) writing is put down to her being too busy.

But, as Stein rightly predicts, she *will* write the cookbook that is going to start her career. From today's perspective, it is possible to read this passage as a prophecy, indicating that Toklas will find time to start a career in writing once Stein's writing, for which she is so indispensable, comes to an end.

Toklas will not let Stein "do" the *Cook Book* for her, then, just as she will not rewrite the story of her own life because her autobiography is "done" by Stein, but she *will* perform an extensive mixing of genres that makes the *Cook Book* eminently eligible not only for the provisional category of a "Toklas autobiography" but also for the category of literary experiment. Without making claims about the political agenda or authorial motivation of the "real" Toklas, it is therefore possible to argue that, after Stein's death, Toklas is able to publish her own life-writing, without trespassing on her husband's territory, through officially staying within the category of cookbook. The way in which autobiographical materials are then *mixed in* with the recipes can then be seen (again, without making truth claims about authorial intention) as a liminal move, the insistent pushing on boundaries and the opening up of a liminal discourse that is almost the same but not quite/not straight in relation to *The Autobiography* as an impossible original and in relation to autobiography as a genre. The *Cook Book* is the paradoxical "reentry" into discourse of an antiautobiography, the "other" of Stein's *Autobiography*. The way in which many "coauthors" have contributed text (recipes) to the *Cook Book* creates a similar ambiguity of authority and authorship as the one produced by the authorial ruse of *The Autobiography*. Consequently, the *Cook Book* can be seen as another autobiography in disguise in a way that largely, but not wholly, parallels *The Autobiography*—again, the relationship can be articulated as almost the same but not quite/not straight.

Despite many important differences, then, *The Autobiography* and the *Cook Book* share an element of *trickery*, a certain renegade quality, not only in relation to each other, but also in relation to generic conventions. Both Stein and Toklas challenge and trouble the borders of autobiography. Hence, a reader or critic may be able to engage in a productive way not only with *The Autobiography* but also with the *Cook Book* through approaching it as a deferred autobiography, thus bringing theories about autobiography to bear upon a liminal case. Texts that trace the outlines of dominant discourse have been recognized in literary critical debates as potentially powerful pointers to the shape and form of literary convention:

"The limits of Western literary structures are abundantly obvious in the powerful elisions, co-optations, and experiments that constitute cultural margins. As counterlaw, or *out-law*, such productions often break most obvious rules of genre. Locating out-law genres enables a deconstruction of the 'master' genres, revealing the power dynamics embedded in literary production, distribution, and reception" (Kaplan, 208). Both *The Autobiography* and the *Cook Book* are "out-law" autobiographies in Caren Kaplan's sense of the term, and as such they constitute potentially useful tools for investigating the hidden grounds of the genre. So far, however, and despite the experimental properties of Toklas's text, it has typically been read and categorized, if at all, simply as a trivial cookbook, while the author is known to literary history primarily as Stein's companion. Of course, it is true that the middle Toklas autobiography *is* a cookbook. It does not pose as high art, it does not introduce itself to the reader as experiment, it does not flaunt its avant-garde potential. It is, in fact, possible to cook by it. Because of its lack of conventional markers of unconventionality, the *Cook Book* is not easily recognizable as experimental writing.

It seems as though *The Autobiography* moves to the category of great art, and therefore a semblance of gender neutrality, through the final twist of authorial identity shift and fictionalization. On the other hand, the *Cook Book*, which in its hybridity could very well be seen as a work of literary experiment, is ignored by literary historians and critics, presumably as a simple recipe collection (a feminine text) and therefore not significant. As I see it, however, the *Cook Book* constitutes as comparable a feat of literary experiment and genre play as *The Autobiography*. In general, the widely disparate status of *The Autobiography* and the *Cook Book* in literary history mirrors the semiprivate distinctions upheld by Stein and Toklas as husband and wife, genius and companion, so that Toklas's invisibility as a writer seems crucially connected to their famously rigid division of labor, in which Stein occupied the role of writer and Toklas performed the part of the secretary-companion. As I have argued above, the one crucial difference between the two texts, even as they relate in similar ways to the expectations of a straight autobiography, is that Stein at the end affirms her text as writing in a move that appears to be directly opposite to Toklas's final exclusion of *her* text from the category of writing. In other words, the distinction between *The Autobiography* as a clever literary experiment and the *Cook Book* as a humble recipe collection was partly established by Stein and Toklas themselves *within* the texts in question and in many intertexts.

Apart from a momentary racket over the drugged fudge recipe, *The Alice B. Toklas Cook Book* attracted little attention when it was published in 1954, and since then it has been the subject of only a feeble trickle of critical commentary and some underground fame as a lesbian cult classic. The fact that the *Cook Book* has been neglected in literary criticism is remarkable, since it can be related to a number of critical conversations, for instance, those concerning literary experiment and autobiography (maybe not simply as "belonging" to one of these categories, but rather as a text in dialogue with such frames, enabling the critic to explore their hidden ground while teasing out the implications of the text). But there are limits to the potential perceptibility of experimental styles. Such limits often run along the lines of the writer's position and status. Toklas is not a Joyce, not a Rabelais, not a Sterne. She is not even a Stein. She is Stein's wife and therefore not easily recognizable as an author, and her writings are likewise not easily recognizable as literary works. Consider Foucault's question: "What is a work? . . . If an individual were not an author, could we say that what [she] wrote . . . could be called a 'work'?" ("What Is an Author?" 103).

The fact that Toklas is not generally considered an "author" makes her invisible to most literary critics. In Traci Marie Kelly's 2001 article "'If I Were a Voodoo Priestess': Women's Culinary Autobiographies," however, the *Cook Book* serves as the model of an autobiographical cookbook and as the very cause of Kelly's interest in the subject in the first place. The account of her discovery of this research topic is rather pertinent as a marker of Toklas's status as a marginal figure in cultural history: "For me, *The Alice B. Toklas Cook Book* was the gateway to thinking about texts that combine recipes and autobiography. I found this cookbook by accident; I was supposed to be researching Gertrude Stein for a graduate course. But in an article about Stein, an interesting passage about Toklas' cookbook and the fury over the marijuana fudge recipe sent me to the cookbook section" (262). Kelly's route to the *Cook Book* is representative. Most critics end up commenting on Toklas, and, rarely, her work, only as an afterthought ("accident") in relation to accounts of Stein's life and analyses of her work.

In a June 1953 letter, Toklas herself touches upon many of the concerns of the present study as she swiftly turns the *Cook Book* into a frustrating excuse for falling behind in her correspondence, questions its status as writing, and decisively establishes its publication as a question of material (or even vital) necessity: "My shameful silence was due to a long boresome attack of pernicious jaundice and to the equally boresome writing (?) of a 75,000 word cook book in half the time—the latter to earn the pennies to pay for the former" (*Dear Sammy*, 203). Having juxtaposed, and, as it were, equated the suffering of an illness and the anguish of commercial text production, Toklas goes on to complain about the strains involved in her situation: "The incompatible combination has exhausted me and tomorrow I go to the hospital for a checkup." It is obvious from comments such as these that Toklas, perhaps not truly but consistently and forcefully, not only when performing her official role but also in personal letters, regarded the *Cook Book* as a low literary endeavor, if at all worthy of being considered writing. In the same letter, Toklas speaks of Stein's character studies in very different terms, as "brilliant beyond words and passionately interesting" (*Dear Sammy*, 203–5). This type of biographical evidence obviously complicates my attempt to recover Toklas as a cultural laborer and a writer while still retaining a firm sense of the material circumstances of production and an adequate amount of respect for the object of investigation. As I emphasize the experimental properties of the *Cook Book* and trace the outlines of its hidden aesthetic, I deliberately disregard Toklas's stated opinion. At the same time, her opinions are accessible to me only in various texts where the real Toklas may have left a trace, an imprint of a certain performance, an echo of a certain role played well, but where she will not dwell long enough to let herself, her *self*, be pinned down and investigated.

Whether Toklas the historical person would have recognized herself as a liminal writer is not an issue in this study, although I imagine that she would have opposed my readings of her autobiographies with great passion. In my engagement with the Toklas autobiographies generally and in this chapter on the *Cook Book* specifically, I am trying to perform critically the "incompatible combination" of extending the words on the page beyond the individual text while acknowledging the possible objections of the author. Hence, I will talk about the experimental qualities of the *Cook Book* without positing as a necessary prerequisite for this focus the category of authorial intention. Another way of saying this would be to once again define my intervention as provisionally deconstructionist, since "deconstructive procedure takes the form of following the line of authorial intention up to the point at which it encountered resistance within the text itself: from this position the resistance can then be turned back against the author to show that [her] text differs from itself, that what [she] wished to say does not dominate what the text says" (Seán Burke, 141).

In the remainder of this chapter, I will perform close readings of the *Cook Book*, specifically in relation to the experimental practice of discursive mixing, which temporarily suspends or collapses conventional binaries such as war/housekeeping, art/cooking, and art/gardening in the text. In relation to the war/housekeeping binary, I will also present an intertextual reading of the *Cook Book* and *What Is Remembered* as unconventional war narratives. I will then discuss certain reversals and destabilizations of domestic roles and functions in the *Cook Book*, specifically, the master/servant relation, which also introduces issues of race, ethnicity, and nationality into the true story of Alice B. Toklas. Finally, I will return to the issue of autobiographical truth, and suggest that, in relation to this elusive category, and in relation to the other two Toklas autobiographies, the *Cook Book* is the odd one out. I will begin, however, with the story of the Mixmaster.

According to Paul Schmidt, Toklas's "endless search" in the *Cook Book* is "to bring together exotic substances—unnaturally, but with such perverse delight that nature itself is ravished in our taste buds, and willingly yields" (193). This is true not only of the recipes contained in the *Cook Book*. The "unnatural" juxtaposition of disparate realms of reality and discourse, the deployment of incompatible combinations, is the modus operandi of this eccentric text in its entirety. Indeed, it is my argument in the present study that all three Toklas autobiographies traverse mixed or mixed-up discursive positions that involve a certain form of mastery at negotiating the jagged boundary between dominant discourse and its eccentric outside. In this chapter, as I discuss the *Cook Book*, I make strategic use of the idea of the Mixmaster to engage critically with the experimental qualities of the middle Toklas autobiography—specifically, generic hybridity (cookbook/autobiography) and the mixing of disparate categories such as war/housekeeping, art/cooking, and art/gardening— alongside a recognition of the irreducible actuality of Toklas's domestic labor, the material necessity behind the publication of the *Cook Book*, and the author's low opinion of her text as possibly not having anything to do with writing.

Samuel "Sammy" Steward, an American professor of English, was a close friend of Stein and Toklas from the 1930s on. He delighted his friends by occasionally sending them various American kitchen gadgets that were not available in France. Even as these gadgets epitomize modernity and serve as American status items in Europe, they also provide a link back to Toklas's family history: "My mother revelled in each year's invention. How she would have enjoyed the present gadget of the week" (*Cook Book*, 97). In the eyes of the recipients, the practical utility of Steward's gifts typically appears secondary to their aesthetic qualities. Having on one occasion received a selection of kitchen devices, among other things "an egg whipper, a garlic squeezer, [and] a lid opener," Stein writes in an animated letter that "Alice is delighted with the gadgets she keeps them on the best Italian furniture in the atelier with the best treasures, and she shows them with so much pride, they are so useful and so beautiful and so pale blue" (*Dear Sammy*, 134). It can be argued that, when Toklas displays shiny new kitchen gadgets from the United States, in a complacent bourgeois version of Duchamp's found art, on the best European furniture in the very atelier that holds some of the most innovative expressions of the burgeoning modernist art movement, she brings two national cultures and two levels of art into critical proximity and moreover claims precedence or at least equal status for her specific position as an American culinary artist.

The story of the most cherished kitchen gadget is recorded in Steward's *Dear Sammy* volume. In the spring of 1940, despite Stein's protest a few months earlier—"No no no, no Mixer, $25 is not cheap it is a helluva lot of francs" (145)—Steward sent a Mixmaster to Stein and Toklas as a house present. The response from Stein, again blurring the line between aesthetic pleasure and domestic utility, and generally emphasizing the former, is characteristically enthusiastic: "The Mix master came Easter Sunday, and we have not had time to more than read the literature put it together and gloat, oh so beautiful is the Mix master, so beautiful and the literature so beautiful" (147). This comment on the aesthetic qualities of the Mixmaster "literature" is intriguing. In conjunction with Stein's sparse use of the period, boundaries between the world of cooking and the world of writing turn increasingly permeable: "the only comfort is the Mix master, who is so at home that it seems just like home well to us and the Mix master, otherwise well otherwise, Yale University is making a show of my ms. this fall" (150). Despite Stein's having declared before the mixer arrived that not only was $25 too pricey but also, "in this particular moment, everybody has time enough to mix by hand all the mixing that needs mixing" (145), playful and frequently ironic references to her and particularly Toklas's (the one who would otherwise have had to do the mixing by hand) delight in the machine recur in several letters, as "Alice all smiles and murmurs in her dreams, Mix master" (148).

One of Stein's letters declares Toklas to be so pleased with the Mixmaster that she could write advertisements for it, again linking the pleasure in a domestic object to a certain textual practice. The letter begins with a catchy rhyming phrase with echoes of commercial marketing discourse, and soon Stein goes on to mention advertising: "Day and night Mix master is a delight. . . . first we had to work it together but now Alice works it all alone and it saves her hours and effort, she can write a whole advertisement for Mix master she is so pleased" (148). In a second letter postmarked the same day, Stein continues the joke, "perhaps we could write a series of adds [sic] for Mix master and get rich that way" (149). The wondrous Mixmaster appliance is described as a source of domestic bliss in the face of any difficulty, even war: "I can't tell you how happy Mix master makes the home. . . . thanks again and again and again for Mix master, three long cheers, neither war not anything could stop it" (148). In July 1940, however, disaster strikes: "Alice dropped the big Mix master green bowl and it fell into little pieces on the kitchen floor, such lovely green little pieces" (151). Even when partly destroyed, the Mixmaster remains aesthetically pleasing. In her next letter from November the same year, Stein admits that the war would temporarily have stopped the Mixmaster's revolution anyway, but the emphasis is on the broken bowl (the original, lost forever) and the (im)possible replacement of it: "it would appear that there is a metal mix master bowl. . . . Alice says she would not like it at all she wants the one that she broke she does not want anything else. . . . you see you can use other bowls but they do not twirl around in that lovely green mix master way . . . and therefore the mix master will have to be a mix master still" (*Dear Sammy*, 151).

In the history of its production, the *Cook Book* emerges from a situation in which Toklas combines her own occupation (cooking) with Stein's (writing) in the composition of an autobiographical cookbook. When Stein tells Steward that she and Toklas started out working their Mixmaster together, before Toklas learned how to handle it herself, she provides us with an instantaneous, but reversed and modified, image of the writing relationship in the Stein–Toklas marriage. When Stein helps Toklas out with the mixer, she is (for once) a guest in Toklas's domain: the kitchen. When Toklas helps Stein out with her writing, she is a (constant) visitor in Stein's realm: the writer's study. After Stein's death, Toklas quietly and humbly combines the two (incompatible) roles, suspending the boundary between the two worlds. The Mixmaster can be usefully employed to conceptualize a number of issues relevant to my reading of the Toklas autobiographies: the intricate combination of Stein's and Toklas's identities and roles in all three texts; the notion of an impossible and irrecoverable original; the mix-up of text and context that muddles and at the same time enables this particular study; and, in relation specifically to the *Cook Book*, the author's ambivalent position, not only between French and American cuisines, but also between the kitchen and the writer's study, as well as a certain experimental practice of culinary and discursive "mixing." The "incompatible combination" is a recurring phenomenon, taking the form of oxymoron, paradox, ambivalence, split loyalties, and possible heresy on all the levels of my engagement with the Toklas autobiographies. In this chapter, the figure of the Mixmaster is a way to acknowledge and at the same time work around the impasse that this incompatibility creates.

The experimental character of the *Cook Book* derives primarily from the mixing of genres and the bringing together or juxtaposition of categories. In view of Toklas's delight in her Mixmaster, it is only fitting that, when she finally starts writing, she dedicates herself to the aesthetic of mixing. The *Cook Book* is a fundamentally mixed text: generically, thematically, and stylistically. This inclination seems eminently appropriate for a person who is American but expatriate, who is a lesbian but at the same time conventionally wifely, who takes part in the avant-garde art movement but remains basically conservative in her values and habits. In the contradictory way characteristic of the Toklas autobiographies, and in line with a certain partiality to convention, the aesthetic of mixing is not immediately or fully endorsed in the text itself. The theme of excess versus propriety, immoderation versus purity, runs through the whole of the *Cook Book* and is never resolved. In one passage, Toklas says: "To cook as the French do one must respect the quality and flavour of the ingredients. Exaggeration is not admissible. Flavours are not all amalgamative. . . . What is sauce for the goose may be sauce for the gander but is not necessarily sauce for the chicken, the duck, the turkey or the guinea hen" (5). Throughout the *Cook Book*, Toklas is particular about good taste and a certain standard of purity: "Abalone has a delicate flavour of its own and requires no barbecue or barbarous adjuncts" (134). And "This is for country cooking; cooking in town does not admit of so much condimenting, or spicing for that matter" (275). "Country cooking" may be seen as analogous to folk art, whereas "cooking in town" is parallel to high art, which must keep close to the code and avoid excess.

At the same time, Toklas, as an American, is willing to sometimes depart from these rigid standards: "We foreigners living in France . . . deplore their too strict observance of a tradition which will not admit the slightest deviation in a seasoning or the suppression of a single ingredient" (3). In relation to her tribute to the rigors of French cooking—"The French never add Tabasco, ketchup or Worcestershire sauce" (4)—the fact that Toklas embraces and celebrates her own culinary experiments and excesses creates a paradox at the heart of the text, and the effect becomes even more complex if we understand Toklas's experiments in the kitchen as analogous to the strategies of mixing in the *Cook Book*: "Gertrude Stein not being able to decide whether she preferred mushrooms, chestnuts or oysters in the dressing, all three were included. The experiment was successful and frequently repeated; it gradually entered into my repertoire, which expanded as I grew experimental and adventurous" (29). In the *Cook Book*, too, more than just one (the "proper") ingredient is included, and the result is both experimental and adventurous.

Toklas's culinary experiments and adventures can be placed in a larger context. The *Cook Book* concerns itself prominently with the bringing together of disparate things, not only in terms of mixing as a cooking technique and a liminal discursive strategy, but also in terms of history and national identity. During World War I, for instance, Stein and Toklas serve as the interface between the United States and France in a very literal sense: "We were asked by some of [the] officers [of the U.S. marines arriving in France after the U.S. declaration of war in 1917] to meet the soldiers that evening and tell them about France. . . . It was their first contact with France and ours with our army" (63). Toklas opens the *Cook Book*, written for Anglo readers primarily on the subject of French cooking, by talking about the ways in which war changes the cooking habits in a country. In relation to this topic, Toklas formulates a specifically American national identity for herself. During the war, the French were forced to use "inferior substitutes" in the kitchen, and after Liberation, Toklas says, "The population had been hungry too long, they had lost their old disciplined appreciation of food and had forgotten or were ignoring their former critical judgment. So that even now French food has not yet returned to its old standard" (3). For an American like herself, however, Toklas says, the effect of the war on her cooking habits was different and more fortunate: "Restrictions aroused our American ingenuity, we found combinations and replacements which pointed in new directions" (4). Toklas deplores the fact that the French "are indifferent to these new discoveries of ours, to the exact science that American cooking has become, to our time- and labour-saving devices. . . . Since the war we Americans have learned a great deal from various sources and as teaching is natural to us we would like to share our knowledge" (4).

At the same time, apropos the difference between "food that emerges stainless from deep freeze" and food that is connected through the chapter "Murder in the Kitchen" to the horror of crime and death, Toklas says that "the marketing and cooking I know are French and it was in France, where freezing units are unknown, that in due course I graduated at the stove" (37). Toklas may know the French cuisine best, but as an American she also makes ownership claims on the specific knowledges, gadgets, and philosophies of American cooking. There are many instances when Toklas's relation to French and American food habits is represented in such a way as to create a sense of discord, a juxtaposition of two separate worlds that will not mix well. A lavish lunch party in the French countryside, "with the endless dishes preceding and following the two courses," is described as "a Gargantuan feast." After the party, however, Stein and Toklas spend the night at a country inn, and Toklas picks her American habits back up: "Providently in my handbag was a little jar of American powdered coffee, which was a blessing for our breakfast and a novelty to our French friends" (25).

Not only do Toklas's French and American culinary affiliations sometimes collide, but moreover she does not remain loyal to either one on its own terms. In the *Cook Book*, part of Toklas's aim is to modify French cooking to suit an American palate, but in her cooking practices she also departs from American culinary traditions: "she cooked what she remembered eating when she was a girl in San Francisco, because [Stein] was homesick for American dishes now and then. . . . But Alice had never been a housewife, in our sense of the word, so that the ways she evolved her down-home dishes stemmed more from nostalgia than kitchen experience, and the longer she lived in France and hired cooks there, the less recognizable her 'corn-pone and apple pie' became" (Fisher, xiii). It is interesting to note that when Fisher says that Toklas "had never been a housewife, in our sense of the word," she pinpoints the way in which Toklas as a lesbian departs from the norm. Toklas remained at home, managing various households, from the tender age of ten and for the rest of her life, but still she does not fit into our conception of a housewife because her domestic labor was not framed by the normative structures of a heterosexual marriage (including procreation). The way in which the Stein–Toklas marriage departs from the heterosexual norm can be said to parallel the way in which Toklas's displaced apple pie departs from the American standard: almost the same but not quite/not straight.

Toklas dilutes, blends, and reformulates her American culinary heritage, even as she advocates certain modern principles of American cooking over the old-fashioned French cuisine, and her overall relation to the two national cuisines is represented not only as an ambivalent position between the two but also as a mix-up in each case. Taken by itself, it is perhaps not very surprising that Toklas enjoys fresh game roasted on a spit over a blazing fire in an ancient French country house *and* American instant coffee for breakfast, and certainly it is only natural that an American expatriate in Paris would occupy a position of ambivalence and hybridity in relation to both national cuisines. These shifts and complexities acquire considerable significance in my reading, however, since the *Cook Book* as a whole operates in a parallel way through the bringing together, unnaturally and with perverse delight, of disparate things. Contrary to what Schmidt seems to be saying about the nature of taste and the unnaturalness of mixing disparate elements, what is natural is only conventionally, not essentially, so. Through a sustained and insistent challenge to the rules of purity, separation, and moderation, and even as it explicitly praises those very standards in cooking, the *Cook Book* exposes and puts pressure on the transparency and naturalness of convention, including the conventions of experiment itself, and should therefore be seen precisely as a literary experiment. Another way of putting it would be to say that, by resisting categorization and mixing genres, the middle Toklas autobiography lends itself (again, authorial intention is not the issue) to a reading that challenges definitions of what is and what is not experiment, autobiography, and, ultimately, writing.

In the *Cook Book*, such widely different spheres of human pursuit as war and housekeeping, art and cooking, and art and gardening are mixed up. In general, the former term in each binary construction is privileged in the sense that it denotes an important public endeavor, whereas the latter term in each pair represents Toklas's domestic occupation and part of her humble private role. Throughout the *Cook Book*, however, these distinctions are unsettled and called into question, in that the text fails/refuses to uphold them and the hierarchies traditionally defining their relation to each other, so that Toklas's domestic labor, at least momentarily, blends into and changes places with the privileged term. In the note that precedes the *Cook Book* proper ("A Word with the Cook"), Toklas points out how both America and France "seem to be" hers, and that she is therefore able to write about differences, not only between those two but between all nations: "And I thought about wars and conquests and how invading or occupying troops carry their habits with them and so in time perhaps modify the national kitchen or table" (xix). Toklas arrives at an understanding of geopolitics and cultural interchange through culinary pursuits: "And here is a note on tracking a soup to its source. It was as a result of eating *gazpacho* in Spain lately that I came to the conclusion that recipes through conquests and occupations have travelled far" (49). Toklas is served a great number of different gazpachos in different parts of Spain and is unable to find the "original" recipe. As if to destabilize the concept of originality, Toklas goes on to present the recipes of seven different "Mediterranean soups" and then indicates that the recipe may have traveled even further: "Did the *conquistadores* take the recipe, along with their horses, to the New World?" (52).

In a sense, the *Cook Book* in its entirety records a process of tracking sources and solving mysteries, a geopolitical account of how recipes and cooking habits travel (through war, conquest, occupation, colonization, or peaceful influences such as traveling and friendship) and at the same time an explicit attempt to bridge the gap between national cuisines. For instance, one of the chapters is called "Little-Known French Dishes Suitable for American and British Kitchens." Relations between colonized and colonizing countries are explicitly mentioned, but without any reference to the political aspects of this contact: "The best foreign cooking is in the homes of the French who have been forced for one reason or another to live in their colonies. . . . [A]fter two or three years in Indo-China or Africa they return not only with the recipes of the local cooking but with the materials unobtainable in France and a knowledge of how to prepare them" (21). Imperialism, colonialism, and global food production enter the text in innocent culinary language: "*Note*. Sesame is an East Indian annual plant cultivated for its seeds which give a delicate faintly sweet oil much used in African and Oriental dishes. Pea-nut oil is a fair substitute" (21). The emphasis is on the Anglo reader's ability to successfully recreate or appropriate an oriental dish. The culinary advantages of doing so have been proven in France: "These Colonial dishes add variety to what are frequently in middle-class French families well-cooked but monotonous menus" (23).[5]

Despite the lack of a stated political awareness or agenda, issues of geopolitical import recur throughout the text. Even as the *Cook Book* appears resolutely apolitical in these matters, or possibly of a rather suspect political attitude, there is one area in particular where certain destabilizations and challenges are effected: Toklas's treatment of war and its effect on (culinary) culture. In the *Cook Book*, the separate occupations of war and housekeeping are located on the same plane and written, as it were, in the same idiom: "When as [Hubert de R.] was leaving I gave him twenty sheets [of gelatine] to take to his wife, he was more grateful than the small gift justified. It was not until some time later that he told us for what he had wanted the gelatine. He had needed it desperately for making false papers" (207). In one of the most famous chapters of the *Cook Book*, "Murder in the Kitchen," the two discourses of war and housekeeping are again explicitly connected: "The only way to learn to cook is to cook, and for me, it suddenly and unexpectedly became a disagreeable necessity to have to do it when war came and Occupation followed. It was in those conditions of rationing and shortage that I learned . . . to cook seriously. . . . It was at this time, then, that murder in the kitchen began" (37). The absurdly humorous tone of light journalism dominates the chapter, for instance, as Toklas assassinates "poor Mr Carp" (38). In the *Cook Book*, however, there is also another possible aspect of this play on the various denotations of murder, a more serious one. As the horror of sudden death goes on in Toklas's kitchen, and her French cook Jeanne tries to convince her that "murder by smothering" is a less "bloodthirsty," more "humane" way of killing a pigeon (39), a striking parallel is created to the situation in the world outside. Even as the *Cook Book* avoids the more concrete and gruesome aspects of the war, the situation must have been deeply distressing for Stein and Toklas as a Jewish-American lesbian couple experiencing war in an occupied country. Toklas learns about "murder in the kitchen" precisely because the war necessitates certain changes in her housekeeping practices, and her comments about culinary "crime" can subsequently be read as obscure references to the killing of humans going on all around her: "I carefully found the spot on poor innocent Dove's throat where I was to press and pressed. The realization had never come to me before that one saw with one's fingertips as well as one's eyes. It was a most unpleasant experience, though as I laid out one by one the sweet young corpses there was no denying one could become accustomed to murdering" (40).

In the *Cook Book* as a whole, the unconventional use of the quintessentially (male) modernist "war story" genre not only alongside but thoroughly mixed up with the description of trivial, domestic aspects of life such as cooking and recipes works to collapse, or at least undermine, the strongly hierarchical distinction between the martial and the domestic arts. In a general sense, history itself appears distorted or paradoxical in the *Cook Book*, because the boundaries between public and domestic concerns have been unsettled or partly erased. This is a challenging move, which has provoked some readers and critics to pronounce the *Cook Book* flippant or crude. For instance, Schmidt suggests that an important aspect of the *Cook Book* is "the notion . . . that life goes on all around the dining table, and death and destruction are there, waiting, without. We are so taken by the charm of Alice B. Toklas' memories and menus that we forget that the major narrative concerns the way two ladies survived the two greatest wars of history in a foreign country. . . . For much of the time span of the book people are being starved, tortured, imprisoned, and killed just off its pages—and once or twice right on them. Yet the two imperturbable Americans go on gardening, hoarding, and scrounging rationed foods." Schmidt adds: "It isn't easy to decide whether to be appalled at such callousness or to admire such sublime detachment. I incline to the latter—it isn't fiction, after all" (193–94).

It is strange that Schmidt does not mention the way in which the *Cook Book* deals explicitly and at length with Stein's and Toklas's work to help soldiers and the wounded during the war. His reaction is also interesting for its vacillation between amusement (in relation to the "charm" of the *Cook Book*) and alarm (in relation to the possible "callousness" of Toklas and Stein). These are the same defensive reactions that we have seen reported by Toklas herself at the very end of the *Cook Book*. It is true, however, that the style and tone of the *Cook Book* is such that the employment of humor and wit, coupled with a certain unreflective acknowledgment of privilege, often creates a sense of detachment from the concrete horrors of war, and perhaps indeed a degree of callousness, even when the subject is war work. "Gertrude Stein confided to me that she was going to show me a tank . . . still in a field on the road to Rheims," Toklas cheerfully says; and she goes on: "Auntie took fields so well. As we went along the national highway, Auntie and her driver were happily swaying and serpentining along. The wine at lunch was undoubtedly to blame for their lack of responsibility. They nevertheless negotiated the field. We saw the tank and got on our way to spend the night with Mildred Aldrich at the Hillcrest. It was from there she had seen the first Battle of the Marne and the German retreat. In her garden that evening I wrote the last report to the *Comité*" (72).

Indeed, as Schmidt indicates, although the war affects and complicates the habits of Stein and Toklas, it does not radically change or prevent them: "Aunt Pauline—Model T, bless her—made no more than thirty miles an hour, so we were always late at inns, hotels and restaurants for meals" (*Cook Book*, 57). In the same way, *What Is Remembered* describes war work in a light, chatty tone, as if it was moderately difficult and mostly enjoyable, despite clearly risky situations: "We were at once in no man's land. The road was desolate and bare, and the fan belt on the truck was broken. Gertrude thought that she would mend it with a hairpin, but that was not successful." Toklas is "disgracefully covered with mud," but she and Stein continue to move, as it seems, effortlessly between the scene of war and their accustomed comfortable existence: "We had a light supper, went to bed, slept, and got up early and toured the battlefield. We lunched at a famous deluxe restaurant, Weber" (*What Is Remembered*, 110). Passages such as these indicate that Stein and Toklas, always relatively privileged and sheltered even when engaged in war work and visiting the battlefield, related to the war going on all around them in the manner of tourists, observers, or voyeurs, something that critics have argued influenced the treatment of war in Stein's writing: "In *The Autobiography* Stein does more than present an analogous relationship between art and war: she claims that war is a 'natural' and 'effective' aesthetic. . . . as [Stein] and Toklas approach the battlefield at the front for the first time, war becomes landscape" (Davis, 35). Paul Alkon similarly expresses disappointment in the treatment of the war theme in Stein's *Autobiography*: "Wars are coldly described as announcements of change. A recourse from disturbing encounters with the unanswered question *why* is concentration on recollections of *what* happened" (866).

Schmidt's reading of the war story in the *Cook Book*, however, is still not convincing. His conventional settling of the question of which narrative (public or domestic) is the major one, and his assumption of detachment as parallel to callousness, are problematic in this context. As a counterargument, I suggest that the strong, multiple *attachments* of private domestic life in a time of war may constitute the major narrative in this particular case, and that this is a legitimate way of relating to the experience of war. Despite the fact that I do not agree fully with Schmidt's analysis of the war narrative in the *Cook Book*, I find his comment that the war happens "just off the page" an excellent description of the distorted and unfamiliar slant on reality that results from a literary experiment of juxtaposition and mixing. Indeed, one of the most important defamiliarizing effects of the *Cook Book* stems from the way in which the text engages with war and occupation.

The very concept of war is undermined or reformulated in the *Cook Book* through a domestic perspective on warfare and occupation and a tendency to close in on details as if using a zoom lens. "Wars change the way of life, habits, markets and so eventually cooking," Toklas says (3). The war stories throughout the *Cook Book* are partly unrecognizable by virtue of their distortion in Toklas's domestic lens; a lens that rewrites history and reorganizes its priorities but does not ignore it. For instance, Hitler is mentioned only twice in the *Cook Book*, despite the fact that his war dominates a great part of the text. One cook, Frederich, tells Toklas and Stein "that he and Hitler had been born in the same village and that anyone in the village was like all the others and that they were all a little strange. This was in 1936 and we already knew Hitler was very strange indeed" (43). Hitler is mentioned a second time in relation to food rationing. Toklas says that the German soldiers were particularly keen on butter, and asks, "Had not Hitler asked them if they wanted butter or guns and had they not given the right answer?" (203). This is as close as she gets to a political statement on the war. On the other hand, the same conflation and mixing of different levels is at work, alongside Toklas's wry sense of humor, in an anecdote about the servant Jeanne: "One day when she sighed, I asked if she was worried. She explained that, Belgium being occupied by the wicked Germans, we would have no endives that winter, since the best endives were imported from Belgium. When a Zeppelin raid had sounded, Jeanne, pointing to the sky, said that something soon would be pelting down on us. To be casual I said, perhaps not on us.

But, Jeanne said, such heavy black clouds meant we were in for a rainstorm" (172).

Instead of judging passages such as these as detached and callous, the framing of serious matters in the style of light journalism and the context of domestic concerns can be rearticulated as a form of literary experiment and analyzed on those grounds. A gendered perspective on this friction between Toklas's chatting and the dramatic world events that impinge on her domestic sphere is crucial. Toklas describes historical events that she has experienced, such as the San Francisco earthquake in 1906 and the German occupation of France in 1940, through an account of the housekeeping measures that she found necessary (30–31). Making provisions for bad times ahead is an act connecting not only the events mentioned but also these two and World War I, and the perspective is kept decidedly personal and intimate, the memories of an eyewitness without omniscient comments about the situation constructed after the fact: "The main road was filled with refugees, just as it had been in 1914 and in 1917. Everything that was happening had already been experienced, like a half-awakening from a nightmare. The firing grew louder and then the first armoured car flew past. Crushed, we took the little dust road back to Bilignin" (31). Throughout the *Cook Book*, Toklas grafts her own story upon the discourse of history in this way and connects her own feminine occupation (cooking and housekeeping) with war and that other kind of occupation, exploding the distinctions between private and public spheres, domesticity and warfare.

The conventions of war literature as a recognizable genre, very much a part of (male) modernism, may not be easily or at all congruent with anecdotes about the weather, cooking, servants, and meals, or with the genre of the recipe, and therefore the result of a sustained juxtaposition is a radical mix-up or the paradox of an "incompatible combination." The same incompatible combination is performed in defiance of the same rules of compatibility in *What Is Remembered*. Like the *Cook Book*, *What Is Remembered* performs a balancing act on the border between various domestic spaces and the battlefield, and the war story is always intimately connected with Toklas's occupation of daily housekeeping chores and the concerns of domestic economy: "The years of the Occupation passed slowly. One of our greatest challenges was the securing of food" (177). War is established as one of the main themes of *What Is Remembered* from the very beginning. As a young woman in California, Toklas "mothers" American troops just like she and Stein would do much later in France: "The cook and I made great quantities of doughnuts for them to take back to distribute in camp." This is significant not only because it introduces the image of Toklas as a maternal nurturing figure in relation to American soldiers going to war, an image that will recur throughout the text and that is commonplace in the legend of Stein and Toklas, but also because it introduces one of the submerged story lines in this true story of Alice B. Toklas: the heterosexual possibility turning into impossibility. "They were the boys with whom I had danced," Toklas says, instead of defining the soldiers as for instance, fellow Americans or brothers (14).

For a large part of *What Is Remembered*, the war theme serves as a backdrop for the narrow concerns of a certain clique, a certain salon, a certain marriage. When World War I begins, it represents an inconvenience, and Toklas remembers someone saying: "I shall not be able to eat figs in Provence this year" (90). Returning to France, however, Stein and Toklas have their "first experience with the eyes of soldiers" (93), and although they are able to continue their privileged and relatively sheltered life, the war is getting closer. Stein and Toklas enlist for war work. *The Autobiography* describes this endeavor as Toklas's idea and places her in command in relation to Stein: "There, said I, that is what we are going to do. At least, said I to Gertrude Stein, you will drive the car and I will do the rest" (229). Stein, although she agrees to learn how to drive, is portrayed as passive in *What Is Remembered* as well: "The next morning I gave Gertrude no time to reflect. We went over to the rue des Pyramides to report to Mrs. Lathrop that we were ready to go to work" (101). In a manner similar to the story of her becoming a skilled publisher in *The Autobiography*, Toklas proudly describes how she becomes a skilled war worker in *What Is Remembered*. "I learned my way with some difficulty until finally I was a professional worker" (103). In this way, Toklas once again invests her own occupation with value.

I have mentioned the way in which Thomson compared Toklas's *What Is Remembered* to Caesar's *De Bello Gallico* and the way in which her sparse style sometimes seems related to Hemingway's. Obviously, both Caesar and Hemingway deal prominently with the masculine matter of war. Toklas's work, too, concerns itself with war to a very considerable extent, but approaches it from a different—domestic or feminine—perspective, or operates on the boundary between the two domains. This liminal discourse is also where the characteristically restrained and compact style of the narrative is most obvious and sometimes brings to mind Hemingway's prose. Sometimes the narrative of *What Is Remembered* displays a level of emotional restraint that approaches the classic Icelandic tale: "Then came some Italians. The war in our corner of the world was nearly over. When news reached the Italians that their country had surrendered, they tore up their military papers. Gertrude Stein said to their officers, You should not have allowed them to do this. They were a kind of protection and you are without any now. You are at the mercy of the Germans. And sure enough . . . the Germans killed them all" (177–78).

The horror of war may not be described or explained in *What Is Remembered*, but it still dominates the text. When World War II begins, Stein and Toklas abandon their apartment and their paintings in Paris and return to their country home. The American consul tells them to leave at once, but a neighbor expresses a contrary opinion: "Oh, don't think of leaving, one is always better where one belongs than hunting a refuge" (175). A couple of eccentric Jewish-American lesbians may not belong unproblematically in the French countryside at this particular moment, despite the fact that "their entire village conspired to keep the presence of the two American Jews there a secret," (Weiss, 87), but they decide to remain, "with the guns getting nearer and nearer" (*What Is Remembered*, 175). As German troops, armored cars, and the Gestapo arrive in Belley, *What Is Remembered* represents the tension and danger in few words and with great emotional restraint: "One day we went to Aix-les-Bains, where Gertrude in her customary voice bought some books. . . . I said to Gertrude, Take care, don't speak English so loud. She said, Nothing counts anymore" (175). For a while the tranquil domestic sphere and the outside world at war are kept reasonably separate. Later, however, the war moves right into the Stein–Toklas household, as German officers and soldiers are billeted with them: "Rooms were hastily prepared for them, and provisions were hidden" (177). The situation must be seen as extreme: Nazi officers actually *moved in* with two Jewish lesbians, one of whom was a writer and had to hide her manuscripts away from them, one of whom was the secretary and had to refrain for a while from typing her partner's handwritten work in order not to make it accessible to the enemy. The unbearable tension created by this arrangement is expressed only indirectly: "When they left, after two weeks, we heaved a deep sigh of relief" (177). The next time Germans are billeted with Stein and Toklas, the text once again downplays the larger context, fails to mention the political implications, and redefines risk and loss in the context of food: "At last they left, though not before helping themselves to our small supplies. One thing they overlooked were my jars of candied fruits, which I had been saving for the Liberation" (178).

Despite the fact that Toklas's writing style can be described as restrained and stripped of emotion in these passages, Schmidt's argument that Stein and Toklas are detached from the reality of war becomes increasingly problematic. During and after the war, Stein and Toklas are *completely* defined by their complicated relationship to the two parties in the conflict. As Jewish lesbians, they have to hide their real identity from the Germans. In relation to the French *Résistance*, however, their position is altogether different. As they travel in the dark back to Paris, they are stopped by the *Résistance* and asked to identify themselves: "They leaned over on to a Picasso portrait and I said, Take care, that is a painting by Picasso, don't disturb it. And they said, We congratulate you, you may go on" (180–81). Moreover, because they are privileged enough to be able to hire housekeeping and gardening help, Stein and Toklas are implicated as employers both on the "right" side and on the "wrong" side of wartime relations (see page 178).

As World War II ends, Stein is finally able to publish her wartime diary, until then carefully hidden from the Germans. As usual, but belatedly and hurriedly, Stein's handwritten words are passed through Toklas's labor at the typewriter. An American soldier "offered to take back Gertrude Stein's manuscript to New York. He was flying back on an American airplane the following day, so that night I sat down and typed everything that Gertrude had been careful to hide during the German Occupation. It was published by Random House as *Wars I Have Seen*" (179). Apart from resuming her duties as a secretary, Toklas also finally gets to make the Liberation fruitcake for General Patch. In other words, she characteristically comments upon the end of the war through celebratory culinary action and through the repetition, copying, transcription of Stein's words. Many years later, in her own autobiographies, Toklas revisits the wars she has seen with an experimental strategy of discursive mixing that similarly suspends the war/housekeeping binary. By reading the *Cook Book* and *What Is Remembered* together in this way, as two Toklas autobiographies, and moreover relating them to *The Autobiography*, it is possible to recover Toklas's work not only as writing, but also as a form of literary experiment.

The *Cook Book* effects a collapse of categories not only in relation to war and housekeeping, but also in relation to art and cooking, again by way of "beautiful soup." "After the first ineffable *gazpacho* was served to us in Malaga and an entirely different but equally exquisite one was presented in Seville," Toklas says, "the recipes for them had unquestionably become of greater importance than Grecos and Zurbarans, than cathedrals and museums" (49). The *Cook Book* opens with an account of the French cuisine, "founded upon the discoveries made in the seventeenth century when suddenly every one who could afford it became interested in food as a fine art" (5). Throughout the *Cook Book*, cooking and art, gastronomy and aesthetics, are pitted against each other, reversed, conflated, and the distinction between the two troubled. About "Madame Loubet's Asparagus Tips," Toklas says: "This is a gastronomic feast. And a thing of beauty" (83). On every level of the text, this motif is ever-present. In the very first sentence of the *Cook Book*, Toklas claims that the French approach to food is entirely on a par with the "appreciation, respect, intelligence and lively interest that they have for the other arts, for painting, for literature and for the theatre" (3). Moreover, and in relation to these "separate spheres," gender roles in the kitchen and outside are immediately problematized: "By French I mean French men as well as French women, for the men in France play a very active part in everything that pertains to the kitchen. Conversation even in a literary or political salon can turn to the subject of menus, food or wine" (3).[6]

Already in the very first few pages of the *Cook Book*, Toklas unsettles a number of hierarchically ordered binaries (high/low, art/cooking, politics/cooking, public/domestic, men/women, necessity/pleasure) in a way that works to modify and enlarge the implications of some subsequent observations. After a preliminary mixing of these key concepts, some of Toklas's observations and comments that seemingly relate *only* to cooking can be read at another level as a critique of existing ideals in writing and art. There are many explicitly aesthetic observations and comments that contribute to the general collapse of distinctions between disparate realms. For instance, Toklas describes Matisse's work as follows: "He used his distorted drawing as a dissonance is used in music or as vinegar or lemons are used in cooking or egg shells in coffee to clarify. I do inevitably take my comparisons from the kitchen because I like food and cooking and know something about it" (54). The comparison of Matisse's "distorted" technique and the trick of clarifying coffee with eggshells creates a sense of continuity between the epistemologies of high art and culinary art. Moreover, Toklas says, "Comparing the cooking of a dish to the painting of a picture, it has always seemed to me that however much the cook or painter did to cover any weakness would not in the least avail. Such devices would only emphasize the weakness" (78–79). A veritable aesthetic theory can be extracted from Toklas's meditations on cooking and/as art in the *Cook Book*: "These dishes . . . are most of them a slow evolution in a new direction, which is the way great art is created—that is, everything about is ready for it, and one person having the vision does it, discarding what he [sic] finds unnecessary in the past. Even a way of cooking an egg can be arrived at in this way. Then that way becomes a classical way. It is a pleasure for us, perhaps for the egg" (139).

A version of this theory appears in "Composition As Explanation," Stein's first public lecture, given in June 1926: "For a very long time everybody refuses and then almost without a pause almost everybody accepts. In the history of the refused in the arts and literature the rapidity of the change is always startling. . . . When the acceptance comes, by that acceptance the thing created becomes a classic. It is a natural phenomena [sic] a rather extraordinary natural phenomena [sic] that a thing accepted becomes a classic" (496). In her rewriting of this passage, Toklas not only describes how change happens in art and cooking but also distinguishes between good and bad innovations in both spheres, marks her own stance as one of taste, again in relation to both spheres, and effectively juxtaposes the two realms so that the hierarchy that traditionally defines them is destabilized or even rendered inseparable: "When treasures are recipes they are less clearly, less distinctly remembered than when they are tangible objects. They evoke however quite as vivid a feeling—that is, to some of us who, considering cooking an art, feel that a way of cooking can produce something that approaches an aesthetic emotion. What more can one say? If one had the choice of again hearing Pachmann play the two Chopin sonatas or dining once more at the Café Anglais, which would one choose?" (*Cook Book*, 100).

A piece of music, like a recipe, is of course not a tangible object. It is interesting to note in this context that Toklas played the piano in her youth and at one time wanted to become a concert pianist. This passage seems to suggest that her subsequent culinary art can make possible equal heights of aesthetic bliss as music, a fundamentally nonutilitarian art form. In the *Cook Book*, Toklas draws upon the aesthetic theory put forward by Stein in her lectures but goes on to extend it to include her own particular form of art—cooking. It is evident that Stein cannot follow her into that domain. In the "Food" section of *Tender Buttons*, Stein, who according to legend never boiled an egg in her life, has the following to say about "EGGS./Kind height, kind in the right stomach with a little sudden mill./Cunning shawl, cunning shawl to be steady./In white in white handkerchiefs with little dots in a white belt all shadows are singular they are singular and procured and relieved" (47).

From the passages quoted here, it seems as though Toklas's aim in the *Cook Book* is to invest her own particular art form—cooking—with more value, similarly to the way in which the anecdote in *The Autobiography* that defines her as superior to Man Ray in the art of photography upsets hierarchies of aesthetic value: "One day [Stein] told [Man Ray] that she liked his photographs of her better than any that had ever been taken except one snap shot I had taken of her recently. This seemed to bother [him]" (268). The picture is more complicated, however, than some of these destabilizations of the art/cooking binary may suggest. Being responsible for cooking and housekeeping is also asserted by Toklas to be the result of unfortunate and extreme circumstances. When her mother died, she was automatically and prematurely placed in charge of her grandfather's and father's household and also helped to raise her younger brother. Already as a young woman keeping house for the male members of her family, Toklas resented domestic duties, and her feelings about cooking are represented as characteristically ambivalent in the *Cook Book*. Later on in France, Stein and Toklas generally kept a cook, but there were exceptional times, primarily during war and occupation, when they had to make do without hired labor: "With the declaration of war we, like everyone else, adapted ourselves as best we could to the new conditions. The old life with servants was finished and over" (*Cook Book*, 199). This experience taught Toklas "not only to cook seriously but to buy food in a restricted market and not to take too much time in doing it, since there were so many more important and more amusing things to do" (*Cook Book*, 37). As Toklas had stepped into the role of her mother when she died, she now out of necessity steps into the role of a servant. Perhaps the low status of domestic labor explains why Toklas sometimes describes cooking as an art form invested with aesthetic values and something that gives her pride and pleasure but sometimes claims to cook only out of necessity.

Despite references to cooking as disagreeable, necessary, trivial, and boring, however, the *Cook Book* as a whole elevates cooking to the level of fine art, which requires inspiration, and equates it with creation: "Can one be inspired by rows of prepared canned meals? Never. One must get nearer to creation to be able to create, even in the kitchen" (131). Moreover, the *Cook Book* describes the way in which Toklas's occupation, cooking and housekeeping, coexists and merges seamlessly with the production of objects of art: "Most of our men guests had their breakfasts served on the terrace. The breakfast trays were my pride, though the linen and porcelain were simple. In the market place in Chambéry we unearthed some amusing coloured glassware, 1840–1850, not at an antique dealer's but in a store that sold glassware. We bought all there was. Berries, fruits, salads and vegetables served in them were subjects for still-life pictures" (268). Of course, Toklas was the one who not only cooked breakfast, laid the breakfast trays, carried them onto the terrace for the benefit of male visitors, and washed up afterward, but also *grew* the berries and vegetables that were turned into art by some of the male guests.

In the *Cook Book* as a whole, Toklas's treatment of great artists, creative geniuses, is typically pragmatic, rather than reverent, thus bringing them down to a culinary and even digestive level. Toklas describes the way in which she would try to take Picasso's diet into account while still creating an attractive menu: "we would have a tender loin of veal preceded by a spinach *soufflé*, spinach having been highly recommended by Picasso's doctor and a *soufflé* being the least objectionable way of preparing it. Could it not be made more interesting by adding a sauce. But what sauce would Picasso's diet permit. I would give him a choice. . . . It was my hope that the tri-coloured sauces would make the spinach *soufflé* look less nourishing. Cruel enigma, said Picasso, when the *soufflé* was served to him" (30). In her account of cooking "bass for Picasso," Toklas also blurs the rigid boundary between herself, the cook, and the artist or painter:

> One day when Picasso was to lunch with us I decorated a fish in a way that I thought would amuse him. I chose a fine striped bass and cooked it according to a theory of my grandmother who had no experience of cooking and who rarely saw her kitchen but who had endless theories about cooking. . . . I covered the fish with . . . mayonnaise and . . . decorated it with a red mayonnaise, not colored with catsup—horror of horrors—but with tomato paste. Then I made a design with sieved hard-boiled eggs, the whites and the yolks apart, with truffles and with finely chopped *fines*

herbes. I was proud of my chef d'oeuvre when it was served and Picasso exclaimed at its beauty. But, said he, should it not rather have been made in honour of Matisse than me. (29–30)

It is significant that Toklas in this instance cooks according to the "theory" of someone who did not herself *practice* cooking, and that she decorates the food so profusely that it must have been almost inedible (*l'art pour l'art*). In this way, she erases the distinction between cooking as a low art form, because of its constitutive pragmatic usefulness, and painting or visual art as a high art form, because of its lack of utilitarian value. This is a parallel to Stein's emphasis on the Mixmaster and various other kitchen gadgets as aesthetically pleasing rather than primarily useful. Describing the dish she made for Picasso, moreover, Toklas once again categorizes her own work as tasteful (using catsup would be a "horror"). At the same time, Picasso's comment that the dish should have been "bass for Matisse" rather than "bass for Picasso" adds a twist to the anecdote and undermines Toklas' construction of herself as an artist *like* Picasso. Picasso and Matisse were rivals, and for Picasso to say that something would be appropriate for Matisse might indicate that he does not consider it particularly tasteful, but rather superficial and decorative.

We have seen that, in reviews of *What Is Remembered*, Toklas is often accused of name-dropping. In my opinion, the *strategy* of name-dropping is a clue to the experimental effect of the *Cook Book*. More often than not, as we have seen in the passages on Picasso above, Toklas punctures the myth of the genius and places famous guests in the Stein–Toklas household firmly in a historical, domestic, and culinary context. In this way, she refuses to replicate the self-aggrandizing gestures of various geniuses and near-geniuses who figure as prominently in the *Cook Book* as they did in *The Autobiography* but in a slightly different perspective. It is true that a famous anecdote in *The Autobiography* creates a similar collapse of the distinction between the sphere of art and artists, on the one hand, and the sphere of cooking and domestic concerns, on the other. At one of his shows, Matisse receives as a tribute "the largest laurel wreath that had ever been made, tied with a beautiful red ribbon. . . . Said Matisse, still more rueful, but I am not dead yet. Madame Matisse, the shock once over said, but Henri look, and leaning down she plucked a leaf and tasted it, it is real laurel, think how good it will be in soup" (126–27). Once again, *The Autobiography* reformulates the story of a genius as the story of his wife.

The *Cook Book*, however, effects the same reversal even more consistently, and more radically, throughout the text. For instance, a dinner with Sherwood Anderson is described as "the happiest of meetings. Of all the delicacies served, it is strange to remark that it was the first time we tasted mint jelly" (128). Some of the included recipes are "interesting . . . for the names attached to them" (117). One recipe from Stephane Mallarmé makes a delicate dessert, Toklas says, "but the syrup must not cook for as long a time as his recipe advised. My dessert was an excellent candy resembling a Chinese sweet long before it was time to add the yolk of the eggs. So now it is made with 1 cup water and boiled to 220°" (117). Apparently, the poet's words are not sacred. Generally speaking, the *Cook Book* claims the right to explode the boundaries between "real" art/writing and the art of cooking, often by means of humor, adding "Ideal for poets with delicate digestions" to a recipe (252).

In scattering famous names around her, representing them not through high discourse but instead through anecdotes, reminiscences, fragments, and recipes, Toklas drops the regime of the proper name and claims for herself the right to name and unname her own world otherwise. In her world, literary and domestic spaces are truly coextensive and embedded in or in bed with each other: "The recipe for the Roast Beef of Mutton is by no less a person than Alexandre Dumas, senior, author not only of the *Three Musketeers* but of *The Large Dictionary of the Kitchen*" (101). Nevertheless, after having searched for a cookbook giving the correct recipe for gazpacho and having been told that "*gazpachos* are only eaten in Spain by peasants and Americans," Toklas hurries "back to Zurbaran and Greco, to museums and cathedrals" (49). Again, the *Cook Book* operates by mixing—not reversal.

We have seen how high and low occupations like war/housekeeping and art/cooking are placed on the same level in the *Cook Book*, in such a way as to collapse boundaries and challenge hierarchies. The last chapter of the *Cook Book* contains reversals and paradoxes that derive from a similar analogy between art and gardening. Gardening is as central a category of labor and knowledge as cooking in "the true story of Alice B. Toklas." At first glance, references to gardening in the *Cook Book* seem to confirm the patriarchal model for the Stein–Toklas hierarchy in which Stein not only exploits Toklas's labor but also trivializes it: "The work in the vegetables . . . was a full-time job and more. Later it became a joke, Gertrude

Stein asking me what I saw when I closed my eyes, and I answered, Weeds. That, she said, was not the answer, and so weeds were changed to strawberries" (*Cook Book*, 266). The way in which Toklas's labor enters very concretely into Stein's writing is obvious when comparing this passage from the *Cook Book* to the opening of Stein's 1936 piece "What Does She See When She Shuts Her Eyes: A Novel": "It is very meritorious to work very hard in a garden. . . . When she shuts her eyes she sees the green things among which she has been working and then as she falls asleep she sees them a little different. The green things then have black roots and the black roots have red stems and then she is exhausted" (63).

In this way, the companion's toil is both glorified and neutralized by the genius, the beneficiary of her labor: "god / bless my baby looks so pretty and / gardening is so good for her" (*Baby Precious*, 124). At the same time, Toklas seems to prefer gardening to any other task: "What a happy life it would be only to cultivate raspberries" (*Cook Book*, 277). The juxtaposition of the drudgery and the pleasure of gardening recurs throughout the text. "It takes a long time to gather enough very young string beans for eight or ten people," Toklas remarks. Then she goes on: "Between the vegetable garden and the rose garden my mornings were happily occupied. To me this pleasure is unequalled" (83). The chapter on "The Vegetable Gardens at Bilignin" opens as follows: "For fourteen successive years the gardens at Bilignin were my joy, working in them during the summers and planning and dreaming of them during the winters" and then goes on: "The weeds remained a tormenting, backbreaking experience all the summers we spent at Bilignin" (265–66). This might seem a perfectly natural ambivalence to any gardener. In the *Cook Book*, however, gardening is not *only* a backbreaking source of pain and pleasure, but also an art form.

It is true that, in certain passages, Toklas seems to distinguish firmly between art and gardening, endowing the former with feelings and complexity, the latter with lack of emotion: "In Paris we had a small room Gertrude Stein called the Salon des Refusés. . . . [It] held the pictures Gertrude Stein refused. . . . In the garden it was simpler. When the *refusés* were rooted up and put on the compost heap, it caused no feeling from anyone involved" (279). At the same time, this distinction is collapsed or at least suspended and called into question by other gestures and assertions in the same chapter. Indeed, the most deeply emotional passage of the entire *Cook Book* concerns Toklas's pleasure in her garden: "The first gathering of the garden in May . . . made me feel like a mother about her baby—how could anything so beautiful be mine. And this emotion of wonder filled me for each vegetable as it was gathered every year" (266). The aesthetic value of Toklas's garden, the creative aspect of her gardening, and her strong affection for this art are completely overwhelming in the text, effectively undermining the distinction she elsewhere makes between art (as emotionally charged) and gardening (as "simpler" because it does not involve feelings). The reversal is perhaps even more apparent in a passage close to the end of the *Cook Book*, where Toklas is strongly linked to the aesthetic and pleasurable and Stein to the practical and economical:

> The day the huge baskets were packed was my proudest in all the year. The cold sun would shine on the orange-coloured carrots, the green, yellow and white pumpkins and squash, the purple egg plants and a few last red tomatoes. They made for me more poignant colour than any post-Impressionist picture. Merely to look at them made all the rest of the year's pleasure insignificant. Gertrude Stein took a more practical attitude. . . . She thought that there were enough vegetables for an institution and reminded me that our household consisted of three people. There was no question that, looking at the harvest as an economic question, it was disastrous, but from the point of view of the satisfaction which work and aesthetic confer, it was sublime. (280)

In this passage, the earlier statement that gardening does not involve emotion is displaced and radically undermined, as gardening ("work") and art ("aesthetic") are placed side by side without hierarchical distinction. There is also a strikingly exact analogy between Toklas's excessive and uneconomical production and hoarding of vegetables, on the one hand, and, on the other, Stein's excessive early production of manuscripts that were not published until after *The Autobiography* or even much later, and thus were "disastrous" if seen as "an economic question." By means of such conflation of levels and mixing of disparate realms, the hierarchical organization that values "real" art more highly than cooking, gardening, and other domestic, utilitarian activities, is unsettled. Indeed, at times it is even reversed. Toklas says that her vegetables provide *more* color than *any* picture. In this double movement of investing domestic labor with value and pleasure and destabilizing the hierarchy and separation that characterizes binaries such as war/housekeeping, art/cooking, and art/gardening, the *Cook Book* engages in a discursive practice of mixing as literary experiment.

Among the Toklas autobiographies, the *Cook Book* in particular thematizes the division of labor in the Stein–Toklas marriage and defines Toklas's labor as Stein's privilege: "Before coming to Paris I was interested in food but not in doing any cooking. When in 1908 I went to live with Gertrude Stein at the rue de Fleurus she said we would have American food for Sunday-evening supper, she had had enough French and Italian cooking; the servant would be out and I should have the kitchen to myself" (29). This passage invites the common analysis of the Stein–Toklas division of labor as asymmetrical and potentially abusive: "No sooner had Leo left 27, rue de Fleurus, than his sister began to imitate some of his worst habits. . . . The routine established after his departure . . . effectively made Alice a domestic" (Benstock, *Women of the Left Bank*, 166). At the same time, as I have mentioned earlier, the strictly defined hierarchical roles of Stein and Toklas are also quite likely to be textual constructs, produced precisely in order to make possible the representation of a lesbian union in acceptable terms. The master–servant image of sadomasochistic erotica has been domesticated, reversed in relation to Hemingway's version of the "same" story, and moved to a different and radically neutralized setting in which Stein says that Toklas "should have the kitchen to [herself]." This transformation of a transgressive sexuality/textuality into relations of labor and domestic organization is ever-present in the legend of Stein and Toklas.

The sexual/textual union of Stein and Toklas takes place in a thoroughly bourgeois structure of comfortable domesticity. The couple normally kept two servants, a cook and a housekeeper, and Toklas occupies an intermediary position in the household as inferior to Stein (as husband) and superior to the servants, although this hierarchy is represented in various texts as strangely fluid and changeable. From the remarkable cook Hélène, for instance, Toklas "learned nothing about cooking. She would have thought such an idea was misplaced. A lady did not cook" (*Cook Book*, 171). It appears, then, that Toklas is a lady who cooks, and therefore not a real lady. In the *Cook Book*, some remarkable reversals and paradoxes are linked specifically to the issue of Toklas's relation with servants and sometimes effect a certain destabilization of their respective positions.

Toklas's position as wife in relation to Stein as husband makes her a borderline or transitional figure. She moves between the realm of art and artists on the one hand and the realm of housekeeping and servants on the other. Her status is exposed as ambiguous not only in terms of gender and sexuality but also in terms of class, in the chapter on servants in the *Cook Book* in particular but also in the other two Toklas autobiographies and elsewhere. Both Toklas and Stein were born into affluent middle-class Jewish-American families. The narrator of *The Autobiography* says, "I led in my childhood and youth the gently bred existence of my class and kind" (7). Simon remarks that Toklas in her early years was expected to "glide quietly into the coming century, comfortable in the Jewish middle class, a well-trained flower of pale Victorian womanhood" (*Biography*, 3). Both Stein and Toklas in their adult life in different ways transgressed the boundaries of their social rank—moving not typically up, but down. Stein was well known for her peasant clothing and her heavy walking boots covered in mud. As a couple, Stein and Toklas experienced a general upheaval in social class in Paris after the war, when they lived "like gypsies": "Our home was filled with people coming and going. We spoke of each other as the chauffeur and the cook. We had no servant. We had largely overdrawn at our banks to supply the needs of soldiers and their families, and now the day of reckoning had come. We would live like gypsies, go everywhere in left-over finery, with a *pot-au-feu* for the many friends we should be seeing" (*Cook Book*, 72). Even before going to Paris and meeting Stein, however, Toklas deviated from the social rank of her "gently bred existence" by willingly positioning herself on the other side of the social boundary separating lady and maid. As a young girl, Toklas reportedly surprised her friends by appearing as the maid at literary gatherings in San Francisco, "jesting in a role she would someday enact seriously" (Simon, *Biography*, 25). The serious performance of the maid's role, of course, refers to Toklas's place in the Stein–Toklas household.

The chapter in the *Cook Book* called "Servants in France" revolves around the recurrent dilemma of finding another good cook whenever one leaves. There is a continuous change of servants, especially women servants. The servants also, however, change employers. For instance, three sisters take turns cooking for Stein and Toklas and arrange the succession among themselves: "What was expected of Caroline was evident. She would take care of the baby [of Cécile who was 'the friend of a married man']. So Margot, the third of the sisters we were to know, was sent for to work for us." Margot, however, soon attends "the Breton balls so success-fully that . . . she married a young man she had met there" (185–86). Several of the female servants, and one or two of the male ones, leave because they are getting married, or having a baby, or because their spouse wants them to. This last reason is true of the famous Hélène, Stein's cook at the time when Toklas first arrived at rue de Fleurus. While in service, Hélène enjoys a position of considerable authority: "It was Hélène who made all the prac-tical decisions. A friend noticing this observed that it was to be hoped that her servant left a free choice of the Picassos to Gertrude Stein" (170–71). The same joke is later repeated in relation to Toklas and her influence on Stein's literary genius. Even Toklas herself reiterates this quip, the comedy of which is based on the collapse of boundaries between high and low, genius and wife, master and servant binaries.

The conventional relation between master and servant is constantly challenged in the *Cook Book*. One servant, Margit from Finland, is ready to work for Stein and Toklas, despite "the disadvantages and inconveniences she would encounter," because of certain "privileges": "Margit was an omnivorous reader—there would be a library in which she would find what she longed for. She saw Gertrude Stein's easy democratic approach-ableness—there would be conversations with her. . . . She said to us one day that she supposed there was no objection to her borrowing auto-graphed volumes if they were not taken to the kitchen." Margit also demands that Toklas draw up the menus: "It was the only thing she expected of me. It was little enough to do in return for the excellence of the way in which she prepared them" (193–94). The demands of other ser-vants are more difficult to put up with. Louise, for instance, "was a *gour-met*, which should include being a good cook. She was not, but enjoyed the cooking I did. This did not flatter me, it bored me." Louise insists upon eat-ing her meals before serving Stein and Toklas. At a Thanksgiving Day lunch party with American guests, Louise expects to be allowed to start on the turkey before it is presented and carved at table. Toklas refuses to allow even a small amputation: Louise "threw her knife and fork on the table and burst into tears, sobbing that it was a cruel thing to do to her. . . . So she departed" (179–80). As we can see, the hierarchical relations between Toklas and the servants are strangely fluent and changeable. When one of the *femmes de ménage* turns out to be a good cook, she and Toklas switch tasks so that "Léonie gradually came to do the greater part of the cooking and I did more of the household work" (173).

The reason Stein and Toklas are only partly plausible in positions of mastery is indicated in the *Cook Book*, but very surreptitiously. In the chapter on servants, it is hinted that Stein and Toklas are not considered ideal employers: "We had certainly luck in finding good cooks, though they had their weaknesses in other ways. Gertrude Stein liked to remind me that if they did not have such faults, they would not be working for us" (173, this quote is also used as an epigraph for Truong's *Book of Salt*). One Austrian servant is perhaps too flawless to stay: "On the third morning she looked at me severely and said that we 'lived French' and that that was not what she had been led to suspect and she was leaving, which she did" (180). This, I believe, is as close as Toklas ever gets to coming out of the closet in writing. Another new servant is left alone cleaning house while Stein and Toklas go out: "The door was opened by a person whose expression was severer and more resolute than I had remembered from the morning. Firmly but not aggressively she announced that she was leaving at once. She found the conditions regarding her work were different from what she had supposed they would be. We did not understand. A friend said the decision was come to after seeing the pictures in the studio. They had frightened her" (180).

Stein's and Toklas's unconventionality, in both sexual and cultural preferences, obviously make them less than ideal employers. The way in which the *Cook Book* openly reveals this to be the case introduces an element of ambiguity in the roles of master and servant as superior and inferior, as dominant and subordinate. Another aspect of the *Cook Book* that similarly contributes to the destabilization of master/servant roles is related to the way in which the text as a whole levels out hierarchies between various art forms, occupations, and people and shows that hierarchically organized binaries such as war and housekeeping, art and cooking, and art and gardening in fact designate areas of human activity that are inextricably related and overlapping. Norris points to some of the most intriguing aspects of Toklas's relation to positions of mastery and servitude: "Eventually, Alice's domestic art was translated into writing—the 1954 *Alice B. Toklas Cook Book*, which remained faithful to the domestic politics of Stein's *Autobiography* in at least one important respect. Alice recognized that her domestic arts were as much a collaborative production as Stein's literary arts. Her chapters [sic] on 'Servants in France' acknowledge the debt that her own domestic art owed to the labor, imagination, and recipes of the domestic workers who stood as wives in relation to her own contribution to the modern art scene" (98, n. 7). In this quote, Norris reiterates the conventional construction of relations of originality and supplementarity among the Toklas autobiographies but also indicates the way in which the *Cook Book*, like *The Autobiography*, can be reconsidered as a collaborative text and, by extension, a literary experiment.

One highly significant aspect of the situation that Norris describes is the fact that many of the domestic workers in the Stein–Toklas household were not domestics in a wider sense of the word, but instead "colonials." As the chapter on servants in the *Cook Book* shows, servants are often defined by Toklas in terms of race and always in terms of nationality, and immigrant servants, exotic recipes, and comments on various foreign ingredients reflect colonial relations. It is true that, in her chatty style of writing, Toklas objectifies Asian cooks (servants in this category are always male) in slightly disturbing ways: "To see Trac, immaculate in white, slicing in lightning quick strokes vegetables and fruits was an appetiser." Trac is also, however, called a "master in his kitchen" and Toklas marvels that "there was no way of knowing how Trac prepared any of his delicious food" (186–87). When Trac leaves temporarily and Nguyen—the only acceptable servant out of the succession of gambling, drinking, womanizing, dishonest, and drugged "Indo-Chinese"—leaves as well, Stein and Toklas move on to Agnel, a Polish-American woman like Toklas herself, but something remarkable soon happens: "Then unexpectedly Trac dropped in on us and said he was ready to come back to work for us, and he would commence the following morning. We explained the delicate situation he was putting us in. He left, saying he would commence to work the following morning. Agnel was overjoyed. She would take a month's vacation on the Côte d'Azur and would find a situation there. We paid her vacation and wages and were able to introduce Trac to her the following morning. They thanked each other. It was ludicrous" (191–92). This procedure resembles the way in which the three Bretonne sisters decide among themselves who is to work for Stein and Toklas at any given point in time. In this way, the all-powerful servants seem to change masters, rather than the other way around, and the master/servant dichotomy is radically unsettled just like other binaries (war/housekeeping, art/cooking, art/gardening) deconstructed in the *Cook Book*.

I have emphasized continuity and repetition among the three Toklas autobiographies throughout the present study. The first and the last

Toklas autobiography can also be measured against the middle one, which in many significant ways differs from the other two. Consider the possibility that the *Cook Book* (not *The Autobiography* because Stein is the author, not *What Is Remembered* because it is not recognizably experimental) is *the odd one out*. The *Cook Book* departs more conspicuously from autobiographical generic conventions than the other two Toklas autobiographies, specifically because it is an autobiographical cookbook as much as it is a culinary autobiography. The paradox, however, is that it can also be said to produce autobiographical truth effects in two ways not shared by *The Autobiography* and *What Is Remembered*. First, the autobiographical material in the *Cook Book* appears to constitute representations of genuine acts of remembering. There is no equivalent to the story of origins in *The Autobiography* and *What Is Remembered*. The *Cook Book* begins very differently from the conventions of autobiography ("I was born"), with an indication of the overall unsettling of the art/cooking binary in this text: "The French approach to food is characteristic; they bring to their consideration of the table the same appreciation, respect, intelligence and lively interest that they have for the other arts, for painting, for literature and for the theatre" (3). The closest you get to a story of origins in the *Cook Book* is *another* form of original memory, what could possibly be called the representation of *remembering*: "What is the first food you remember, remember seeing it if not eating it? Well, the first food I remember from my early childhood in San Francisco in the early 'eighties was breakfast food: cracked wheat with sugar and cream, corn meal with molasses and farina with honey" (97). The reason I call this a representation of remembering is that the text refers to these breakfast foods as the first foods that *can be recalled*. Obviously, there were other dishes served in Toklas's early childhood, but she personally cannot remember them. If we compare this story of origins in *The Autobiography* and *What Is Remembered*, the difference is obvious but important. Of course, Toklas (and certainly Stein) cannot "remember" what her grandparents did before she was born, her mother's birth, or, for that matter, her own. What is "remembered" in these cases, then, are the *stories* of her background, secondhand memories as it were. The same thing goes for the sections on Stein before she came to Paris and before she met Toklas, if we read *The Autobiography* without the authorial twist, and for the sections on Toklas before she met Stein, if we read it as *Stein's* autobiography. The *Cook Book*, on the other hand, is dominated by representations of what seems to be *actual memories*. Note the fact that the "first" memory in this case is described almost a hundred pages into the text.

The exclusion of secondhand memories in the *Cook Book* and the inclusion of them in *What Is Remembered* may have been a perfectly conscious and deliberate decision in the writing process. Toklas would have been well aware of this predicament in autobiographical writing, since Stein begins *Wars I Have Seen* (1945) as follows: "I do not know whether to put in the things I do not remember as well as the things I do remember. To begin with I was born, that I do not remember but I was told about it quite often." A little later, she goes on: "And now [as a young child in Vienna] there was something I could remember as well as some things I could be helped to remember by hearing them told again and again, then and later" (1). Traditionally, memories that an autobiographer needs help to remember are often included in the autobiography, and generic differences become quite important in this respect. There is no demand for a coherent, complete, or particularly orderly narrative in a cookbook, no need to rehearse the official story of one's childhood or describe what happened in someone else's life before her story became intertwined with yours. Indeed, there is no demand for linear narrative or a stable autobiographical persona (supposedly reflecting a "whole" person) at all. Instead, the autobiographical anecdotes, which can be seen as extra-generic supplements to recipes and cooking instructions if the *Cook Book* is categorized as an autobiographical cookbook, are at liberty to be grounded in Toklas's nonchronological memories of travel, meals, cooking experiences, servants, and people with whom she has shared meals. Between those memories, there are gaps and blanks and instructions for the preparation of Singapore Ice Cream and Nameless Cookies.

Second, if the *Cook Book* is instead conceptualized as a culinary autobiography, the inclusion of recipes in an autobiographical text creates a strong connection between the textual level and the real world, a link to material nourishment for material bodies. Typically, this activates the assumption that the text, its recipes linking it to materiality, is telling the truth. Kelly develops this assumption as follows: "Recipes can't be fiction. The concept that recipes reproduced in a book are ones that *work* is an essential element of the implied contract between the reader and the author of cookery books." She goes on to argue that "Intriguing questions begin to arise when we look at the culinary autobiography functioning like any other autobiography" and proposes an interesting connection between the autobiographical contract as defined by Lejeune and the contract implied in the recipe-sharing tradition: "Recipes, when included with autobiographical assertions, transform the autobiography. If we believe that the recipes will work (that they are 'real'), will we have more faith that the autobiography is a faithful recounting of a life? . . . Is this a 'real' recipe? Is this how events in this person's life really happened?" (265–66).

In the context of the present study, the possibility that the inclusion of recipes in an autobiography may be said to enhance the truth effect of the autobiographical material is quite significant. In the *Cook Book*, however, recipes and culinary reminiscences also function as a *substitute* for real-life nourishment. Toklas composed the middle Toklas autobiography while severely ill, and "while she waited for her insides to stop heaving and churning at the thought of food, she satisfied her emptiness by remembering better days" (Fisher, xiv). Toklas admits in her note "A Word with the Cook," preceding the text of the *Cook Book* proper, that this work represents "an escape from the narrow diet and monotony of illness" (xix). Similarly, the *reading* of cookbooks provided escape and sustenance for Toklas during war and occupation, when she and Stein lived in a "protracted, even a perpetual lent" (*Cook Book*, 214). Fisher points out that it is possible to nourish oneself "in many ways from . . . printed rations" (xvii). The *Cook Book* spells out the way in which books about cooking can be used primarily for reading, like any other literature: "Cook-books have always intrigued and seduced me. When I was still a dilettante in the kitchen they held my attention, even the dull ones, from cover to cover, the way crime and murder stories did Gertrude Stein" (37). In this way, the textual category of the recipe, typically considered a utilitarian discourse secondary to material reality, can take precedence over the actual dish represented by it. World and word part company once again, as the signified (food) becomes unwanted (because of an illness) or unavailable (because of war and occupation), and attention shifts over to the signifier (recipes, narratives concerning food), now to some extent separated from the former: almost the same but not quite.

With this caveat in mind, let us dwell for a moment on the *Cook Book*'s possibly privileged relation to autobiographical truth as an instance of the subgenre autobiographical cookbook or culinary autobiography. If Kelly's suggestion is valid, it could be argued that the *Cook Book*, offering presumably truthful instructions for the preparation of real-life nourishment, is indeed more directly or *honestly* autobiographical than *The Autobiography* or *What Is Remembered*, despite the fact that it neither calls itself an autobiography nor looks like one. Even though I find this conception of the culinary autobiography as a bridge between textuality and reality intriguing and useful, I do not wish to reinstate the traditional (gendered) binary of truth and lies in relation to autobiography. In *Autobiographics*, Gilmore "read[s] autobiography to discern how it engages with 'truth' telling and 'lying,' those determinants of autobiographical authority, how it participates in linking identity to gender, and how it politicizes and aestheticizes that connection." Gilmore's ambition is to "break the link between 'women' and 'lying'" (*Autobiographics*, ix–x). I would not want to argue that the *Cook Book*, in a paradoxical way because recipes are typically seen as a specifically feminine form of writing, represents universal/androcentric truth in relation to *The Autobiography* and *What Is Remembered* as women's gossip, "lesbian lies."

Finally, we might return to the famous passage in *The Autobiography* where Toklas argues that her own way of relating to art and literature (dusting and typing) is superior, in terms of knowledge and aesthetic sensation, to Stein's way (looking and reading). Perhaps the *Cook Book* cannot be appropriately analyzed until the critic, trusting or even *consuming* Toklas as author and autobiographer (this is another way of saying "eat Pussy"), has prepared and ingested "Crème Marquise," "Scheherezade's Melon," "Bass for Picasso," and, indeed, "Haschich Fudge" "(which anyone could whip up on a rainy day)." Therefore, the effect of the famous brownies, as reported by Brion Gysin, can be placed here as a possibly heretical and positively licentious suggestion about some of the potential gains of a critical reconsideration of the Stein–Toklas literary heritage, which includes three Toklas autobiographies: "Euphoria and brilliant storms of laughter; ecstatic reveries and extensions of one's personality on several simultaneous planes are to be complacently expected" (*Cook Book*, 259).

Conclusion

The True Story of Alice B. Toklas?

*She appears to the world to be profoundly giving, wholly selfless,
graciously volunteering. She appears to the world an empty page
inventing a narrative, even if it is not her own. Miss Toklas fools the
world because it is populated with fools who do not bother to look
at the light in her eyes, the crisscrossing lines of steel.*
MONIQUE TRUONG, *Book of Salt*, 158

*Now this is the end of this story, not the end of [her] story,
but the end of this story of [her] story.*
GERTRUDE STEIN, *Picasso*, 532

Because of the way in which the focus of the present study has
undergone a radical expansion rather than a narrowing down, it seems
fitting to end my discussion of the Toklas autobiographies not with an
attempt at closure, but instead with a strategic opening up of the critical
perspective to include another intertext drawing upon and contributing
to "the true story of Alice B. Toklas": Truong's *Book of Salt: A Novel* (2003).
As I see it, and despite its generic designation, *The Book of Salt* must be
considered an intertext of the Toklas autobiographies and a contribution
to (reiteration or rearticulation of) the ongoing legend of Alice B. Toklas.
It is consequently also an intertext in relation to the present study.
Indeed, Truong makes the protagonist repeat one of the claims at the center of my own argument: "Miss Toklas has long since made herself indispensable to GertrudeStein [sic]" (30). This movement, away from texts
written by Stein and Toklas and forward in time to the present century, is
at the same time a passage across the border to (what seems like) fiction,
a gesture toward the issue of race and ethnicity that is only touched upon
in the *Cook Book* and in literary critical debates on Stein and Toklas, an
expansion of the "not quite/not straight" concept to include the gay male,
and a plunge even deeper into the domestic realm where Toklas spent a
great deal of her time: the kitchen at 27 rue de Fleurus.

The Book of Salt is the story of Bình, Stein's and Toklas's Vietnamese live-in cook, a young gay male. His story is relevant in relation to the Toklas autobiographies not only because the issue of a certain domestic hierarchy is so prominent in Toklas's life and writing, but also because it is an example of the way in which the legend of Stein and Toklas has been transferred to discourses other than literary criticism and biography. Bình's perspective on Toklas is constructed out of various recognizable biographical and critical sources. As a semifictional character, he himself seems based both upon Trac (who calls a pineapple "a pear not a pear," Cook Book 186, Book of Salt, 35) and upon Nguyen (who had been a servant in the household of the French governor-general of Indo-China and who cooks for a bachelor on Sundays—in The Book of Salt his services extend beyond the culinary realm) from the chapter on servants in the Cook Book (Trac also figures quite prominently in Everybody's Autobiography, see for instance 124–25, 155–65, 297). His portrayal of Toklas—moustache and all—is clearly a modification for the novel of her looks as they have been described in various biographical sources (Book of Salt, 25–26).

Bình goes on to recount various parts of the Stein–Toklas legend as known from their own writings and many other sources. For instance, he mentions that even in good times, Toklas would cook for Stein on Sundays, the cook's day off. She would then serve American food to soothe Stein's "periodic hankering for her childhood" (26). But the traditional recipes would be corrupted by French influences and too much culinary knowledge—"Her menus can map the world" (27). He rehearses the common conception of Toklas's unconventional style of dress by mentioning that she would be wearing woolen socks and sandals in the kitchen. But then of course, Truong also makes her protagonist embroider somewhat upon the biographical discourse as he enters into the minds of the two eccentric ladies: "GertrudeStein thinks it is unfathomably erotic that the food she is about to eat has been washed, pared, kneaded, touched, by the hands of her lover. She is overwhelmed by desire when she finds the faint impressions of Miss Toklas' fingerprints decorating the crimped edges of a pie crust" (27). Bình goes on to imagine the way that many well-known events in Stein's and Toklas's lives happened, for instance, the purchase of the made-to-order armchairs (for Toklas not to have to dangle her feet) and Stein's decision to have her hair cut short. Clearly, Bình presumes to know Toklas in ways that the reader of her and Stein's own work would not: "Miss Toklas likes the wind in her face . . . [and] the smell of fresh ink on fingertips" (30). Throughout Truong's novel, Toklas strikes the reader as the more intriguing character out of Bình's two "Mesdames." As Bình puts it, "Miss Toklas, believe me, is a package worth unwrapping. An artichoke, if you know what I mean" (184).

Liberated by a certain dimension of generic license (which perhaps matches the license in relation to *gender* of Bình as a gay man), Truong modifies specific passages from the *Cook Book* for her novel, as it were recycling and extending some of the anecdotes that recur in the Toklas autobiographies and many other sources. For instance, she makes Toklas teach Bình how to kill pigeons the way that Jeanne teaches Toklas how to do it in the *Cook Book* (*Book of Salt*, 67, *Cook Book*, 40) and also tell him Hélène's schema for the way in which eggs can be prepared according to the message the cook wishes to deliver to the dining guests (*Book of Salt*, 101–2, *Cook Book*, 171). Truong also provides some creative interpretations of the Stein–Toklas legend that speak to my own concerns in this book. For instance, she troubles the gift/theft dichotomy that I discussed earlier and that riddles *The Autobiography* in particular: "Leo wrote a note . . . accusing Miss Toklas of stealing [his sister] away from him. When Miss Toklas read this, she laughed, and wrote back: 'Your sister gave herself to me.' How true, I think. A gift or a theft depends on who is holding the pen" (215).

In this way, the novelist provides the literary critic with an image of the way in which it is possible to say not only that *The Autobiography* can be reconsidered as a gift from Toklas to Stein, but also that Stein can be seen as having given her life, her work, and her genius to her companion to nurture, cherish, and control. The flow of power between the two women becomes radically indeterminate at this point. It is true that Toklas devoted her life to serving Stein. At the same time, Stein dedicated all her writing from 1907 onward to her "little Jew." Typically, these dedications, a ceremonial part of Stein's notebook drafts (see Dydo, *Gertrude Stein*, 28), never became part of the published material, but there are exceptions: "Thank you very much, how often I have thanked you, how often I have cause to thank you. How often I do thank you. / Thank you very much. / And what would you have me do. / I would have you sing songs to your little Jew" ("A Sonatina Followed by Another," 287). Toklas, as Stein's "little jew," approaches the "you" addressed by Stein's playful rhyming comment on the flexibility of pronouns—not only do "she" and "I" merge but also "she" (Toklas, the "jew") and "you"—and the way in which discourse turns obscure, *turns upon obscurity*, even in moments of great transparency and insistence: "*I say it to you.*" And still you are unable to hear it. In the final analysis, it becomes impossible to fix the relationship between masters and servants, between Stein and Toklas, and between the three Toklas autobiographies, in a stable hierarchical form. This is part of "the true story of Alice B. Toklas"—an autobiographical truth that departs from the expected properties of unity and stability and instead develops continually in a series of incompatible combinations and heretical (im)possibilities.

It is time to once again revisit "the true story of Alice B. Toklas," a conception now transformed into a question or a riddle, a recognition of the abyss between critical desire and critical power, and more specifically an uncomfortable but necessary inquiry into the justification and value of the present study. These concluding remarks should be seen as thoroughly relativized by a certain proliferation of question marks. At the same time, there are also declaratory statements to be made. In this study, I have brought three Toklas autobiographies together for analysis in order to conceptualize the Stein–Toklas sexual/textual relationship as fundamentally reciprocal, Toklas as indispensable to Stein's literary production, and Toklas as a cultural laborer and a writer of her own books. This agenda has motivated a critical practice characterized by an "incompatible combination": the simultaneous postulation of a historical and biographical context, on the one hand, and the strategic privileging of textual and intertextual conjecture, on the other. I have tested and argued my hypothesis that, in the Toklas autobiographies, "the true story of Alice B. Toklas" resides in the destabilization, multiplication, and textualization or fictionalization of autobiographical truth, and in the strategic deauthorization of the author. Instead of looking for autobiographical truth, I have argued, it is possible to reconsider these texts otherwise, as practices of writing, as commodities, and in relation to the legendary division of labor in the Stein–Toklas marriage. Moreover, I have made the claim that instead of looking for the author or lamenting the fact that she is missing from the text, these texts can be constructed as indications that Toklas's authorial agency resides in a certain reverse discourse of absence.

The way in which Toklas remains absent, even from her own autobiographies, brings to mind the story in *The Autobiography* of Picasso painting Stein's portrait and fretting about the difficulty of "capturing" her: "All of a sudden one day Picasso painted out the whole head. I can't see you any longer when I look, he said irritably. And so the picture was left like that" (71). Returning from a trip, however, Picasso "sat down and out of his head painted [Stein's] head in without having seen [her] again. . . . It is very strange but neither can remember at all what the head looked like when he painted it out" (76–77). As is well known, Toklas later crops Stein's hair, and Picasso reacts to her new haircut with great emotion: "he caught sight of her through two doorways and approaching her quickly called out, Gertrude, what is it, what is it. What is what, Pablo, she said. Let me see, he said. She let him see. And my portrait, said he sternly. Then his face softening he added, mais, quand même tout y est, all the same it is all there" (77). This anecdote illustrates the approach that I have taken in order to conceptualize "the true story of Alice B. Toklas." Trying to "capture" Toklas will result in frustration and a critical impasse, the realization that "I can't see [her] any longer when I look." The only way to move forward then is to "out of [one's own] head" trace the contours of Toklas's likeness "without having seen [her]." She will move away from this provisional rendition, multiply, change, and dodge any attempt to pin her down, so that the only thinkable saving grace of the portrait resides in a strategic reformulation of Toklas as (that) text—"all the same it is all there."

My quest for the "true story of Alice B. Toklas," all over the legend of Stein and Toklas and especially in the Toklas autobiographies, has provided me not so much with a clear picture of who Toklas "really" was, but rather with a sharpened sense of the way in which these texts and/as intertexts shift the emphasis from the *truth* of the story to the *story* of autobiographical truth, and indeed to the telling or writing of it. The fact that there are many different stories concerning the same life, or perhaps rather many versions of the same (life) story, creates a distance between the concept of autobiographical truth and the expected properties of transparency, correspondence, referentiality, and unity in autobiography. At long last, then, autobiography acquires a much-needed stress on its last constituent—in Sidonie Smith's words, and as opposed to the question of woman's *bios*, "the larger and more complex issues of . . . woman's *graphia*" (*Poetics*, 7). In other words, autobiography turns into a practice of *writing*. This is perhaps not so much a telling of li(v)es as a writing of death, or the written life as the death of the fantasy of autobiographical presence and/as truth. As Derrida argues in his deconstruction of Rousseau: "Death by writing also inaugurates life. . . . As soon as one determines it within the system of this economy, is not the sacrifice—the 'literary suicide'—dissipated in the *appearance*? . . . We would be obliged to decide that a ruse and an appearance are necessary if in fact we were to abide by these concepts . . . which determine what we here call economy in terms of truth and appearance, starting from the opposition presence/absence" (*Of Grammatology*, 143).

A certain ruse and a certain "appearance," *despite everything*, govern the semblance of a "true story of Alice B. Toklas" in all three Toklas autobiographies and in the general legend of Stein and Toklas. A reformulation of the "true story" as a function of writing involves a reconsideration of binaries such as presence/absence, truth/lies, and world/word. Moreover, the writing of the (autobiographical) truth about Alice B. Toklas is an ongoing and ever-changing process, which involves many intertextual relationships beyond those that I have privileged in the present study. The *reading* of autobiographical truth is equally convoluted and always situated in a specific context, and I have placed emphasis throughout on my own engagement with the Toklas autobiographies *as* a reading, more specifically as *one* particular reading among many actual and potential readings, none of which can be established unconditionally as the truth, or even as more truthful than other readings. The only possible justification for the present study, then, lies in its provisional and utterly situated *articulation*, not in its relative correspondence to some preexisting "true story." Indeed, the true story exists only in someone's discursive engagement with it, and this is true even when considerations of material reality and authorial intention enter into the equation. At this point, it might be interesting to return to Gilmore's concept of autobiographics as an "other [position] from which to tell the 'truth,'" inhabited by "women who intervene in the linkage of 'lying' and 'women,' who refuse the violence of gender identity compelled by dominant discourses of self-representation in order to put themselves into their texts through the agency of remembering" (239).

Gilmore's theory seems to present possibilities for the reconsideration of autobiographical truth (in women's writing) as relative and plural. Where, if at all, can the alternative "true story" of Alice B. Toklas be found, the one that is told from another position? Perhaps in a consideration of her own power over the discourses that (fail to) define her, along the lines of Gilmore's notion of an intervention into the connection between women and lying. Since Toklas can be grasped only momentarily, however, as the eternally escaping referent for an unusually unstable autobiographical "I," is it at all possible to imagine her in a position of agency? In this study, I have found it useful to articulate both truth and agency *negatively* in relation to Toklas and her story. Instead of necessarily investing these concepts with essence and presence, it is possible to rethink them in terms of a reverse discourse of absence. One example is the emptying out of the category of remembering in *What Is Remembered* and in White's conception of this text as autobiographical failure. The "true story of Alice B. Toklas" seen from another perspective can also be imagined through recourse to various marginal—unauthorized and deauthorizing—discourses. Toklas's true opinions may not be available in the Toklas autobiographies, but they can be provisionally reconstructed from her corrections of and comments on various *other* texts presumably telling the "true story" of her and Stein. This is not to say that I consider Toklas's version truer than these other texts, or my own reading closer to the truth than previous articulations. The opposite of truth is perhaps not lies anymore, but instead the very assumption that truth is stable, singular, and universal, in other words, that it cannot be told from other positions.

Toklas's copy of *The Third Rose* (1959) by John Malcolm Brinnin (YCAL MSS 76, Folder 3325) contains multiple corrections and comments, exclamation marks, and other signs that indicate various "critical moments" at which Toklas disagrees with Brinnin's interpretation of Stein's life and work (in the following, brackets indicate words crossed out). Some of the comments seem to fit the description of Toklas as someone who wanted to remain anonymous, and whose most cherished task was to protect the literary reputation of Stein. In a chapter centering on her (something which must have annoyed her immensely), Toklas crosses out the words "[upper-middle-class] gentility" and "[domestic] servitude," and then, in a paragraph that deals with the result of "domestic boredom" and Toklas's escape from it, corrects the following sentence: "In the [advanced state of her spinsterhood], she was not, as it turned out, unresponsive to the tenderness and friendship which, in lieu of marriage, would soon determine the course of her existence" (104–5). Toklas disagrees by exclamation mark with Brinnin's claim that "*Three Lives* belongs to the literary area marked out by French naturalism" (124), and when Brinnin suggests that Stein's word portraits were partial self-portraits, Toklas writes in the margin "no no no!" (149). Indications of political sentiments can be detected as well in Toklas's reaction to Brinnin's claims. In a section on the Nazi soldiers staying at their home, and Stein's opinions on this arrangement, she crosses out the sentence "She even came to feel a little sorry for them" (368). In a 1959 letter to Steward, Toklas mentions "a very unpleasant book by Brinnin. He sent me a copy which I spent a month correcting to send to Yale for reference, not for circulation" (*Dear Sammy*, 232).

It is tempting to draw the conclusion that Toklas's reaction to Brinnin's text is an old woman's attempt to soothe herself and to reconstruct her own gilded version of the story, in which she is not a poor old spinster and Stein is not fat. Sometimes, however, the corrections indicate that Brinnin in fact embellishes and alters reality far more extensively than Toklas does as the guardian of Stein's memory. For instance, at one point in Brinnin's text, Toklas changes "the hotel whose window gave out on groves of whispering cypresses" to "the hotel whose window gave out on an avenue" (154). It seems fair to assume that Toklas would know about the hotel and its views, since she was there. Furthermore, when Brinnin talks about Toklas typing Stein's work at the Villa Curonia, Toklas laconically remarks "no typewriter" (167). Moreover, Toklas marks with an X an obviously erroneous description of Stein in her Radcliffe days as short-haired, mannish, and uncorseted (27)—indeed photos of Stein from that time show her most visibly corseted and with elaborately arranged long hair. It is true that Toklas sometimes seems to cross out "truths" (to which she herself testifies elsewhere): "Things were always going wrong with 'Auntie'" (220). But elsewhere, she gives the impression of quiet sincerity in her corrections. For instance, she does not deny Brinnin's claim that she became hard of hearing and would break into interviews with irrelevancies that indicated that she had not been able to follow the flow of conversation, but just says in the margin: "much later" (396).

Some of Toklas's marginal interventions in Brinnin's text are interesting because they are ambiguous and depart from the way in which she generally comments. In a passage on the famously infected relations between Toklas, Gertrude Stein, Leo Stein, and Mabel Dodge Luhan, Toklas *underlines* rather than crosses out parts of the text. For instance, as Brinnin quotes Luhan on Leo Stein's "neuroticism," Toklas adds emphasis to the comment that "when *Alice supplanted him* he was cut off from [human contact with life] completely." Moreover: "Some friends of his and Gertrude's, among them *Mabel Dodge*, felt that the attachment between Gertrude and *Alice had* very much to do with his leaving. It was their feeling that by having relieved Gertrude of every onerous activity, by assuming all secretarial duties, and by protecting her from every undesirable and annoying contact with people, Alice had made herself *indispensable to Gertrude's comfort.*

Gertrude, growing helpless, less inclined to do anything for herself, had begun to seem foolish in Leo's eyes. The vine, they felt, was beginning to strangle and vitiate the tree" (198, Toklas's emphases). There are no comments in the margin, and nothing crossed out. Toklas's practice of underlining here, as opposed to her crossing out and openly disagreeing with certain claims elsewhere, seems to affirm rather than question the overall content of this particular passage. It is as if Toklas is saying, yes, I *was* indispensable to her, and they did not like it. The same message can be surmised in another correction, a sentence where Toklas crosses out three words: "It was Alice Toklas, [of all people], who redeemed the sad situation and fulfilled the long hope by herself becoming the 'adventurous publisher' of the works of Gertrude Stein" (296). Here it seems as though Toklas is saying, *who else if not me?*

The comments and corrections in Toklas's copy of Elizabeth Sprigge's *Gertrude Stein* (1957) (YCAL MSS 76, Box 140, Folder 3292) are considerably more poisonous, with frequent harsh remarks about Sprigge as a person and her methods, as well as recurrent inscriptions in the margin of "not so," "nonsense," "never," and "oh dear no!" It is true that Sprigge makes a few remarkable mistakes, for instance, saying it was *Stein* who learned to knit for the soldiers during the war (109–10). Quite understandably, Toklas fumes in the margin: "knitted! nonsense." In a way that pleases the literary critic, Toklas seems to indirectly answer back to Meyerowitz's homophobic comments on *Tender Buttons* when she crosses out Sprigge's note on the title of the work "so called because of her predilection for buttons" and adds an exclamation mark in the margin. At the same time, taking a look at Toklas's reaction to Sprigge's work makes me aware of the way in which she would most probably have reacted to mine. For instance, most words are crossed out and "nonsense" again written in the margin when Sprigge writes of *The Autobiography* "Told in the first person the conversational style is that of [Miss Toklas]; on every page [one hears her turn of phrase, recognizes her sharp or gentle observation, her swift sizing up of everything and everybody]" (173).

What is really interesting about this conflict between Toklas and the woman who claims the right to tell her story is the fact that Sprigge's version of the background for her book exists side by side in the Yale collection with serious counterclaims in Toklas's corrected copy of it. Sprigge's "Journal in quest of Gertrude Stein" (YCAL MSS 77, Box 18, Folder 306) begins with the account of an April 1954 lunch meeting that indicates that

Toklas had "encouraged" Sprigge to "undertake the biography" but also acknowledges Toklas's refusal to even be mentioned, except perhaps as publisher of the Plain Edition (2–3). In Sprigge's version of the story, Toklas is fickle and unreliable, one day telling her to go ahead and write whatever she wants, and then the next day, "prickly as a hedgehog" (65), prohibiting her from going into certain areas. One of the areas not even mentioned, of course, is the issue of Stein's and Toklas's sexuality, which makes Sprigge wake up trembling in the middle of the night, although she dares not speak it aloud in her book. As a whole, Sprigge's journal indicates a bitter falling-out between her and Toklas, similar to the one between Toklas and White, the prospective ghostwriter for *What Is Remembered*. Sprigge, however, goes on to write and publish her book without Toklas's blessing. And this is what brings us back to the predicament of these concluding remarks, the demand for critical introspection. What is the point of the present articulation of "the true story of Alice B. Toklas"? Wherein lies its value? How can it be justified? And by whom? Certainly the object of investigation would not have authorized it.

Although researched and written several decades after Toklas's death by someone who was not even born when she died, and completed exactly fifty years after Sprigge had lunch with Toklas and was discouraged from even *mentioning* her role in Stein's work, the present study similarly but far more extensively pushes on the boundaries of respect for Toklas's desire to remain under cover and determination *not* to end up between book covers. The one and only "true story of Alice B. Toklas" cannot be found in this study, despite its seemingly pretentious title, nor the story that Toklas would have liked to have told about herself (that is, no story at all). The least I can do to provisionally displace the violation in this book of my object of study is to grant her, the "other woman," *the last word* (as was her predilection while alive), albeit recontextualized to signify as a comment on the present study. The "true story of Alice B. Toklas" is out of my reach, as is the possibility that Toklas would have approved of my work, had she been alive. But, in a critical endeavor that serves to recover a cultural laborer and a writer of vast importance to the literary discourses of the twentieth century, "cant one count and build upon conviction—prejudice and passion—my inadequate equipment?"

Notes

References to the Yale Collection of American Literature at the Beinecke Rare Book and Manuscript Library at Yale University, New Haven, Connecticut, are given as YCAL in the Notes.

INTRODUCTION

1. Toklas specifies this arrangement in her own will, which is preserved in the Yale collection (YCAL MSS 77, Box 18, Folder 312). It should also be noted that Stein's part of the headstone, that is, the front, is not an unproblematic "master narrative": "Ironically, since Gertrude had always teased French officials with the spelling of Allegheny, Pennsylvania, the name of her birthplace is misspelled and the date of her death is given incorrectly as July 29, the day of Leo's death" (Mellow, 471).

2. In Luhan's *Intimate Memories*, there is a famous passage that describes a potentially explosive love triangle: "one day at lunch, Gertrude . . . sent me such a strong look over the table that it seemed to cut across the air to me in a band of electrified steel—a smile traveling across on it—powerful—Heavens! I remember it *now* so keenly! At that Alice arose hastily and ran out of the room onto the terrace. From that time on Alice began to separate Gertrude and me" (93–94).

3. Tom Hachtman provides the most creative and hilarious comment on this incident and Hemingway's reaction to it in a *Gertrude's Follies* comic strip from 1979. It begins by Toklas asking "Have you noticed how Hemingway bristles when you call me Pussy?" "No Pussy no," Stein replies. Toklas goes on: "Have you seen my gloves?" "No Pussy." "Wanna help with the trash?" "No pussy no." "Bananas on your cereal?" "No, please, pussy, don't." The comic strip ends with an image of Hemingway in the street going crazy and running off as he overhears the "no Pussy no Pussy" chorus from a "big dance number" performed by Stein, Toklas, and friends (Picasso, Matisse, Fitzgerald, and others).

4. Stein herself denies the "twin" image in a love note to Toklas: "my baby / is just so little and tall, she is so / fat and neat and thin, *she is not / my twin she is my all* and lively / like a ball and tender as the / fall and lovely as a wall" (Turner, 150, my emphasis).

CHAPTER I

1. This formulation has been used in relation to Stein's writing by, for instance, Shari Benstock: "Her writing first revises the relation between word and a determining world of objects (*The Making of Americans*, *Tender Buttons*,

the word portraits) and later breaks entirely the assumed connection between word and world (*Lucy Church Amiably, Stanzas in Meditation, Four Saints in Three Acts*, etc.)" (*Women of the Left Bank*, 161).

2. Norris borrows the term "technology of gender" from Teresa de Lauretis's highly influential rethinking of gender in relation to Foucauldian theory and North American feminist identity politics in *Technologies of Gender: Essays on Theory, Film, and Fiction*. De Lauretis's four propositions on gender suggest a certain affinity with Butler's views: "(1) Gender is (a) representation. . . . (2) The representation of gender *is* its construction. . . . (3) The construction of gender goes on as busily today as it did in earlier times. . . . (4) [T]he construction of gender is also effected by its deconstruction" (3).

3. The way in which the Toklas autobiographies lend themselves to a Butlerian reading of (gender) identity as (discursive) performance is illustrated, for instance, in an anecdote in *The Autobiography* concerning Toklas's correspondence with T. S. Eliot's secretary: "We each addressed the other as Sir, I signing myself A. B. Toklas and she signing initials. It was only considerably afterwards that I found out that his secretary was not a young man. I don't know whether she ever found out that I was not" (273). At the same time, it must be noted that the present study applies only a very limited part of Butler's theoretical *oeuvre* to my reading of the primary material, specifically the basic assumptions of *Gender Trouble*, concerning repetition and the possibility of a variation on the repetition as a provisional category of agency. Rather than a decision to adopt a wholesale Butlerian perspective, my interest in the issue of performativity should be seen as an attempt to articulate the position of my study in relation to an ongoing critical conversation and a wish to push on the boundaries of the critical debate as it has been played out so far. For instance, Sidonie Smith in her discussion of autobiographical performativity speaks briefly of Stein's *Autobiography*, but despite the fact that she has mentioned Butler's concept of the "possibility of a variation on [the] repetition" ("Performativity," 20) as the unsteady foundation for performative identity and agency, she fails to mention that the story of Alice B. Toklas has been repeated (indeed, with significant variations) in several autobiographical works in a way that brings to mind Butler's argument that "the task is not whether to repeat, but how to repeat or, indeed, to repeat and, through a radical proliferation . . . *to displace* the very . . . norms that enable the repetition itself" (*Gender Trouble*, 148, emphasis in original).

CHAPTER 2

1. In relation to my own attempt to suspend considerations of "high" and "low" literary genres, it is interesting to note that Adams finds it necessary to add the following caveat to his characterization of Stein's text: "Although *The Autobiography of Alice B. Toklas* can be considered an example of the American tall tale, . . . this fact does not subtract from its importance as literature or as a picture of 'The Lost Generation'" (12–15).

2. This *Vanity Fair* piece can be seen as an alternative follow-up on *The*

Autobiography. Dydo talks about a work planned by Stein and the publisher, "spoken of as the 'Confessions' or 'Confessions of the writer of the Autobiography of Alice B. Toklas,' [which] was to be a second autobiographical volume in the voice of the *Autobiography*. An aborted affair, it became only a short piece published as 'And Now.' The two works involve different writing ideas but share important ideas" (*Gertrude Stein*, 572–73). It is intriguing to imagine yet another level of autobiographical truth telling, the *confessions* of the writer of the (unreliable?) previous autobiography, and also the idea that these confessions would be spoken in the "same" voice.

3. The *transition* crowd reacts violently to the fact that an American woman pretends to know something about modern art in Europe and focuses primarily on perceived "errors" on the level of content. But it can be imagined that *The Autobiography* was also challenging because it was almost the same but not quite/not straight in relation to certain conventions of authority and authorship. When Tzara complains about *The Autobiography* in terms of "lie" and "pretention," he is presumably talking about the provocative double-voicing tactics of this text. The fact that Tzara and the other contributors to "Testimony against Gertrude Stein" react negatively to such transgressions is surprising. It seems as though Stein's challenge should have attracted praise from other great modernists, who were not only used to, but also themselves promoted and deployed challenges in art and literature.

4. Incidentally, the passage on Madame Matisse is among the most valuable in Stein's entire production for feminist criticism. The way in which the artist's wife is in charge of this particular narrative is emphasized: "This is the way Madame Matisse used to tell the story" (52). Moreover, it is not only the story of the buying/selling of this particular painting, but in fact is the story of the way in which Madame Matisse has always supported and made possible her husband's art: "And so, Madame Matisse used to end up the story triumphantly, you see it was I, and I was right to insist upon the original price, and Mademoiselle Gertrude, who insisted upon buying it, who arranged the whole matter" (54). The great modernist painter is all but excluded from the picture, as the woman who makes his art possible through posing for all his paintings and being the breadwinner of the family and the woman who makes his art possible through buying his paintings come to an agreement on the value of his work.

5. It is interesting, and in line with many other reversals and conflations in the Stein–Toklas legend, that Fisher suggests that Toklas caused bells to ring in people's minds, too: "People have told me that when this small ugly woman was in a room they were keenly aware of her, before they even recognized her as Miss Toklas. She seemed to send out waves of inaudible sound, like bells clanging somewhere in another space than ours" (Fisher, ix–x).

CHAPTER 3

1. It is interesting to note that when Toklas wrote her memoir, she carried her life up through the 1950s, but then she dropped the final chapter in its published

form and concluded her book at Stein's death. There are indications, however, that Toklas was not entirely happy with the ending as it stands in the published version. In a 1962 letter to Steward she complains, "It doesn't end as it should. . . . It should have ended more gaily" (242).

2. Stein's death is only one of those important events in the legend of Stein and Toklas for which there are multiple conflicting versions of the "same" story. Toklas's copy of *The Third Rose* (1959) by John Malcolm Brinnin (YCAL MSS 76, Folder 3325) contains multiple corrections and comments in her handwriting. There are lots of changes in the last few pages, especially concerning Stein's illness and death. An interesting note is that Toklas here crosses out everything concerning the two famous questions and leaves in only the following sentences (brackets indicate words crossed out): "Doctors worked [for an hour] to revive her, but her death at 6:30 ended their efforts. At her bedside were Alice [and her niece and nephew, Mr. and Mrs. Dan Raffel]" (404). I discuss Toklas's corrections of Brinnin's text in the conclusion. In a 1953 letter to Carl Van Vechten, Toklas apparently answers a question about the famous last words: "She said upon waking from a sleep—What is the question. And I didnt answer thinking she was not completely awakened. Then she said again—What is the question and before I could speak she went on—If there is no question then there is no answer. And she turned and went to sleep again. Were [these last words] not a summing up of her life and perhaps a vision of the future" (*Staying On Alone*, 276–77).

3. This reading is not entirely supported by the history of the book's production, however. Toklas suggested as titles for her memoir *Gertrude's Manner* and later *Things I Have Seen*, but the publisher changed the title without consulting her to *What Is Remembered*. According to Simon, Toklas found this move "ill-mannered" (*Biography*, 246). The title *Gertrude's Manner* would perhaps have deterred critics and reviewers from expecting to find Toklas "herself" in the text. *Things I Have Seen* would correspond better with White's conceptualization of Toklas's process of remembering as watching a silent movie, and also with the common characterization of *The Autobiography* as "literary cubism." Moreover, it would constitute obvious "repetition with a difference" in relation to the title for Stein's *Wars I Have Seen*, and as such bring to mind the implications of Bloom's argument about repetition: "By the very nature of its form, autobiography-by-*Doppelgänger* veritably precludes repetition or imitation. The wit intrinsic in the initial endeavor becomes a joke progressively more stale with each repetition, guaranteed to annoy the readers of successive works. . . . Imagine the third volume of Stein's autobiography, *Wars I Have Seen*, rewritten as *Wars Alice B. Toklas Has Seen*! Once is genius; twice is gimmickry; thrice is boredom. The form itself is almost self-destructing" (82). Twice and thrice need not be bad if the "imitation" produces a text that is almost the same but not quite/not straight. In this context it is interesting to note that *Wars I Have Seen* was originally called "Civil Domestic and Foreign Wars" (preliminary version, typescript) and then *Wars I Remember* (written on the front of manuscript notebooks).

4. This event is described elsewhere as well. In the Duncan interview, Toklas says "I met her the day I arrived [in Paris]. . . . [W]e came in in the very early morning and we cleaned up and had lunch and then went over to see the Steins, and I told you, it was Gertrude. That's registered. In fact, I remember" (97). Toklas here indicates that this story as it is "registered" and as she "remembers" it is the "same." But the very distinction between two types of autobiographical truth (the record and the reminiscence) speaks to a dimension of ambiguity at the center of the present study.

CHAPTER 4

1. In fact, all three Toklas autobiographies can be seen as deferred autobiographies. *What Is Remembered* is perhaps the *ultimate* deferred autobiography, if analyzed in relation to the famous ending of *The Autobiography*. After all those years, in her old age, Toklas finally "find[s] time" to write "My Twenty-Five Years with Gertrude Stein." *What Is Remembered* could even be said to replace the forever deferred autobiography that is prior even to *The Autobiography*, namely the autobiography that *Stein* refused to write before she decided to write Toklas's autobiography: "For some time now many people, and publishers, have been asking Gertrude Stein to write her autobiography and she had always replied, not possibly" (*The Autobiography*, 341). In relation to all three Toklas autobiographies, the other definition of "defer" also comes into play. In the first deferred autobiography, Toklas can be said to defer/yield to Stein's authority/authorship, and Stein can be said to defer/give in to the pressure on her to produce a commercially viable text as well as the necessity to speak Toklas's story in Toklas's conversational style. In the second deferred autobiography, Toklas defers/agrees to write some sort of autobiographical text ("a cook book . . . with memories") despite her claim that her autobiography is "done" already. In the third deferred autobiography, Toklas defers/complies with the official story of her own life and the Stein–Toklas relationship as it was articulated by Stein in *The Autobiography*.

2. For a number of interesting essays on recipes and the recipe collection as a genre, see *The Recipe Reader: Narratives—Contexts—Traditions*, edited by Janet Floyd and Laurel Forster. In their introduction, Floyd and Forster touch upon several of the assumptions at the heart of the present study, for instance the fact that "Personal histories or pasts, constructed through memory, or the process of remembering with others, are often centered on food" (7).

3. This is a complex situation, since the autobiography that elevates the husband's work is traditionally the wife's responsibility—thus, Toklas's failure to perform her wifely duty is the impetus for Stein to take on the wifely role in *The Autobiography* (see Smith, "Performativity," 29).

4. In fact, Stein and Toklas may have planned a cookbook together in quite some detail, and slightly more seriously than this anecdote indicates. On the inside cover of Stein's copy of James Fenimore Cooper's *Pilot* (kept in the Yale collection), there is a partly unreadable sentence in Stein's handwriting that

suggests collaboration or a piece of writing in two voices, and on the flyleaf opposite, there is also an outline for the seven chapters of an imaginary cookbook. The first chapter is called "My Life with Cookbooks" and the last chapter "Eating and Not Eating, an Occupation" (YCAL MSS 76). It is not unlikely that Toklas may have had this prospective cookbook in mind when she wrote the *Cook Book* many years later.

5. For essays on "cross-cultural consumption, or what happens to commodities when they cross cultural borders" (1), see *Cross-Cultural Consumption*, edited by David Howes.

6. This collapse of categories characterizes all three Toklas autobiographies. Although *The Autobiography* seems to present a strict hierarchical system separating geniuses from wives and art from more mundane aspects of life, the text also collapses these dichotomies and offers a strikingly "flat" rendition of all the various components of Stein's and Toklas's world. One example of this fluidity in the text of high and low categories is the beginning of the third chapter, "Gertrude Stein in Paris: 1903–1907." This chapter begins by enumerating the art dealers operating in Montmartre as Gertrude and Leo Stein begin their famous collection of modernist paintings and especially those on the rue Laffitte (for instance, Vollard, the "huge dark man" who provided them with their first Cézanne works). The narrator continues the description of the street as follows: "Also on the rue Laffitte was the confectioner Fouquet where one could console oneself with delicious honey cakes and nut candies and once in a while *instead of a picture* buy oneself strawberry jam in a glass bowl" (38–39, my emphasis). Indeed, later we are told that Gertrude and Leo Stein consume quite a few of Fouquet's honey cakes (to "refresh themselves") while trying to decide which Cézanne portrait to buy (44). These gastronomical observations, juxtaposed with reminiscences of paintings, art galleries, and the burgeoning modernist art movement, may not seem very remarkable, but they should be considered alongside a general collapse of high/low categories in Stein's and Toklas's literary imagination. To cite one of the most extreme examples, one of the wartime love notes from Stein to Toklas included in *Baby Precious* reads "As surely as Life publishes / me and we get material / and baby has a cow so / surely will the allies / win. You think so" (83). As I have already mentioned, Turner, seriously and convincingly adopting the "the excretory point of view" (33), reveals "cows" in Stein's writing to be Toklas's stools rather than her orgasms. In this short private love poem, then, Stein brings her own literary success, Toklas's digestive "success," and the military success of the allied forces into radical proximity and also suggests that Toklas is the one who believes in such flattening out of hierarchical divisions between high and low, public and private, cerebral and corporeal realities: "You think so."

Bibliography

Acton, Harold. *Memoirs of an Aesthete 1939–1969*. Excerpted in *Gertrude Stein Remembered*. Edited by Linda Simon. Lincoln: University of Nebraska Press, 1994: 109–16.

Adams, Timothy Dow. "'She Will Be Me When This You See': Gertrude Stein's Mock-Autobiography of Alice B. Toklas." *Publications of the Arkansas Philological Association* 6, 1 (1980): 1–18.

Alkon, Paul K. "Visual Rhetoric in *The Autobiography of Alice B. Toklas*." *Critical Inquiry* (1 June 1975): 849–81.

Barney, Natalie. "Foreword to *As Fine As Melanchta*." Excerpted in *Gertrude Stein Remembered*. Edited by Linda Simon. Lincoln: University of Nebraska Press, 1994: 28–36.

Beach, Sylvia. *Shakespeare and Company*. Excerpted in *Gertrude Stein Remembered*. Edited by Linda Simon. Lincoln: University of Nebraska Press, 1994: 49–57.

Beaton, Cecil. *Photobiography*. Excerpted in *Gertrude Stein Remembered*. Edited by Linda Simon. Lincoln: University of Nebraska Press, 1994: 137–40.

Benstock, Shari. *Textualizing the Feminine: On the Limits of Genre*. Norman: University of Oklahoma Press, 1991.

———. *Women of the Left Bank: Paris, 1900–1940*. London: Virago Press, 1987.

Berry, Ellen E. *Curved Thought and Textual Wandering: Gertrude Stein's Postmodernism*. Ann Arbor: University of Michigan Press, 1992.

Bhabha, Homi K. "Of Mimicry and Man: The Ambivalence of Colonial Discourse." *The Location of Culture*. London: Routledge, 1994: 85–92.

Blair, Sara. "Home Truths: Gertrude Stein, 27 Rue de Fleurus, and the Place of the Avant-Garde." *American Literary History* 12, 3 (Fall 2000): 417–37.

Blanchot, Maurice. *La Folie du Jour*. Saint Clément-la-Rivière, France: Fata Morgana, 1973.

Bloom, Lynn Z. "Gertrude Is Alice Is Everybody: Innovation and Point of View in Gertrude Stein's Autobiographies." *Twentieth Century Literature* 24, 1 (1978): 81–93.

Bodart, Anne. *The Blue Dog and Other Fables for the French*. Translated with an introduction by Alice B. Toklas. Boston: Houghton Mifflin, 1956.

Bollinger, Laurel. "'One As One Not Mistaken but Interrupted': Gertrude Stein's Exploration of Identity in the 1930s." *Centennial Review* 43, 2 (Spring 1999): 227–58.

Breslin, James E. "Gertrude Stein and the Problems of Autobiography." *Women's*

Autobiography: Essays in Criticism. Edited by Estelle C. Jelinek. Bloomington: Indiana University Press, 1980: 149–62.

Bridgman, Richard. *Gertrude Stein in Pieces*. New York: Oxford University Press, 1970.

Brinnin, John Malcolm. *The Third Rose*. Boston: Little, Brown, 1959.

Brodzki, Bella, and Celeste Schenck (eds.). Introduction to *Life/Lines: Theorizing Women's Autobiography*. Ithaca, N.Y.: Cornell University Press, 1988.

Broughton, T. L. "Women's Autobiography: The Self at Stake?" *Prose Studies* 14, 2 (1991): 76–94.

Burke, Carolyn. "Getting Spliced: Modernism and Sexual Difference." *American Quarterly* 39 (1987): 98–121.

Burke, Seán. *The Death and Return of the Author: Criticism and Subjectivity in Barthes, Foucault, and Derrida*. Edinburgh, U.K.: Edinburgh University Press, 1998.

Butler, Judith. *Gender Trouble: Feminism and the Subversion of Identity*. New York: Routledge, 1990.

Chessman, Harriet Scott. *The Public Is Invited to Dance: Representation, the Body, and Dialogue in Gertrude Stein*. Stanford, Calif.: Stanford University Press, 1989.

Cixous, Hélène. "Laugh of the Medusa." *The Routledge Language and Cultural Theory Reader*. Edited by Lucy Burke, Tony Crowley, and Alan Girvin. London: Routledge, 2001: 161–66.

Cope, Karin. "'Moral Deviancy' and Contemporary Feminism: The Judgment of Gertrude Stein." *Feminism beside Itself*. Edited by Diane Elam and Robyn Wiegman. New York: Routledge, 1995: 155–78.

Curnutt, Kirk. "'In the Temps de Gertrude': Hemingway, Stein, and the Scene of Instruction at 27, Rue de Fleurus." *French Connections: Hemingway and Fitzgerald Abroad*. Edited by J. Gerald Kennedy and Jackson R. Bryer. London: Macmillan, 1998: 121–39.

Davis, Phoebe. "Subjectivity and the Aesthetics of National Identity in Gertrude Stein's *The Autobiography of Alice B. Toklas*." *Twentieth Century Literature* 45, 1 (Spring 1999): 18–45.

de Lauretis, Teresa. *Technologies of Gender: Essays on Theory, Film, and Fiction*. Bloomington: Indiana University Press, 1987.

Dellamora, Richard. "Responsibilities: Deconstruction, Feminism, and Lesbian Erotics." *Canadian Review of Comparative Literature* 21 (March–June 1994): 221–42.

de Man, Paul. "Autobiography as De-Facement." *Modern Language Notes* 94 (1979): 919–30.

Derrida, Jacques. "The Law of Genre." *Critical Inquiry* 7 (1980): 55–81.

———. *Of Grammatology*. Translated by Gayatri Chakravorty Spivak. Baltimore: Johns Hopkins University Press, 1997.

———. *Margins of Philosophy*. Chicago: University of Chicago Press, 1982.

Duncan, Roland E. "Miss Alice B. Toklas Interview." (1952). Transcript from tapes. Interview for the Oral History Department, the Bancroft Library, University of California at Berkeley.

Dydo, Ulla E., with William Rice. *Gertrude Stein: The Language That Rises. 1923–1934*. Evanston, Ill.: Northwestern University Press, 2003.

———. "*Stanzas in Meditation*: The Other Autobiography." *Chicago Review* 35, 2 (1985): 4–20.

——— (ed.). *A Stein Reader*. Evanston: Northwestern University Press, 1993.

Fisher, M. F. K. "Foreword." *The Alice B. Toklas Cook Book*. New York: Harper and Row, 1984: ix–xvii.

Flanner, Janet. "Letter from Paris." *The Critical Response to Gertrude Stein*. Edited by Kirk Curnutt. Westport, Conn.: Greenwood Press, 2000: 280–81.

Floyd, Janet, and Laurel Forster (eds.). *The Recipe Reader: Narratives— Contexts—Traditions*. Aldershot, U.K.: Ashgate, 2003.

Foucault, Michel. "What Is an Author?" *The Foucault Reader*. Edited by Paul Rabinow. New York: Pantheon Books, 1984: 101–20.

Gilbert, Sandra M., and Susan Gubar. *No Man's Land: The Place of the Woman Writer in the Twentieth Century. Vol. 2: Sexchanges*. New Haven, Conn.: Yale University Press, 1989.

Gilmore, Leigh. "An Anatomy of Absence: *Written on the Body*, the *Lesbian Body*, and Autobiography without Names." *The Gay '90's: Disciplinary and Interdisciplinary Formations in Queer Studies*. Edited by Thomas Foster, Carol Siegel, and Ellen E. Berry. New York: New York University Press, 1997: 224–51.

———. *Autobiographics: A Feminist Theory of Women's Self-Representation*. Ithaca, N.Y.: Cornell University Press, 1994.

———. "A Signature of Lesbian Autobiography: 'Gertrice/Altrude.'" *Autobiography and Questions of Gender*. Edited by Shirley Neuman. London: Cass, 1992: 56–75.

Gilmore, Leigh, Kathleen Ashley, and Gerald Peters. "Policing Truth." *Autobiography and Postmodernism*. Edited by Leigh Gilmore, Kathleen Ashley, and Gerald Peters. Amherst: University of Massachusetts Press, 1995: 54–78.

Gilot, Françoise. *Life with Picasso*. Excerpted in *Gertrude Stein Remembered*. Edited by Linda Simon. Lincoln: University of Nebraska Press, 1994: 170–75.

Grahn, Judy. *Really Reading Gertrude Stein: A Selected Anthology with Essays*. Freedom, Calif.: Crossing Press, 1989.

Gygax, Franziska. *Gender and Genre in Gertrude Stein*. Westport, Conn.: Greenwood Press, 1998.

Hachtman, Tom. *Gertrude's Follies: An Irreverent Look at the Life and Times of Gertrude Stein and Her Faithful Companion, Alice B. Toklas*. New York: St. Martin's Press, 1980.

Hall, Lynda. "Lorde, Anzaldua, and Tropicana Performatively Embody the Written Self." *a/b: Auto/Biography Studies* 15, 1 (Summer 2000): 96–122.

Hardack, Richard. "The Franklin-Stein Monster: Ventriloquism and Missing Persons in American Autobiography." *Writing Lives: American Biography and*

Autobiography. Edited by Hans Bak and Hans Krabbendam. Amsterdam: Vrije Universiteit University Press, 1998: 16–28.

Hemingway, Ernest. "The Autobiography of Alice B. Hemingway." Unpublished. Item 256. Hemingway Collection, John F. Kennedy Library, Boston.

———. *A Moveable Feast: Sketches of the Author's Life in Paris in the Twenties*. New York: Scribner, 1964.

———. "The True Story of My Break with Gertrude Stein." *The Critical Response to Gertrude Stein*. Edited by Kirk Curnutt. Westport, Conn.: Greenwood Press, 2000: 254–55.

Hilti, Gabriela. "'That Dangerous Supplement,' Intertextuality: Gossip As History in Michael Ondaatje's *Running in the Family*." *Henry Street* 7, 2 (Fall 1998): 36–52.

Hoffman, Michael J. (ed.). *Critical Essays on Gertrude Stein*. Boston: G. K. Hall, 1986.

Howes, David (ed.). *Cross-Cultural Consumption: Global Markets, Local Realities*. London: Routledge, 1996.

Imbs, Bravig. *Confessions of Another Young Man*. Excerpted in *Gertrude Stein Remembered*. Edited by Linda Simon. Lincoln: University of Nebraska Press, 1994: 117–28.

Irigaray, Luce. *Speculum of the Other Woman*. Translated by Gillian C. Gill. Ithaca, N.Y.: Cornell University Press, 1985.

———. *This Sex Which Is Not One*. Translated by Catherine Porter with Carolyn Burke. Ithaca, N.Y.: Cornell University Press, 1985.

Jelinek, Estelle C. (ed.) *Women's Autobiography: Essays in Criticism*. Bloomington: Indiana University Press, 1980.

Johnston, Georgia. "Narratologies of Pleasure: Gertrude Stein's *The Autobiography of Alice B. Toklas*." *Modern Fiction Studies* 42, 3 (Fall 1996): 590–606.

Kaplan, Caren. "Resisting Autobiography: Out-Law Genres and Transnational Feminist Subjects." *Women, Autobiography, Theory: A Reader*. Edited by Sidonie Smith and Julia Watson. Madison: University of Wisconsin Press, 1998: 208–16.

Kellner, Bruce (ed.). *A Gertrude Stein Companion: Content with the Example*. Westport, Conn.: Greenwood Press, 1988.

Kelly, Traci Marie. "'If I Were a Voodoo Priestess': Women's Culinary Autobiographies." *Kitchen Culture in America: Popular Representations of Food, Gender, and Race*. Edited by Sherrie A. Inness. Philadelphia: University of Pennsylvania Press, 2001: 251–69.

Lejeune, Philippe. *On Autobiography*. Edited by Paul John Eakin, translated by Katherine M. Leary. Minneapolis: University of Minnesota Press, 1989.

Loulan, JoAnn, with Sherry Thomas. *The Lesbian Erotic Dance: Butch Femme Androgyny and Other Rhythms*. San Francisco: Spinsters, 1990.

Luhan, Mabel Dodge. *European Experiences*. New York: Harcourt and Brace, 1935.

————. *Intimate Memories: The Autobiography of Mabel Dodge Luhan*. Edited by Lois Palken Rudnick. Albuquerque: University of New Mexico Press, 1999.

Marcus, Laura. *Auto/Biographical Discourses: Theory, Criticism, Practice*. Manchester, U.K.: Manchester University Press, 1994.

Martin, Biddy. "Lesbian Identity and Autobiographical Difference(s)." *Women, Autobiography, Theory: A Reader*. Edited by Sidonie Smith and Julia Watson. Madison: University of Wisconsin Press, 1998: 380–92.

Mellow, James R. *Charmed Circle: Gertrude Stein and Company*. New York: Praeger, 1974.

Meyerowitz, Patricia. "Lesbianism—Never." *New York Review of Books*, 7 October 1971. Accessed at http://www.nybooks.com/articles/10426/ on 8 September 2005.

Moore-Gilbert, Bart. *Postcolonial Theory: Contexts, Practices, Politics*. London: Verso, 1997.

Munt, Sally (ed.). *Butch/Femme: Inside Lesbian Gender*. London: Cassell, 1998.

Murphy, Karla. "The 'Convincing Lies' of Gertrude Stein: Cubism in *The Autobiography of Alice B. Toklas*." *Platte Valley Review* 22, 2 (Spring 1994): 5–20.

Neuman, Shirley. *Gertrude Stein: Autobiography and the Problem of Narration*. Victoria, B.C.: University of Victoria Press, 1979.

————— (ed.). Introduction to *Autobiography and Questions of Gender*. London: Cass, 1992.

Norris, Margot. "The 'Wife' and the 'Genius': Domesticating Modern Art in Stein's *Autobiography of Alice B. Toklas*." *Modernism, Gender, and Culture: A Cultural Studies Approach*. Edited by Lisa Rado. New York: Garland, 1997: 79–99.

Rogers, W. G. *When This You See Remember Me: Gertrude Stein in Person* (1948). Indianapolis: Charter Books, 1964.

Roof, Judith. "1970s Lesbian Feminism Meets 1990s Butch-Femme." *Butch/Femme: Inside Lesbian Gender*. Edited by Sally Munt. London: Cassell, 1998: 27–36.

Rousseau, Jean-Jacques. *On the Origin of Languages*. Translated with an afterword by John H. Moran and Alexander Gode. Chicago: University of Chicago Press, 1966.

Sceats, Sarah. *Food, Consumption, and the Body in Contemporary Women's Fiction*. Cambridge, Eng.: Cambridge University Press, 2000.

Schmidt, Paul. "As If a Cookbook Had Anything to Do with Writing." *Prose* 8 (1974): 179–203.

Scobie, Stephen. "'I Is Another': Autobiography and the Appropriation of Voice." *American Modernism across the Arts*. Edited by Jay Bochner and Justin D. Edwards. New York: Peter Lang, 1999: 124–36.

Simon, Linda. *The Biography of Alice B. Toklas*. New York: Doubleday, 1977.

Smith, Robert. *Derrida and Autobiography*. Cambridge, Eng.: Cambridge University Press, 1995.

Smith, Sidonie. "The Autobiographical Manifesto: Identities, Temporalities, Poetics." *Autobiography and the Questions of Gender*. Edited by Shirley Neuman. London: Frank Cass, 1991: 186–212.

———. "Performativity, Autobiographical Practice, Resistance." *a/b: Autobiography Studies* 10, 1 (Spring 1995): 17–33.

———. *A Poetics of Women's Autobiography: Marginality and the Fictions of Self-Representation*. Bloomington: Indiana University Press, 1989.

Souhami, Diana. *Gertrude and Alice*. London: Pandora Press, 1991.

Spivak, Gayatri Chakravorty. *A Critique of Postcolonial Reason: Toward a History of the Vanishing Present*. Cambridge, Mass.: Harvard University Press, 1999.

Sprigge, Elizabeth. *Gertrude Stein: Her Life and Work*. New York: Harper's, 1957.

Stanton, Domna C. "Autogynography: Is the Subject Different?" *Women, Autobiography, Theory: A Reader*. Edited by Sidonie Smith and Julia Watson. Madison: University of Wisconsin Press, 1998: 131–44.

Stein, Gertrude. "Ada." *A Stein Reader*. Edited by Ulla E. Dydo. Evanston, Ill.: Northwestern University Press, 1993: 100–103.

———. *The Autobiography of Alice B. Toklas*. New York: Random House, 1993.

———. 'A Birthday Book." *The Yale Gertrude Stein*. Selections with an introduction by Richard Kostelanetz. New Haven, Conn.: Yale University Press, 1980: 73–97.

———. "Composition As Explanation." *A Stein Reader*. Edited by Ulla E. Dydo. Evanston: Northwestern University Press, 1993: 493–503.

———. *Everybody's Autobiography*. New York: Cooper Square, 1971.

———. *Geography and Plays*. Boston: Four Seas, 1922.

———. "Lifting Belly." *The Yale Gertrude Stein*. Selections with an introduction by Richard Kostelanetz. New Haven, Conn.: Yale University Press, 1980: 4–54.

———. "Patriarchal Poetry." *The Yale Gertrude Stein*. Selections with an introduction by Richard Kostelanetz. New Haven, Conn.: Yale University Press, 1980: 106–46.

———. "*Picasso*." *Gertrude Stein: Writings 1932–1946*. Edited by Catharine R. Stimpson and Harriet Chessman. New York: Library of America, 1998: 495–533.

———. "A Sonatina Followed by Another." *The Yale Gertrude Stein*. Selections with an introduction by Richard Kostelanetz. New Haven, Conn.: Yale University Press, 1980: 287–315.

———. *Stanzas in Meditation*. *The Yale Gertrude Stein*. Selections with an introduction by Richard Kostelanetz. New Haven, Conn.: Yale University Press, 1980: 316–464.

———. *Tender Buttons: Objects, Food, Rooms*. New York: Haskell House, 1970.

———. *Wars I Have Seen*. London: Batsford, 1945.

———. "What Are Master-pieces and Why Are There So Few of Them." *Gertrude Stein: Writings 1932–1946*. Edited by Catharine R. Stimpson and Harriet Chessman. New York: Library of America, 1998: 353–63.

———. *What Does She See When She Shuts Her Eyes: A Novel*. *The Yale Gertrude*

Stein. Selections with an introduction by Richard Kostelanetz. New Haven, Conn.: Yale University Press, 1980: 63–65.

Stein, Leo. *Journey into the Self: Being the Letters, Papers and Journals of Leo Stein*. Edited by Edmund Fuller. New York: Crown, 1950.

Steward, Samuel M. *Dear Sammy: Letters from Gertrude Stein and Alice B. Toklas*. Boston: Houghton Mifflin, 1977.

Stewart, Lawrence D. "Hemingway and the Autobiographies of Alice B. Toklas." *Fitzgerald/Hemingway Annual 1970*. Washington, D.C.: NCR/Microcard Eds, 1970: 117–23.

Stimpson, Catharine R. "Gertrice/Altrude: Stein, Toklas, and the Paradox of the Happy Marriage." *Mothering the Mind: Twelve Studies of Writers and Their Silent Partners*. Edited by Ruth Perry and Martine Watson Brownley. New York: Holmes and Meier, 1984: 122–39.

———. "Gertrude Stein and the Lesbian Lie." *American Women's Autobiography: Fea(s)ts of Memory*. Edited and introduced by Margo Culley. Madison: University of Wisconsin Press, 1992: 152–66.

"Testimony against Gertrude Stein." Henri Matisse, Tristan Tzara, Maria Jolas, Georges Braque, Eugene Jolas, and André Salmon. Pamphlet #1, supplement to *transition* 23 (1935).

Thomson, Virgil. *Virgil Thomson*. London: Weidenfeld and Nicolson, 1967.

Toklas, Alice B. *The Alice B. Toklas Cook Book*. Foreword by M. F. K. Fisher. New York: Harper and Row, 1984.

———. *Staying On Alone: Letters of Alice B. Toklas*. Edited by Edward Burns. London: Angus and Robertson, 1974.

———. *What Is Remembered*. London: Michael Joseph, 1963.

Trinh Minh-ha. *Woman, Native, Other: Writing Postcoloniality and Feminism*. Bloomington: Indiana University Press, 1989.

Truong, Monique. *The Book of Salt: A Novel*. Boston: Houghton Mifflin, 2003.

Turner, Kay (ed.). *Baby Precious Always Shines: Selected Love Notes between Gertrude Stein and Alice B. Toklas*. New York: St. Martin's Press, 1999.

Watson, Julia. "Unspeakable Differences: The Politics of Gender in Lesbian and Heterosexual Women's Autobiographies." *Women, Autobiography, Theory: A Reader*. Edited by Sidonie Smith and Julia Watson. Madison: University of Wisconsin Press, 1998: 393–402.

Weiss, Andrea. *Paris Was a Woman: Portraits from the Left Bank*. London: Pandora, 1995.

White, Ray Lewis. *Gertrude Stein and Alice B. Toklas: A Reference Guide*. Boston: G. K. Hall, 1984.

Index